*Dedicated to all whose life, fate and DNA is somehow
intertwined to the inmates of one-time occupants of one
particular pigeon hole in the sky which they called home....
and it is priceless to have friends with the same mental illness!*

Inside the twisted mind
of
Rifle Range Boy

Farouk Gulsara

https://www.facebook.com/RifleRangeBoyBook

Inside the twisted mind of Rifle Range Boy
Copyright © Asokan Shamuganathan; 2014

The moral right of the author has been asserted.
All rights reserved.

No part of this book may be used or reproduced in any manner whatsoever
without permission from author except for critical reviews.

This write up is the work of imagination with frequent reference to pop culture.
It had previously appeared in the author's blog, 'Rifle Range Boy'.

First Edition: December 2014.
Reprint: 2015
ISBN: 978-967-13153-0-9

Publisher: Asokan Shamuganathan,
           Cheras, Kuala Lumpur, Malaysia.
           asokan@hotmail.co.uk

Illustrations: http://www.prom-ad.com.my
https://www.facebook.com/RifleRangeBoyBook

Printed in Malaysia by:
I-Colour Separation Sdn Bhd
No. 58 Jalan Tembaga SD 5/2B,
Bandar Sri Damansara, 52200 Kuala Lumpur.
T : 03-62748668 F : 03-62749668
E : icolourprint@gmail.com

Rifle Range Boy (asokan63.blogspot.com) A site about growing up in Penang, Malaysia in the 70s, the blogger's thought, unique (weird) sense of humour and train of thoughts on current events! A dreamer, occasional running junkie with an unshakable TV addiction living in his own hermit-like safe cocoon! Like an ant perched upon a dry leaf being led by the whirling currents of water on rainy day and trying to make sense of the twirling world around it,trying to make sense of things around him...

Content

Preface

I grew up in a family which believed that there is only one way to do things. It is either black or white, no two ways about it. When you were a child, you are expected to study, excel in your examinations and that is it — your life is made. And that is what we did. After growing up with blinkers accepting their guide as the gospel truth, with the benefit of tertiary education and age on your side, you begin to realise that many roads do indeed lead to Rome.

The idea of penning one's thoughts has never been our culture. We, of the timid species, have been contented to be in the sidelines, being followers and not wanting to rock the boat.

Now seated in the comforts of not worrying too much of your next meal, you only naturally want to reappraise your thoughts. As you start analysing things that you were taught throughout life to be the only way, the more you realise that there must be more than one way of doing it.

As it has often been said, things in life are in shades of grey. The more you look at a certain event, the more you realise that there could be more than one way of looking at it. The advent of information technology is shot in the arm for us to look at alternative views on the myriad of subjects.

This collection of thoughts is taken my blog, Rifle Range Boy. At various instances at various life events, I put on my analytical and sometimes devils' advocates horned-helmet to stimulate discussion with the followers of the blog.

The idea of creating the blog came about back in the 90s when I discovered the magic of Microsoft Words. As in many Malaysian families who started life in the tough days of early Malaya, my parents family too had many heart-wrenching stories to tell. I saw this outlet as an opportunity for future generations to come to appreciate that we too, albeit a small one, had a small role in the history of nation - Not as a legislator but as small men in small roles. Only when I started inking my experiences in the pigeon hole in the sky called home in Rifle Range Flats in Penang did I realise that I actually had a memorable childhood. This is a stark contrast to how we, my sisters and I, actually felt when we were growing up. We dreaded being cooped in the confines of the four walls immersed in melancholia and financial misery.

On being vegetarian....

Being vegetarian is a highly overstated virtue propagated by its proponents to put the fear of God into the non-believers and cow them into submission. The same people will say "eat to live" not "live to eat", but they lead their whole life by analysing what they eat. When you eat to live, you also logically should eat whatever food that comes your way, vegetarian or otherwise! Eat to live may include being careful in what you indulge in — whether it is clean (prepared in a hygienic fashion, halal if you are a Moslem), laden with cholesterol (to clog up the arteries), rich with carbohydrates (which will increase your abdominal girth and place you at high risk of getting a coronary event) etc. etc...

Maybe if you were Gautama Buddha, you would eat whatever is served to you, whether on a platter or on a leaf so as not to offend the feeder. According to the Mahayana sect, the Enlightened one was fed contaminated (?tainted) pork meat which he consumed willingly as he knew his time to attain Nirvana was imminent. Of course, there is always two sides of the coin. The Hinayana sect, on the other hand, believe that he succumbed to mesenteric infarction which may be a common occurrence for his advanced age of 80! I digress... way off tangent...

The story of veganism is the story of affluence of man. When Man is a beggar, he would scavenge on leftovers at the bin. Life would be blissful, a full stomach and a warm place would be Shangri-La for him. As his stature (the beggar, no longer a vagabond but has an abode) improves, he will be picky on his food. He would want his food clean and unpolluted by other people and animal's body secretion! Later, he would long for food to be prepared in a certain fashion – Chicken ala Kiev, tikka style, Duck Peking style and the list goes on and on... He would later be "enlightened", he will suddenly realise that he has been doing it all wrong all this while. He will have the compulsion to be a vegetarian. Then, the need to go organic and so on and so on...

There is a thin line between ingenuity and insanity. The heights of idiosyncrasy to stay vegan took new meanings when my daughter actually refused the *"roti canai"* offered at the temple, assuming that egg is an inherent ingredient of this Malaysian dish!

Man is an animal of convenience. He will alter rules and regulations to suit his whims and fancies. For instance, Brahmins are generally accepted as epitomes of vegetarianism. But wait a minute, Brahmins residing around the Bay of Bengal actually consume fish and their counterpart in the Kashmir Valley enjoy mutton. On a personal note, I know of a Brahmin who likes his steak rare! FG.18.1.10.

Contradiction of man

Man, an animal created by God, is full of contradictions. He will claim to be a vegetarian because he cannot stomach cruelty imposed on animals culled for meat but has no qualms about abusing the small men, maids, pets or other animals. He would go to great lengths to fulfil his religious obligations but cannot bear the sight or see eye to eye with his siblings or offspring. He would insist that his food must be 'pure' (free of any animal contaminants of any kind — be it of trace elements or seasoning) but has no problem throwing food, over-indulging, hurting and traumatising the feelings of the servant who, through his ignorance or feeble-mindedness, may have added oyster sauce or shrimp paste to his master's stirred fried vegetables to earn extra brownie points! He does not realise that his original reason to be vegetarian is to be in control of his inborn inner animal desire to be carnivorous but he craves for vegetarian chicken, vegetarian mutton or vegetarian prawns. Anyway, most animals eaten by men were vegetarian prior to their demise!

It is like a famous soothsayer, regularly featured on TV predicting the fortune for the country on the birth of a new year and advising people on their horoscope but unfortunately has a miserable family life himself-married twice, with second wife being slightly hypochondriac with histrionic personality. It is ironic that he could not predict his own life!

It is like restricting the cholesterol-laden sweet food for an 80-year-old diabetic just to serve these same foods on the prayer of his death anniversary. It is like some radicals proclaiming the greatness of God but in the same breath express fears being charmed by djinn, talisman and black magic. It is like in George Orwell's 1984, where all men are born equal but some are born 'more equal' than others! It is like Malaysia trying to bring back its brains from abroad but has no brains to keep its applications user-friendly. Contradictions...contradictions...FG.14.1.10

The fish stinks from the head...

The RTD chief was recently reported to have been appalled by the way Malaysians drive. This, he discovered during one of his *'balik kampong'* trips the last CNY holidays. He had taken snapshots of traffic offenders from his car and plans to issue summons to them. This, he discovered after 19 years at the helm of the RTD!

That is the problem, is it not? Day in day out you can see benign looking (including young housewives fetching their kids from schools) Malaysians blatantly disregarding traffic rules in broad daylight.

Does the RTD head not drive to work? Does he drive with blinkers? Does he sleep when he is driven around? Come on, wake up! Whatever happens on the roads is your bread and butter. You get paid with a fat cheque of a salary at the end of the month for it (sometimes earlier during the festive season).

Are you like an average "uncivil" Malaysian civil servant whose sole purpose of life revolves around clocking in and clocking out, collecting your fat paycheck at the end of the month and find solace in chit-chatting in workplace comparing dinner menu and their nocturnal activities! You should be looking out for ways to improve your department and what it works for even if it is outside normal working hours.

I suppose I (and my colleagues) were idiots when we were employed as Government servants for 12 years! I thought I was there to serve others because we were classified servants just like how my mother was a servant to the colonial masters back in the 60's! All those missed lunch breaks, missed mandatory midday civil servant tea break, working way past office hours, all those post-operative rounds in the night, the never ending outpatient clinics and the list goes on and on.

I suppose we will go on living and hoping that we will be remunerated accordingly in our after-life or better karma, definitely not with 40 virgins!!!FG.8.3.10.

Are you OK, Annie? Who knows?

In the course of our conversation, I casually asked my accountant about his health. To this he replied, "Oh, I did my medicals and the doctors told me that my results were fantastic. The doctor was so happy with the result and told me that my results were better than his, a cardiologist'." That's P, my accountant, the ever optimistic chap who looks at the world through very positive lenses. You ask him about his son who was studying in Ukraine, he would say the lecturers were so impressed with his performance and so are the Consultants he is working for now as a house officer. And his daughter is so happily married in the cold mountains of Germany!

Well, good for him. If only everyone in this world is as contented as him, the world would be a better place.

On one hand, I feel happy for him for his good results as it gives him a sense of satiety to enjoy his happy life as it is. On the other hand, it gives him a false sense of security. That started me thinking...

One of my friend's sister was diagnosed by a professor in UHKL to have a lethal form of lymphoma back in the 80's. Her prognosis was grave and her days were numbered, so she was told. As the Americans say, when the going gets tough, the tough gets going, she went on various traditional medical treatment modalities – Indonesian, Chinese, Japanese and Indian. The testimony of her endeavour is that she is still standing and has outlived the professor by a good 15 years so far. So, did another renowned professor who was afflicted with Chronic Renal Failure in the 1980s, embraced the new millennia, lived past 80 and outlived the physician who gave him the bad news!

Nobody knows how healthy or sick a person is! An able body can just collapse just like that with a ruptured brain aneurysm. Nobody can say for certain what is in store for him. Every living day is a divine gift and all of us are living on borrowed time. We should be glad that we can actually get up in the morning and continue with life. Que sera sera, whatever will be will be...Obladi Oblada! Life goes on bra...FG6.3.10

Too late for Happy New Year?

And a happy new year... But 2010 started 4 months ago! The Gregorian calendar, yes, but for many cultures and civilisations the year starts in mid-April. For the Zoroastrians and those of the Bahai faith, it starts on the March equinox. The Telugus commence the New Year a month after this date as well. The Christian Churches decided long ago that the single most important event in their religion (i.e., The Resurrection) will be celebrated on the first Sunday after the first full moon on or after the March equinox as Easter Sunday depending whether the church follows the Gregorian or Julian calendar. The Malayalees, Sindhis and Sikhs celebrate their respective New Years (Vishu, Cheti Chand and Vaisakhi) around now. Not to forget the Red Shirts in Thailand who called it truce to honour their Songkhran and at least the Sinhalese and Jaffnese celebrate something together on the same day. The Laotians, Cambodians, Myanmarese and the Dais of Yunnan celebrate similar function at about the similar times. I vaguely remember that the Balinese start their New Year in March by fasting, observing silence and meditation for 24 hours on Nyepi. All Hindus and Indians generally all over the world celebrate New Year today.

The buck stops here, so to speak. This is how far the similarities go. Unlike their Chinese counterparts who celebrate their Chinese New Lunar Year irrespective of their practicing religion with their traditional mandatory reunion dinner, for a Tamilian who professes any other monolithic religion (e.g., Christianity or Islam), the Tamil New Year would be a non-event. Rather than being a cultural event, Tamil New Year is so intertwined with religion that it is now viewed as a religious event. Instead of looking at the similarities, people are going all out alienating each other from a fellow homo sapien!FG14.4.10

Malaysian Indian, Indian Malaysian or Malaysian?

Dear Thelma,

I am confused. I am at a crossroads. I was born in Malaysia some almost half a century ago in a government hospital to two Malaysian parents whose parents were also born in Malaysia. My parents and grandparents contributed in their own way (albeit their low status in the rung of the social ladder) to put Malaysia on the world map so at least some Americans now know that there is no void space between Thailand and Singapore; and Himalaya and Malaya is not interchangeable; or Malaya is not a female equivalent of He-Malaya!

I started my primary education with Malaysian Language as the medium of instruction even though other countries in the region were keeping up with the Joneses and emphasised on the English Language because our leaders told us that it would unite the people and stop internal squabbling. All my subjects from Standard 1 to Upper Six were taught in Bahasa Malaysia, even though we did not have enough reference books at the higher levels and we had to translate (in our head) what we read in English before writing it on our examination papers. I only learned my mother tongue from my mother (duh!) and the POL classes. I obtained a distinction in Bahasa Malaysia at 'O' levels. I speak the Malay Language, English, more than smattering of *Hockkein* and Cantonese dialects (also swear in these dialects as well) and Hindi/Punjabi. I can understand the Malay in its different dialects – *Apo nak dikato* (Negri); also a Malay song by the local group, Blues Gang; *Hangpa pi sana 'ngan sapa?* (Northern); *Kecek Kelantan gak gewek* (Kelantan); Makang ikang (Terengganu), etcetera. I have many Malaysian friends of various ethnic and religious backgrounds. I also rejoice during their merry making cultural and religious events.

I furthered my studies at a Malaysian university, spent 2 years living and dining amongst people of Kelantan. I started working with the Malaysian Ministry of Health (12 years altogether), serving people of all races in various states in Malaysia. I pay my dues as a responsible citizen by paying hefty taxes regularly and vote in the General Elections. I know the lyrics of the Malaysian anthem (Negara Ku) by hard and stand at attention when the Jalur Gemilang is hoisted or Negara Ku is played. I cheer my Malaysian team whenever they are competing even though they are losing. When I am overseas and foreigners asked me whether I am Indian, I proudly tell them I am Malaysian. That reminds of the 80s' song by 'Men at Work' titled 'Down Under'...

Buying bread from a man in Brussels
He was six foot four and full of muscle
I said, "Do you speak-a my language?"
He just smiled and gave me a vegemite sandwich
And he said,
"I come from a land down under
Where beer does flow and men chunder
Can't you hear, can't you hear the thunder?
You better run, you better take cover." Yeahhh!...

But now, my Deputy Prime Minister (and Prime Minister) say I am Indian first then only I am Malaysian. How can I call myself Indian when I have not set foot on Indian soil and have no plans to do so either? I am sure the Indian Government has no interest in me too. Maybe they and their people may want our economic support via the well-orchestrated guise of temples. Thelma, I am going ravaging mad. I need an answer now. Please help me fast. I can hear the paramedics entering my house to strap the straight jacket on me!

FG.

Dear FG,

I will see you in person in the psychiatry ward after you are more lucid with your insight intact and after the doctors have medicated, stabilised and rehabilitated you. You see, I do not want to lose my publication licence. Please fight your own battles as I have been fighting mine.

Thelma.FG.27.4.10

My brush with the Other side*...Mariska Hargitay™**

Over the weekend, I was roped in (probably by divine intervention) to be an interpreter to a pious man who was addressing a predominantly non Tamil speaking congregation at a home cleansing (house warming) ceremony.

I arrived there with a lot of fanfare. As it was pouring cats and dogs en route to function, my family and I arrived fashionably late. Another faux pas moment happened here. I honked as I parked at the porch to get help to bring in the food and cutlery from the car, not knowing that the prayers were already in session! (Probably to the annoyance of the attendees, I suppose). Only after parking the car and entering the house did I realise the foot in the mouth moment.

Upon entry to the abode, I was whisked in like some kind of VIP to sit beside the holy man to help him address the audience, as an interpreter. And the sacrificial fire started burning...

The joist of the teaching of the day was (as interpreted by my unenlightened, non-vegetarian mind):

- *From time in memoriam, man has awed by creations around him and was puzzled about its origin and its creator. The elders and the learned told that the black rock (the Shivling) is the original rock representative of the creator. And so our forefathers decided that it should be our guiding light.*

-I have learnt from other sources that the *Shivling* also signifies the union of the two basic union of nature-the male and female components-Shiva and Shakthi. Not to forget the monolithic structure in Stanley Kubrick's 'Space Odyssey 2001'.

- *That the Shivling is within us. Through meditation and guidance, one can achieve a state of mind where one can be in control of his humanly desires, temptations and knowing what is right and wrong. And the Shivling will follow you wherever you go like the sun and the moon that can be seen at the four corners of the world.*

- *That the sound of the universe is the same as our breath – Aum -but, but...my simple mind says the universe is vacuum and sound waves need air to transmit!*

- *That life is a gamble. Everything you do involves risks, your daily duties, your marriage, your spouse from a different background, your relationships, etcetera. All this will progress well via divine intervention and through guided intervention of man and woman.-via religion discipline and self control can be instilled, I suppose.*

I guess we all know all of the above, but when a third person tells you it all makes sense. Just like when a piece of news gets repeated repeatedly, this piece of news becomes a fact of life and when it is mentioned by a person in power, it becomes a doctrine! And when it whispered by a holy man, it becomes the divine truth. Amen.

Live and let live

During my posting in Johor Bahru, I was fascinated listening to the BBC World Radio FM transmissions from Singapore, in particular, its weekly editorials. A 15-minute rendition of some mundane topic like 'The pros and cons of Daylight Saving Time' was really intriguing. That got me thinking — that there are always two sides of the stories to everything in life, even something as pure as Mothers' Day.

Mothers' Day is joyously celebrated by mothers and people in the business community on the second Sunday in the month of May annually. Mothers naturally are overjoyed as they are glorified as the centre of attention, especially when she is in a community where women are always considered second-class citizens, a burden whose opinion do not count and female infants are considered curses. Of course it is heart warming to hear and see Rajnikanth singing praises and carrying his stroke-stricken mother to temples to cure in the movies (reel), but in real life?

Well, and fine. Mothers become mothers because of nature's unstoppable clock work of continuation of species, the society expects her to be a mother sometime in her life cycle. Of course some women are impregnated via unscrupulous man and divine intervention of Act of God through Man. I read somewhere of an immaculate conception without man as an accomplice a century ago (circa 3 AD).

True. Nature, through its progestogenic effect, has primed and prepared mothers into motherhood. While fathers sleep through the night like a log (or like a baby), mothers will be instinctively be awoken by a slight jolt or squeak of her infant even late into the night or wee slumbering hours of morning in spite of her back breaking feats nurturing these brats (and possibly other brats too) in the daytime. Have we not heard of mothers running into burning houses in desperate attempts to save their offspring and instead perish in the fire themselves? Or the real live events of mothers who cannot swim drown to save their struggling toddlers? No mother would give a second thought to sacrificing their meal, appearances, entertainment, worldly pleasures or even partners to ensure their children are sufficiently prepared to sail through into adulthood. Or would they not? We generalise.

Having done all these over the years and guiding them through the shark infested ocean of life, these same warm hands that rock the cradle, pulled us off the rocky roads, rock and roll to our antics may also rock families or wreck families altogether! This is especially so with domineering Indian mothers who think that their sons are still clinging on to breasts for milk and their sons have no mind of their own with just mud between the two ears and the world is out there just out pollute, manipulate and mystify their mind! Sometimes they blame it on black magic. Or are they just reminiscing their own devious mischievous earlier deeds? They expect payback time for all the earlier sacrifices all these years. They expect royal treatment in the shadows of Cleopatra and Jhansi Rani and everyone should dance to their fancy tunes and pick their crumbs. They have no qualms about everybody else feeling miserable. They would continue doing all these without an iota of guilt but instead plead self-pity through emotional blackmail. And they would seek solace, eternal peace from the Almighty after this long path of destruction by attending prayers and temple soul cleansing rituals. I think I have been watching way too many M. R. Radha and Manorama movies!

Girls are born daily, they become mothers and they die to complete the cycle of life on earth. Mothers should learn to live and let live. They should learn to let go of their sons and let him live his life. They should not stick to the dictum 'My way or no way!' Diplomacy is the essence of civilised living and above all common sense should prevail. Like what a not so famous guru once said, 'Expectation only leads to disappointment but acceptance brings contentment." He was not so famous hence nobody has heard his sayings and he was so insignificant that I cannot remember his name!

All of the above are just rumblings of a fool with artistic and writing licence. Of course, I love my mother for all her sacrifices and undying devotion. And I pray for her health and long happy life. I love you, Amma. Happy Mothers' Day. Now, can you take the dagger off my jugular?

She broke the bread into two fragments and gave them to the children, who ate with avidity.

"She hath kept none for herself," grumbled the sergeant.

"Because she is not hungry," said a soldier.

"Because she is a mother," said the sergeant. **Victor Hugo (1802-1885)**

The Hand that rocks the cradle is the hand that rules the world.

William Ross Wallace (1819-1881), U.S. Poet and Songwriter.FG.11.5.10

Going somewhere?

Anywhere but India!

Warning: Readers' discretion and common sense should prevail. This description is of personal nature and is not a travel advisory and should be used as a guide under any circumstances! And Indian Tourism Board should not be offended by this article as it not directed at them and I am sure it must be administered by level headed officials .

After 47 years of living on planet Earth, I have not stepped on Indian soil and do not plan to do it in any near future. Why not, you may ask. Why should I, I ask.

I am Malaysian, born, bred and hope to die here in my motherland (*tanah tumpah darah ku*). I will go there when I want to go there, i.e., when there is a calling. From young, all the teasings and name calling must have left its effect on my psyche. Even in the mid twenties after burning the midnight oil and burning the candle at both (or if possible at three) ends and toiling day and night to successfully complete medical studies in USM, when people see an Indian doctor they would invariably ask, "So, you studied in Manipal, ah?" Maybe it is because I do not look intelligent lack the charisma or the X factor is sorely missing! In this way, I can still tell them how I could not have studied in a place I have never set foot on.

Why visit India? The temples? Well, sages say God is everywhere, even in the tiniest of the crack and in our heart. So, why go so far to worship God. Mother Theresa once said that God lives amongst the poor, so why go to a temple where the priest do an 8-hour shift counting money and donations. Furthermore, this particular temple has a branch in Malaysia.

Why visit India? The people? We have of Indian expatriates for us to see if you want to. They also look like us. The poverty? Do you really want to spend so much money to see poverty? We have it in our own backyard.

Or do you want to see it to show gratitude to your long-lost ancestors who literally made living hell to force mass immigration of my forefathers to Malaya?

Why visit India? The food? Really? Have you not seen enough people walking around with two important things close to their body? Their passports for fear of being duped or pick pocketed and their mineral water bottle for fear of tropical sprue. That too, the seal on the mineral water bottle cap had to be checked to eliminate possibility of tap water contamination or recycling of bottles.

Anyway, scenes from *Makkal* TV are real turn offs to visit India. If you insist, there is always Discovery Channel to view the sanitised views of India. As for me, I am still waiting for the calling. No, thanks, no need to pay for a visa either! And I do not think India is missing me.FG20.5.10

Amnesty and Gotong-Royong

What amnesty has got to do with *gotong-royong*, you may ask. Amnesty usually refers to affairs between countries whilst *gotong-royong* involves things at the village level. If you have a criminally and cynically critical mind like mine, then you would probably correlate these two phenomena and skewer them together in the same BBQ pit in a negative light.

Amnesty here refers to the recurrent government amnesty (grace period) to allow illegal immigrants to go back to their countries of origin before the long arm of the law goes on a blitz to nap illegal immigrants. This will predictably start a slowdown in nation's economic activities as all our nitty gritty work of cleaning our homes to building mansions are manned by immigrants (legal and otherwise). Pressure groups in the form of politicians and businessmen, like a knee-jerk reaction, will start pressing the enforcers to go lenient on the wrongdoers who in turn will temporarily slow down the whole wheel of enforcement, yet to start churning again sometime in the future.

Gotong-royong is a cultural entity among the Malay community where after one whole year of dirtying their village and not bothering about cleanliness and hygiene, a wake-up call will come in the form morbidity or mortality due to communicable disease. Villagers will then get together to embark on a spring cleaning drive.

The striking similarity between these two scenarios is that, in both instances, after months of malaise and lackadaisical attitude (of lax enforcement and not taking care of own backyard), efforts are made to right the wrong. When the load gets too heavy and dangerous, they call for everyone else to do their dirty jobs. If the Immigration Department officials were not sleeping on their jobs, the number of illegal immigrants in this country would not have skyrocketed to levels that make Malaysian Indians (who had toiled their blood and sweat to prosper early Malaya) a minor minority! If the villagers had taken care of their own backyard, the need for *gotong-royong* would not arise at all.

Giving amnesty to illegal immigrants and performing large scale *gotong-royong* is not something to be proud of. Neighbouring countries from where these illegals originate from is not going to be eternally grateful for not charging their citizens. Instead, they will be sneering at our inefficiencies. Just like the *gotong-royong* which just reveal our lethargy of the people in power.FG24.5.10

Petroleum and Civilization (or end of?)

I remember visiting *Petrosains* at KL City Centre few years ago. I had an uneasy feeling on exiting that the visitors to the venue had been hoodwinked into believing (via its exhibits and messages) that petroleum had indeed made Mother Earth a nicer place to live in. Really? Sorry, I cannot buy your story!

Recently one of my friends emailed me an article narrating the potential devastation waiting to happen as a result of BP's misadventure of oil exploration in the Gulf of Mexico. The damage to the environment is said to be in gargantuan proportions as evidenced by the 22,000 people and 10,000 vessels deployed in rescue plan making it the largest effort in the history of disaster recovery. That got me thinking...

Actually, petroleum seems to me like a curse or the root of all evil rather than our saviour. Most of the world catastrophes are somehow linked it- e.g. Twin Tower incident, Iraq War, etc., etc.

The Second Industrial Revolution, fuelled by the discovery of Colonel Edwin Drake helped to jump start the modernisation of the world as we see it today. We can build mammoth structures and architectural marvels at a fraction of time used by our ancestors. Anyway, the Incas and the Egyptians build these too, but at the expense of much human (slave) sufferings and lives. We are not much further now after so many years — we have sweat shops! I digress.

I am not a proponent of anti-modernity and that we should all be moving from point A to point B on a bullock cart or that we should all don cavemen hides and be stoned in Stone Age - also, I am too lazy to hunt for my meals!

Revolutionary ways of extracting petroleum deeper into the ground rather than scooping it off Earth's surface made kerosene replace whale oil in lamp fuels in Northern America at the turn of the 19th century. This, with many other innovations, made petrol the most sort after commodity creating strings of obnoxious billionaires especially in the US who worshiped the God of Capitalism. Over time, money seems to justify and compensate all our deficiencies and inadequacies. The ferocious appetite of these billionaires seems insatiable that they have ventured beyond their shores, influencing governments and warlords towards this end. The ugly side of Man of is revealed by his fixation of expanding his arsenal of nuclear heads to achieve his goal.

In the early 70's, the oil cartels held the world at its throat by fixing the oil prices. It then showed us how important petroleum was to mankind. It is also quite evident to us by now how George W. Bush and Tony Blair smoke-screened us into believing on the existence of weapons of mass destruction, hence justifying their march into and colonisation of a sovereign nation, all in the name of the completing the missing link between the Siberian-Caspian pipeline! As a result of these, air travel had never been more cumbersome. Human beings, who had been quite accommodating of each other, (are you sure?) have started staring at each other with suspicion, especially at those who believe that they should cover the religion-sanctioned areas of their bodies.

Do not even bother talking about the environmental damage caused by oil spillage and the carbon footprints left by this fossil fuel. Marine biologists working in the tropical waters off the coast of US in the 80's actually found extinction of the male gender in a group of marine life some ten years after a massive oil spill. So, petroleum has changed mankind in a big way. Right! Even my toes are not laughing.

@Thanks to SC for the email. Now I am more confused now than ever and have been put on suicide alert! There I see it now, the shadow that had been following me all day....FG27.5.10

'Wealth is Health' or 'Health is Wealth'?

That is a good question. From the time I can remember, the age old adage of 'Health is Wealth' had been ingrained in our impressionable minds to be the ultimate truth. Is it really the elusive truth that everyone is looking for?

In the pre-industrial era when most people led simple lives toiling on the wonders provided by nature, e.g., farming, hunting or any work which involve indentured labourers or bondage slavery. Here, a healthy fit body will ensure ability to endure the hardship of calamities of nature to bring home the bacon! An unhealthy invalid or an ageing senile individual will be a burden to family and society unless a social safety net is in place.

If you were the servant of the palace or a sorcerer in the dawn of human civilisation, (as if we are more civilised now), health is of paramount importance for survival. Is this adage still of relevance at this present date and time?

Let me look at how health brings wealth to an individual. As a cynic, first look at how many caregivers in the healthcare services generate wealth from other people's ill-health. Then there are the giants in the healthcare industries, HMO's and insurance companies who managed to build a conglomerate from people's sickness. I have seen so many friends whose family and generations have been escalated the rung of ladder of strata of society via acquiring medical studies either via pure hard work or via a short cut. Medical studies have become affordable, no longer the domain of the high achievers alone. Advertisements are often seen in the local dailies showing SPM as the requirement for entry to some of these so-called Government-approved medical institutions.

It is no secret that the cost of healthcare all over the world has leapt by bounds over the years. It will literally cost a leg or an arm to afford cutting-edge medical care in a private hospital anywhere in the world. So, to acquire good health, one has to have some wealth and be willing to part with it. I remember a relative of mine, who during a routine screening procedure, who was told to have a small benign looking renal cyst. It kept on reappearing on repeated subsequent screening. Being not satisfied with reassurances by his doctors, he seeks advice of various experts for more invasive diagnostic procedures. To cut the story short, he underwent a nephrectomy after biopsies showed slow growing renal cell carcinoma. Here, it is apparent that this individual acquired good bill of health after paying a hefty bill of wealth! Of course critics will say that it is a slow-growing tumour anyway which would have been picked up anyway by subsequent regular screenings. To the patient, however, as far as he is concerned, his local doctors have failed to detect cancer and he would always be wary of their treatment modalities and advice.

Many diseases that use to plague mankind (e.g., smallpox and poliomyelitis to a certain extent) have been literally wiped out from the surface of earth, save some kept in the laboratories (which may be used as a biological weapon when the time is ripe). Beri-beri which used to plague bonded labourers in the middle of the 20th century is unheard of in modern Malaysia. Eradication happened with improvement of economic climate and affordability of vaccines and proper balanced nutrition. On the other hand, wealth has brought with it some lifestyle related diseases as well — obesity, diabetes, hypertension, coronary events, etc.

Fearing for their health, wealth affluent societies no longer believe in curative medicine but rather concentrate on preventive medicine. This has been instrumental in mushrooming of numerous health sanctuaries. Here, absolutely normal individuals of various ages are subjected to various tests just to find a result which would deviate from norm so that more tests can be done, all in the pretext of finding sickness in a healthy person. Business is generated — healthcare providers are happy - they got a job; insurance companies are happy — they have got low-risk individuals tied down with their policies and are laughing all the way to the bank; the 'patients' are happy — they have taken care of their health so that they can continue acquiring wealth! And continue their way of life, for good or bad... Now which side are you on?FG 25.5.10

Excited over small pricks!

This pointless discussion is on some of the meaningless celebrations that we as Tamilians honour. It caught my attention when one of the neighbours in my housing estate erected a canopy across the road blocking half of the road just to officiate the erection the small Muniswar statuette in his house compound. From my life experiences, I can say with conviction that the usual justification of such an erection is usually as part of fulfilling the demand of a dream. The Gods (or some of their representation of them, e.g., dog, whip or an apparition with a big moustache) would have manifested during their sleep and demanded or hinted for something of that nature. You cannot say this is something new or nonsensical as others have also known to have done this in the name of religion. Abraham almost put his son to the slaughter as God supposedly manifested in his dream to test his faith. Just as the unthinkable was about to happen, the 'sacrificial lamb' was replaced with a ram via miraculous work of God and now a good proportion of the world population rejoice this event. The ceremony (at the neighbour's newly built mini temple) started at the heat of noon sun with chanting of high pitch hymns accompanied by beating of loud drums. Just to clarify, I was not there witnessing the brouhaha. The obvious pandemonium was clearly audible to whole Taman! Interestingly, the sounds of the drums were the same as the one used in Tamil Nadu village funerals! The climax of the event was the billy goat sacrifice. From my limited knowledge of religion, this practice is not ordained by any of the reputable Hindu bodies anywhere in the world. In fact, such a similar sacrificial practice is one of the reasons Siddhartha Gautama started his brand of religion which is really an off-shoot of Hinduism.

How the mass of human race is conned with hearsay! A convincing preacher has managed and will continue eluding mass hypnotism on his subordinates to achieve his self egomaniacal self-interest by one day bringing homo sapiens to the brink of extinction following the same road as the mammoths, T-Rexes and Sabre-toothed tigers!

Right up to the mid 20th century, only two groups of the world population pierce their ears – Indians and aboriginal head hunting people (e.g., Borneo, Africa, Papua New Guinea). Fast forward to the late 20th century and ear piercing became a fashion statement and an art. Many other body parts, visible and otherwise, got pricked as well. Together with this, other traditionally South Indian practices like nose ring and toe rings have become synonymous with the rebellious youth of the 21st century just like the pelvis gyrating and bra burning counterparts of the 50s and 70s respectively. The ear-piercing ceremony in the Tamil society came about as a status symbol and became a hallmark of culture among the society as gold (in the earring) has had a special place in their society. It also created an avenue for relatives to meet and mingle as the society had determined that certain relatives had specific roles in this ceremony and would be frowned upon if they fail in their undertakings. A few months ago, I was invited for such an event. It was hosted in a 5-star restaurant with soothing ambience complete with traditional musicians and paraphernalia. For a few moments, the venue was immersed in a cheerful festive mood, with the baby hoisted on the shoulder and the highlight of the event was the piercing of the baby's ear lobes by the traditional Indian jeweller with the seated on the maternal uncle's lap! There was a designated master of ceremony who was giving a running commentary of the events and the significance of each step of the occasion. One particular comment that struck me was the reason for such a big fanfare on the ear-piercing ceremony. If one were to look at the ear auricle, it is supposed to resemble the divine letter 'Aum' or 'Om' in the Tamil alphabet. Piercing the earlobe is said to complete the letter by putting a dot where it is due. (Is this for real, rationalisation or artistic creation, I wonder?)

How something frowned upon as a practice of the 'less cultured' as assimilated in to world culture and is considered trendy and hip. Harrison Ford was once spotted donning ear-stud on his left ear. Why left ear? If worn on the right ear, it is a subtle announcement of the wearer coming out of the closet. I wonder if it applies on both sides of the Atlantic, bearing in the mind that the traffic is reversed on the either side of the Atlantic!

One of the functions that had outlived its usefulness in the 'coming of age' ceremony. It is done to announce to the world that their female child has attained menarche. During this time, probably the only time, the girl is given special diet rich is proteins and mineral so as ensure her future fecundity. (As if fertility is determined by the female factor alone!)

In the era when child marriages were accepted as the norm, this ceremony hailed as a perfect way to announce to the world around them that a maiden is available for continuation of species. At present times where the female is destined to rule the world with their academic and career ambitions, this ceremony appears totally irrelevant. Ladies mostly choose their life partners way past the teenage years and their exposure to the outside via education and work makes 'coming of age' ceremony unnecessary. The society, however has given many religious significances to this event and even the position of the stars at time of menarche is said to of high significance towards the fecundity and even her obstetric performance in her future childbearing years!FG8.6.10

Tamil school, anyone?

In my humble opinion on the existence of Malaysian Tamil schools is that they should not exist. Period. The existence of these schools in this country is defeating the purpose of disseminating quality education to the masses but gives a false sense of satiety and security to the community. It makes its students 'jaguh kampung' (local champions) with no secure standing in facing the real world. The real world is competing with people of many expertise and background whilst able to blend and understand each others' whims and fancies. In that aspect, the Tamil schools have failed miserably as it only attracts pupils of a particular community and to top it all, only from a particular stratum of the community.

Let me give you an example. When I was in primary school, I was invariably in the first five top students' of the form without fail without really putting much effort. All these changed when I was placed in one of the premier schools during my secondary school years. Suddenly, excelling in studies was no more a stroll in the park but a Herculean task needing much effort and willpower. The drive to compete and other external factors has placed me where I am today. Language is an important tool helped me in this endeavour. Pupils from Tamil school, far in between, are handicapped in this aspect, no matter when the educators may say and justify their positions by statistics and number.

There is no continuity in Tamil school education. Learning mostly in their mother tongue, venturing into a different language in the secondary school is not easy. This scenario is, however not the case in Chinese medium schools. Chinese school students can continue their seamless education to right to tertiary levels!

I am not saying we should bundle Tamil language to our museums and forget about it. On the contrary, we should strive to bring the language to a higher level by making it a lesson in the mainstream schooling system and offer it as compulsory third language to the students (besides English and Bahasa Malaysia).

In the meantime, let Tamil medium schools thrive only in Tamil Nadu, India.FG22.6.1o

Life lessons learnt from FIFA World Cup 2010

(under the hypnotising hum of the vuvuzelas...)

A living day is a learning day in the voyage of life. We all sail, somewhere. Some wade along aimlessly, some claim to know the way whilst others follow blindly but there is no Google map to follow.... The destination may be variable but end-point is the same!

Now, what can we learn from the FIFA World Cup 2010.

- France: if there is no mutual respect between coach (leader) and player (citizens), the team (country) is bound to go nowhere.

  Just like that, the 1998 world champions fizzled out after the first round with its dismal performance.

- Argentina: do not write off people too easily. Everybody deserves a second chance. In the qualifying stage, Argentina just managed to scrape through as a representative of South America. In the first and second match, they showed the world the real way to play football, shutting up their critics.

- •Prima-donnas never shine: Look at Italy (the last WC winners) and their humbling 2-3 defeat to Slovakia, all at once eliminating them at the first rounds! The arms that hoisted the World Cup in 2006 is now supporting their fellow sobbing team mates!

- Mind the minnows! Knowing that the Japanese are inferior in physique and stature, they excelled in speed and 'never-say-die' samurai spirit. South Koreans, out to prove that their last outing was no fluke and a flash in the pan, are giving their opponents a run for their money in this dogfight! (could not resist the pun). Do not forget the Fern-leaf country with more sheep than human, New Zealand! Even though they had part time footballers and no big guns to shout about, they exited the 1st round without losing a single game!
- Team spirit is important. Just like the previous WC, the African teams did not do so well. No, thanks to their internal squabbling.

The football pundits say, "Life's a pitch". If that is true, we can learn a thing or two of lessons in life from the football pitch (field). Well, it is not over yet. The World Cup action is just heating up and the best is yet to come!FG25.6.10

Don't cha wish your girlfriend was hot like me?

Just the other day, my eldest daughter asked me if I still found my wife (her mother) hot after all these years. A simple yes or no answer will suffice, right? Well, life is not so black or white. That's lesson in Life 101!
Finding a wife is just like ordering food in a Chinese restaurant. After ordering your food, only then you discover that the food served on the next table seem to look nicer. Or like buying the latest mobile phone — just after weeks of buying your smart-phone and still getting familiar with its applications, comes a newer and smarter phone with many newer features and is the talk of the town.

Love just happens! At the correct time and correct position of the stars, things just happen. Whatever changes that affect the couple does not affect either partner unilaterally. Everything happens in unison, naturally, in accordance to the law of nature. Just like the redistribution and increase of adipose tissues as well as climacteric changes that affect the female partner over time, their male counterpart also undergo various metamorphoses. They not only grow older, grey, and slower in response time, reduced chivalrous gestures to familiar partner with increased abdominal girth. They also become grumpier and develop peculiar idiosyncrasies. Both parties must accept each other's shortcomings and let it be.

Do not wish for the moon and the stars, you will be zapped by a meteorite.

So, the answer to the question is an emphatic YES. Period.FG7.7.10

Jai Hanuman Ji

Two things happened today that got me thinking. Both the two events were totally unrelated, but were they?

In the first incident, a stray monkey entered the study room and helped itself with some cookies placed on the study table and scooted off upon being spotted. The second one happened when I was waiting for my kids to finish their music class. There I saw an unkempt handicapped Indian (immigrant, probably illegal) man limping around spitting on the road with no care in the world. The hawk-eyed can always smell out a non-Malaysian Indian. They are the ones who wear a singlet under their T-shirt or wear a long-sleeved shirt in the heat of the afternoon sun or like donning chequered shirts with a thick lock of curly hair.

This guy was walking back to his makeshift quarters built at the corner lot of a terrace house. I was fuming as he was spitting on spreading germs to be distributed among fellow Malaysians and fuming as misfits like him were allowed to roam the streets of Malaysia due to lax enforcement of the Immigration Department which was given the broom award by the previous State government .

I am getting angry because the serenity of my living space has been invaded and my way of life has disturbed. This is probably how the monkey must have felt. His ancestors must have been swinging without a care in the world until the bulldozers came marching in to bulldoze their playing fields. We are looking at them as invaders of our privacy. We are wary of their presence because of fear of rabies and other communicable diseases.

This is also probably how the Malays felt in 1946 when the question of citizenship arose. They must felt that it is appropriate to get special treatment as they were here earlier!

With time, all the migrant population will assimilate into the country. Just like the other day, a Bangladeshi family drove to the pasar malam in their Proton Wira to buy their favourite meal from the nasi lemak stall!

Looks like we also have learnt to live with the monkeys, too. Learn? Am already!FG7.7.10

I shot the sheriff but I killed no deputy!

Today there was an uninvited guest to the house this morning. Out of nowhere, I sighted a little mouse scooting off across the room. I followed it and it appeared again! As a reflex, I stepped hard on it! And hold behold, I killed it instantaneously.

Then it fell on me. The Hindu sages say that a visit by a mouse is a visit by Lord Ganesha himself! And a bad host I have been. That would explain why they have a Rat Temple in Rajasthan which shelters thousands of rats. They would say the same thing if a snake should enter your house. One should not harm the reptile as its partner would come back with sweet revenge. And legend has it that cobras are supposed to have a real elephantine memory! If fact, 10 years ago when there were plenty of constructions around the housing estate, I found a baby cobra in one of my jogging shoes! This, I found it the hard way when I slipped in my foot into the shoe just to kick it out thinking that there was a cockroach in my shoe. And out slithered out a black baby cobra and stood out looking at me like as if it was taking a photo-shot of me!

I guess the religious people will say that it is time I had a special prayer for Vinayakar and Nagamah! And the priests will be more than willing to carry it out for a small fee, all in praise of God... And to forget the Hanuman whose manifestation appeared a few weeks ago in the study room to squander some cookies. And the believers of Muniswar will call for his appreciation as many dogs wander the road in front of my house to answer nature's call cum territorial markings when their owners decide to let them feel the joy of running against the wind! What about the Persian cat? Egyptian prayers for Cleopatra, perhaps? May be with human sacrifice?FG21.7.10

Matha Pitha Guru Theivam

The Tamil language is famous with its many saying and quotations. The critics will also complain that its literary circle is only full of talk with no action! Not only they just talk, there is also so much of emotion and gestures to complement this. Just like the joke that has been circulating in the Klang Valley...

The Police once arrested an Indian man to help them in their investigations. This handcuffed suspect was brought in to the interrogation room for questioning. In spite of repeated attempts by the junior policemen at questioning, the suspect just would not speak! In frustration, they called in their superior for help. Their seasoned superior just walked in, removed the handcuffs from the suspect and off went the suspect, rattling away complete with hand gestures and facial expressions until the cops told him to shut up.

Another proof of this statement is evidenced in the 'Arratai Arangam' (அரட்டை அரங்கம்) - a Tamil talk show (from Tamil Nadu) on Malaysian cable TV. Speakers on this show, who would normally be discussing social issues relevant to Tamil Nadu would sometimes be so emotional and loud that the moderator has to step in to put the house in order. The outbursts, however, are puny by Jerry Springer Show's standards! Another favourite topic of their discussion is the glory of old Tamil movies, which just goes on to show how important the celluloid make-believe world is in the Indian culture.

I digress...

The saying 'Matha Pitha Guru Theivam' is taught to most elementary students in Tamil school, Tamil language classes and Hindu devotional classes. The words translate to 'Mother, Father, Teacher and God' — that is the easy part.

There are many interpretations of this elementary saying. At a glimpse, the phrase seems to denote the hierarchy of importance in a person's life: Matha (Mother) is at the pinnacle of importance, source of unconditional and unassuming love; followed by Pitha (Father) — the provider; then comes the Guru (teacher) — who would open our eyes and mind to the world outside; and finally Theivam (God) for divine guidance.

Another interpretation would be that this is the order in which an individual goes through from cradle to adulthood. And another is that God is the final destination, and all the others are our vehicle to reach our destiny. Some say that our mother, father and teachers are the God that we can see. The bottom line is that all the above-mentioned people deserve our undying respect and support. That would bring us to another topic — filial piety.FG27.7.10

Situational comedy (Sitcom): Not funny no more!

Just the other day, I was watching two sitcoms back to back in the morning — episodes of '2 and a half men' and 'How I met your mother'. For the inhabitants of the Stone Age who are not familiar with these shows — '2 and a half men' is acted by the dysfunctional Charlie Sheen as a drunkard womaniser who shares his house with his 'forever broke' dysfunctional and gullible divorced brother with a pre-teen son who sometimes stays with him. They have a sarcastic housekeeper with an attitude and a nymphomaniac daughter who is a single mother. On the episode that I watched, the subject revolved around what the son overheard from his mother's bedroom when she was with her current live-in partner!

'How I met your mother' is a story of 5 late 20s friends - 3 guys and 2 girls; 1 couple is a pair who are living together, another couple use to date but have separated and the remaining fornicates with anyone who carries the XX chromosome! This group will forever be discussing facts of lives in a pub sipping alcoholic beverages. On that episode that I saw, the dilemma was that the promiscuous friend had bedded the other friend's ex-girlfriend, hence had broken the brotherhood code (bro code).

The glaring similarity between the two episodes was in their themes of adult nature. First of all, the sitcoms are hardly suitable for daytime viewing. The script (conversation) was not sexual innuendos but in fact point blank in your face. This is coming from a country which boasts of being a Christian nation in God they trust and would go into crusades to live their way of living. And a country which has a large so-called 'Bible belt' states. Is it not ironic?

Whatever happened to sitcoms of yesteryears, albeit churned from Hollywood with canned laughter but carves a smile or two on its audience without stooping so low (sic) as to talk about sex, sex and sex all the time. The above-mentioned sitcoms make the old sitcoms look like episodes from 'Sesame Street' and 'The Electric Company'. In fact, the teenage Disney sitcoms today are like sitcoms of the 70s and 80s. Am I missing something here? I feel like I have been through a time warp or cocoon and the world just slipped by. I miss real situational comedies like 'Gilligan's Island', 'Beverly Hillbillies', 'I love Lucy', 'I dream of Jeannie', 'Bewitched', 'MASH', 'Gomer Pyle', 'Happy Days', 'Laverne and Shirley', 'One day at a time', 'Different Strokes', 'Facts of life' and 'Brady Bunch'. Does it mean that as the lady's swimming suit gets smaller over the years, we have fewer things to hide and nothing is taboo anymore and anything can be out in the open? Is taboo a taboo word now?

It does not take a rocket scientist to pen jokes of sexual nature but it takes a lot wit and brain matter to come up with witty real funny situational comedies as it used to be in most British comedies. In that sense, their trans-Atlantic counterparts fared much better with their evergreen efforts like 'Yes, Minister', 'Black Adder', 'Mr Bean' and more.

True, we should move with the times like Bob Dylan said, 'Times are a changing'. However, certain things are better left mysterious and the search for it more gratifying!FG2.8.10

Mad about myself?

There I was minding my own business without disturbing anybody, quietly typing my two sens worth of worthless opinions which was not going to change the destiny of mankind but to provide light comic relief to my die-hard followers. Sometimes I do wonder if they are smiling (?laughing) with or at me!

Anyway, after last StarMag's column in the Sunday Star newspaper, my family members have unanimously decided that my appropriate place is in the loony bin. They have collectively diagnosed me to suffer from NPDS (Narcissistic Personality Disorder Syndrome). Sufferers of this disorder are said to be self-absorbing individuals who think very highly of themselves, put themselves on a self-made pedestal and forever think themselves as being better than others and find gratification and satisfaction by other's praises.

That is the problem, isn't it? There is a thin line between ingenuity and lunacy. Some professions survive because of narcissistic attributes-movie industry, beauty pageant, maybe law too! Modern society has also encouraged its young by praising their effort even if it is the most horrendous painting or singing. Blind criticism is discouraged as it retards imagination and development of inner potentials. The child who has been thinking very highly of himself, not knowing where he actually stands because grading and placing in classes are taboo (so old school). So, in a way, the society actually encourages narcissism. On top of that, the Western society encourages individualism. Everybody is talking about 'my right', 'my life', 'my wish', unlike the traditional Eastern cultures that were set to continue the status quo, to serve and care the elders and society at large.

Anyway, modern medicine is known to create diseases that non-existent. Oh, you are 80 and you don't have a good sex life — you must having erectile dysfunction, then you will need Viagra. Oh, you are 70 and your knees ache, the synovial fluids must have reduced — you need Viatril-S. Oh, you are 60 and you have wrinkles — you need Botox. Oh, you are 50 and you have been eating like a pig all your life and your belly is hanging like an apron — you need a tummy tuck. And have you noticed how the recommended cholesterol levels at which medications are instituted have reduced over the years and the big drug companies are laughing all the way to the bank?

And how the medical (especially psychologists) have labelled certain defence mechanism at various professions — e.g. murderers sublimate to be surgeons, robbers become bank tellers, sexual perverts become gynaecologists, people who find it hard to communicate with fellow human become animal right activists!

And do not forget how anyone who opposes the Kremlin is labelled as schizophrenic in the iron curtain days.

Well, anyone can say what they want. Don't worry die-hard followers, the hits will keep on rolling....like the number of new diseases that they are going to come up with!FG26.8.10

Caught in a time warp

On a quiet Friday afternoon, I dropped in my relative's office as I was passing by that area. Something like how a mafia henchman drops in at the boss' place to show respect! Anyway, just to say 'hi' and 'bye'. The Man was not in so I ended up with a tete-a-tete with his high-society daughter. After the usual pleasantries, the conversation swayed on to her two children's education in an international school. The high heeled Madame managed to enlighten the poor relative on the latest happenings in an international school these days. It was indeed an eye opener!

The catch phrase these days in the educators' circle seem to be to protect the psyche of the students and to refrain from creating an aversion to school. In other words, bend over backwards to keep the children happy and to put up with all their tantrums. It is a cardinal sin to ever upset their feelings. Learning should be a pleasurable experience for them with no dent in their individual self-esteem (ego). Students cannot be reprimanded for making mistakes in class and in their worksheet. They are not required to do corrections for errors in their school work. They do not have to sit for dictation. Red ink cannot be used to mark books as again it will upset them and maybe they would not like to come to school. At the end of the term test, they would not be given placing in class as again it may crush their little egos and may retard their self-development. It appears to me that we are dealing with whiny spoilt bred babies and the educators are retarding their growth to adulthood with the ability to endure trials, tribulations, competitions, failures and what not which is seen in the real dog eat dog world!

The good thing offered by the school is the exposure that the students get in the fields of games, drama and music. Being dissatisfied with the pace and depth of studies, the family members and private tutors were roped in to provide patch up work to fill up the deficiencies in the private school system so as to prepare a well-rounded education for her kids to face the real world. And mind you, both kids have not reached double digits in their ages yet!

Hey! Looks like things have not changed much from RRF days. You still depended on tuition teachers and tuition classes even if you are in international schools. And guess what; even tertiary students in college and universities in the Klang Valley employ tuition teachers to teach them. These tuition-teacher dependent varsity students are going to lead some multinational companies and perhaps rule the country one day. Scary!!!FG5.9.10

"Mr. Watson, come here! I need you!"

The famous first words spoken by Dr Alexander Graham Bell to his assistant, Mr. Thomas Watson on the first phone.

A mobile phone rings when a lady is undergoing a gynaecological examination in a gynae clinic. What would a normal warm blooded vertebrate educated of a Malaysian lady worth of her salt do in a delicate and personal situation as this? Well, pick up the phone and start yakking while the good doctor finishes his work, what else (duh!).

In another instance, after waiting for 40 minutes to see a doctor for a 2-minute consultation, the phone rings. Again the good Malaysian says, "Sorry ah!" and goes into a frenzy answering his call walking aimlessly around the consultation room talking on top of his voice oblivious to happenings of the surroundings. I am just waiting for a day for someone to walk out his house or clinic naked as most people go into a trance once their cell phone rings. In fact at one juncture,the Mayor of New York was contemplating banning the usage of cell phones in its streets due to abnormally high incidences of road vehicle accidents involving pedestrians-on-phones who tend to forget the cardinal rule of crossing the road — look before you leap!

In the cozy ambiance of a cineplex in Kuala Lumpur, a cell phone rings at the height of the climax before the intermission of a Hindi movie. A Bangladeshi answers his call on top of his voice telling directions to his caller trying to outdo the decibels emitted by the crying heroine in the movie. How do I know he is giving directions? It cannot be anything else when he says right, left, *Puduraya* and *Leboh Ampang* in the same breath.

Recently it was heard on RTM *Minnal* news that the Malaysian Hindu Sangam had advised all temple committees all over the country to ban the use of mobile phones in temples. Its president reiterated that some ringtones are obviously too sultry to be heard in public, what more in the divine house of God. In my humble opinion, it is aimed at the humble servants of God who decided to give up everything in life for service of God. The priests, being human as they are, are sometimes tempted to answer his ringing phone while performing his religious obligations at the altar as curiosity takes the better of them! Somehow the idiot phone can be a nuisance as it always seems to ring at the most inconvenient time.

Taking about ringing at an embarrassing moment, I once received a phone call while answering nature's call on the other end (pun not intended). In midst of the conversation, I used the flush. The caller on the other side of the line was curious on the sound to which I replied, "You do not want to know!"

These days everyone is clinging on to a cell phone from a vagabond and a pauper to a CEO. To them, every call is a billion dollar deal struck and they have to answer it against all odds. The sales assistants at the departmental stores and the security guards seem more interested in cyber-friend than giving undivided attention to their jobs — i.e. answering to customers' demands or manning their sentry posts respectively.

I am sure Dr Alexander Graham Bell, his assistant Mr. Thomas Watson and Elisha Gray (who invented the telephone about the same time, but lost in the patent ownership after a long legal battle) did not envisage these problems when they embarked on their discovery.

That just reminds us of the Digi newspaper Chinese New Year advertisement where all the family members at the dinner table are busy tied to their phones on their ears giving two hoots to the true spirit of the reunion.

Every technology will eventually find its true place in society. Whatever happened to the ever popular spiralling toy of the 70s, Yoyo? It used to be every child's dream birthday or Christmas present just to be lost in the annals of time. This time around the new found toy seems to excite not only the young but the grown-ups alike, with internet facilities tied to it. It looks set to revolutionise the way we live in (for good or worse) and helps to satisfy our ever increasing appetite for instant gratifications! One guy in New York actually delivered his child in the traffic jam stranded cab with things he picked up on 'You Tube'.

Maybe the way we, Asians, are acting with the phone issue is because we are the nouveau riche and are becoming self-centred. With time and education, phone etiquette may eventually be second nature.FG9.9.10.

Nice to hear but... in reality?

Here we are talking about equality and that we are all one. It is nice to talk when your next meal is non-brainer and your children and family is in the pink of health and the price increase of sugar by 20 sen means nothing to you. But, to a manual worker or a security guard who earns RM 2 per hour toiling day and night, everyday is survival!

Take a look at the example of one of the security guards working in Hospital TAR, Klang who was gunned down by a not so friendly fire by his working colleague recently. Instead of upholding serenity in the hospital, there themselves appear to need hospitalisation. The deceased 22-year-old guard and his 37-year-old mother were employed by the same company as colleagues. This 22-year-old man actually supports his mother and his siblings as well as being married to a bank teller with a 14-year-old daughter. In the newspaper interview, the mother of the victim described the debilitated state of her financial status — the family was depending on the son's security guard pay to service the house loan monthly. Even with his paycheque, their utility bills have been outstanding for many months.

This event also reminded me a scenario which I witnessed many years ago in the same hospital. It involved two hospital attendants — an Indian and a Malay. The Indian lady was waiting impatiently for her bus which was late as usual. Along came her colleague, a Malay attendant, in her spanking new *Kancil* to offer her a ride. I am sure the first attendant will be wondering, "How come both of us are of the same strata at work, she can afford a car while I can't?" Of course there may be many reasons for this. Her husband could be earning well, well-planned family finances, perpetually living on credit, keeping up with the Joneses or just plain show off! It is very easy to complain along racial lines and how the Government is forever helping 'them' from cradle to grave. But then, you must ask why the foreigners who come here menial work are doing so well with their finances.

It is easy to whine. We should never forget that the Nazis' hatred of the Jews stemmed from the fact that their frugal calculative way of living managed to weather even the worse of the depressive times. In spite of the various restrictions in doing business, they got around the system to excel through sheer hard work.

Anywhere in this world, we have marginalised groups of citizens who are forever at the bottom rung of the society. It is up to them to give a kick to themselves to jump start into a new future.

We are one if we chose to be, for better for worse. Simone Groove*

*Simone Groove - Zulu. African National Congress' (ANC) call to all South Africans to unite when apartheid ended in 1994. Of course, it was a political slogan, much like 1Malaysia, meaning we are all one. In 1997, when my sister in law got married in Durban, South Africa, I delivered a speech on behalf of the Malaysian entourage. This term was included in the closing remarks of my speech much to the delight of the audience who were mainly ANC supporters! FG12.9.10.

Behind the veil

Recently, one of email buddies sent me a powerpoint presentation on the ordeals of the ladies behind the meshed veil of the burqa had to endure in a male dominated society all in the name of man's own interpretation of the religion. Their voices are muffled by the sobbing sounds of their unheard cries in the dark.

That got me thinking....

In fact, in our own everyday world close to us, there are many amongst us who walk around putting up a front covering the sorrows that they carry behind the mask that they wear on their faces. Just like they say in show business, "Honey, the show has to go on!", life has to go on...

I know a general practitioner, who is forever ready with his pearly white teethed smile, was diagnosed with cancer of the urinary bladder about 2 years previously. He is still smiling these days after enduring 12 hours of radical surgery, nauseating chemotherapy afterwards, losing erectile and ejaculatory functions, losing his bladder and using a stomal bag for urinary functions. And he is still practicing medicine to treat others as well as to provide for his young family.

Just like a lady that I know who only moves in high society, attending one party after another. Her younger sister is an equally high-heeled jet trotting executive in a successful multinational company. The youngest sibling, unable to live up to the sisters' mark lost the rat race and was labelled a schizophrenic. Struggling to manage himself, he needs the help of his ailing mother for guidance. But how long? So much of anxiety...

So the next time when you are in a situation where someone is hogging the road and you are in a hurry, take a step back and ponder. You do not know what hopeless situation he may be in. His wife could have died or something worse. You do not know what trouble he is in. Maybe you do not want to be in his shoes.

Or the annoying man who is talking on top of his voice in a school concert in an unknown language. Maybe it is not because he lacks common phone etiquette or common sense, he may be in hot soup. Like they say, "I was complaining that I have no nice shoes to wear till I saw a man with no legs!"

Everybody wears a mask to face the real world. Do you seriously think that the runners-up in the Miss World is all joy and smiles for losing the crown or the worker who laughs it away when his boss reprimands him?

We want everything to be perfect for us but in reality we have to live with the imperfection that is endowed upon us and to get the best out of the less than perfect to newer heights.FG5.10.10

Legacy Lost?

Early this morning, S, our local pious man, (vegetarian, bearded and forever in a kurta, a practical Indian wear) dropped at our gates to request for a place to host the *Navarathri* prayers at our house. I politely declined as it was a last minute request and the house was raging with exam fever!

Since we started living in this Taman more than 10 years ago, a *bhajan* group comprising some adults but mostly school children equipped with musical instruments and percussions, under the auspices of S's father (*Masterji*, as he known as he taught classical Indian singing and could speak Hindi, as well), went from selected house to house singing devotional song on the 9 days of Navarathri (the 9 auspicious days to worship the Goddesses Durga, Lakshmi and Saraswati). Coincidentally, the Chinese people have a similar 9-day celebration for Goddess Kwan Ying, the Goddess of Mercy! The reception for 'carolling' group used to be so overwhelming that the sessions used to go on till past midnight. That was then... *Masterji* and his right-hand man, NS, passed on a couple of years ago. And the *Navarathri bhajan* group has come to this. All dressed up and nowhere to go!

What happened? Has S failed in continuing his father's legacy or have people changed their priorities? Have achieving good results and enjoying worldly comfort superseded the need to improve our karma standings in the afterlife?

We have to remember that *Masterji* was a retired man with time in his hands. S has a full-time job to attend to and a young and growing family to be fed and educated. Charity and divine deeds start at home first!

Talking about continuing the old man's legacy, I just remembered my old barber, Lingam who succumbed to a heart attack 3 or 4 years ago. When he was alive, he ran a small barber shop near our Taman. He was a mild-mannered man who had only nice things to say about everything. This is a stark anomaly to most of the Indian barbers that we are accustomed to, who are strongly opinionated and you tend to agree with them as they would be holding a blade at your jugular!

Lingam's had a small following of loyal customers who actually sang praises of his simpleton way of life and his cordialness in a letter to the editor of our national newspaper. As always, all good things came to an end. Like Joni Mitchell sang in Big Yellow Taxi..."Don't it always seem to go, that you don't know what you've got till it's gone...They paved paradise, And put up a parking lot...." Lingam died after his first fatal attack at the age of 54. (What do you know, you cannot have a second fatal attack, can you? You only live once. He had been a diabetic but kept himself trim. His morbidly over-sized chronically lethargic wife with a plethora of diseases has outlived him thus far. Perhaps, God wanted Lingam to be by his side to meet to his tonsorial needs up in heaven!

Lingam sudden demise caught the family by surprise. His heir was a 17-year-old teenager who had bigger plans on his mind — undergraduate and law studies and so forth. So, the widow hired some young punks to continue the business. After some disagreement, she got an elderly man to run the show. After a few no-shows by the replacement barber, the premises is now permanently shut. And all the loyal followers have moved on to other barbers around there. Life goes on...another legacy lost! I suppose that is why many renowned figures around the world are grooming their young ones to take over their legacy.FG12.10.10.

Public declaration of private intent!

Most of the time wedding reception dinner speeches are boring. Nobody, except maybe the bride and the groom actually pay attention to what the speaker has to say. I suppose that is why I distinctly remember what my brother-in-law spoke on the occasion, the beginning at least! He started his speech by saying that a wise man once said that a wedding is actually a public declaration of private intentions. Though deemed unpalatable to be spoken in public, this 'tongue-in-cheek' kind of dictum may not hold water anymore.

Most young couples of the 21st century, have private intent on their mind first when casually meeting someone and like to get away as soon as it is over. Making a declaration, what more a public one, is the last thing on their minds! Wedding celebrations as it stays now remain a public declaration of private intentions by legitimising private activities behind closed doors.

I remember hearing a joke many years ago of how a sociology student was conducting a study in a small town. Part of his task was to fill up a questionnaire about the number of children and marital status of ladies in that town. He approached the first lady to ask, "Are you married?" She replied, "Not yet." And the next question was, "How many children?" BAM!!! He got a slap on his face! Obviously shaken by the encounter, he changed his strategy when he interviewed his next subject. He asked, "Any children?" The interviewee replied, "Yeah, 3 children!" And then he asked, "Are you married?" BAM!!! Came another slap on the other cheek! The student dropped his papers and abandoned the research altogether. Apparently, in that conservative society, it seems blasphemous to mention about having kids out of wedlock. In most societies, within a single generation, how things have changed!

Now, the British tabloids and citizens alike, have gone agape over the recent announcement of the imminent royal wedding between Prince William and a commoner with just as many limbs and appendages by the name of Kate Middleton, as if they have nothing else better to look forward to in life. Their parents too went 'gaga' in 1981 during the Charles-Diana union which eventually came to zilch with mentions of adultery, infidelity and fornication. But it was all right since it was done by the blue-blooded.

People of my generation would have a sense of déjà vu looking at the recent turn of events. Almost 30 years ago, every teenage girls dream was to have a wedding like Diana's, long pristine white dress with long bevy of toddlers following faithfully behind, horse carriage, roses and all. It looks like history is going to repeat itself, that is, if you believe what soothsayers of many beliefs have to say. In unison, they all see gloom and doom of the marriage which would not last more than 7 years. Hey, life is not that easy. We have to work hard to make it happen. That will be a wee bit difficult for the royal family - They do not work for a living!!! Anyway, some private things are better left private to the privacy of consenting adult and their private lives behind closed doors or closets... FG25.11.10

What's TRUTH got to do with it

Many a time all of us may have been caught in a betwixt and between situations where we are in the middle of two warring factions. Most of the time, we are at a lost as both factions seem to have some justifications in the way they behaved and the way the other did!
The truth of the matter must lie somewhere in the middle as I have come to understand that things in life are neither black nor white. It is usually in shades of grey. I was caught in a similar situation not too long ago.
A was happily employed by B for many years with both parties respecting each other, enjoying each other's company and the relationship was more than just an employer-employee one but rather to that of close friends' one. A was single handedly running and taking care of the company as if it were his own. It was during this time I came to know A and B. I got along well with both parties. Over the years, things soured up between A and B. By B's standards, A was becoming laggard and slip shot in his work and cutting corners. According to A, on the other hand, B was easily irritable and petty, made worse when his business hit a rough patch and things were generally slow moving and income was dwindling. From A's point of view, B was becoming a fussy old man with an unpredictable predicament. After many ugly incidences, both decided to go different ways. A quit and another employee took over A's post. Towards the tail end of the employment, I was caught in the middle with each party trying to tell their side of the story and try to get me to see

their side of the story in the hope of condoning their respective actions. I managed with occasional non-committed "Oh!"s, "Is it?"s and half hearted "Yeah"s. It managed to have worked as I am still friends with both parties, one year down the line.

Misunderstandings are bound to happen in any relationships, to err is human; to forgive but divine! Innocent bystanders should not take sides. We should not enjoy the side show but rather just savour the good moments. The last thing that you want is both the warring factions teaming up and pointing their arsenal at your direction! Sometimes it is better to be like the weeds (*lallang*) in the meadows that sway and play to the tune of the direction of the winds. Do not take sides, just enjoy the good moments and stock up in the huge memory bank and savour it later. What has truth got to do with it at all? That's all!FG16.12.10.

The ballad of Amoi and Thangachi

We finally collected the framed picture from Ms Loh's shop. Over the years, we have seen Ms Loh mature and prosper from a petite 17-year-old girl who started working as a clerk in a shop which made photo frames and mirrors. After learning the nooks and corners of the business while working in the same premises over the past 10 years, she has finally opened a new shop after renting a shop lot in a new housing estate. Ms Loh is now running the business with her husband who is also giving a helping hand. She seems quite excited about the business and we wish her all the best for her boldness in entering the shark eat shark world of business!

Ms Laxmi also completed her studies at the same year as Ms Loh. Not performing as well as she should, to continue her studies; she started to work as an assistant nurse in a clinic. Over the next 10 years, she got hitched, started her family, become a mother of 3 children but remained put in her place of employment (her employer is so nice!), performing the same job but with more experience but a leader among her peers. Her salary had increased marginally to commensurate her years of faithful employment, but she sees herself at a sort of dead end. She would probably be doing the same job till she decides to call it quits.

Here you can see the different paths taken by two individuals after secondary education. One has become an entrepreneur of sorts whilst the other remains contended with her simple job. We have seen many Ms Lohs and Ms Laxmis in daily lives.

People who are not bold enough to improve their living standards or are constantly expecting handouts from the others or living on self-pity will and are always complaining that the powers that be is not doing enough to help them or that the community is not doing enough to help their ethnic group. At the end of the day, the western movies' words of wisdom come to mind — 'a man got to do what a man got to do'. FG25.1.11

A giant step into the past?

Neil Armstrong's' famous lines as he set foot on the moon (that is if you believed that he actually did) on 21st July 1969 were, 'A small step for mankind, a giant step for mankind!'

The newspaper today complains about men hogging the ladies-only LRT coaches in the city. I remember watching Tamil movies where they apparently had public buses only meant for ladies in Chennai after the ladies there had been constantly disturbed, cat-called, groped and touched inappropriately by the highly sex-strung Indian men who could not keep their hands to themselves. Or maybe the ladies were so conceited (they thought that they were such ravaging beauties) that they thought every man on the street were out get them under! They also had Police Station manned (or rather womaned) by an all female crew so that women would not shy away from reporting sexual crimes. The powers that be did not want the female complainant to be sexually disadvantaged and be seen as being sexually harassed by the male police personnel.

Malaysian ladies think that by successfully getting an all female LRT or bus service in the city, it is a feather in the cap for the bra-burners and is seen as an advancement as far as progression of species is concerned. I am sorry, but I beg to differ.

From time in memoriam, women had been playing second fiddle to men, at least in the eye of the public. What happens behind closed is left to individual's own interpretation. They were never seen to be in the limelight but rather play their roles subtly in the background. Decisions concerning communities and countries were left to the male gender. Only in the early 20th century were women considered mature enough to cast their votes to elect their leaders in elections. That is if you do not believe Dan Brown's proposition in the 'Da Vinci Code' of the world before Christianity ruled. He argues that in the pagan world, man offered special status to women due to their ability to generate life within their bodies. The modern religions of the world apparently changed all that and women lost everything.

Slowly but surely with time, the fairer sex have made their presence felt and their voices have been starting to be heard louder and louder over the globe. They have made their way to the universities, held high esteemed positions rivalling men eye to eye and even led big democracies demanding society to treat them as equal partners rather than upon whom they trampled upon.

All these victories and achievements appear to have come to zilch. It seems that now they have to be protected from prancing males who looks like not seem to be giving due respects but instead treat them as toys to satisfy their visual and tactile gratifications.

The more they are protected, the more the predators will yearn for the forbidden fruit. Get real! Women are smart enough to take care of themselves. What I want to know is that whether they are going to have special transportation for the third sex soon?FG27.1.11

Puppets on a string....

"Not bad," I thought to myself. After being unconscious for a month since first day of *Aidilfitri*, being in the twilight of things in a world of paranoia, delusions and hallucinations afterwards, recovering from nosocomial infections, recovering from cellulitis after a poorly set infusion line, pressure sores and still recovering from weakness of both upper and lower limbs, it is nice to see FM alert, jovial and poking fun at himself after five months of hospitalisation! And I have not got to the point of asking of his experience after 12 cardiac arrests. And he has not even completed his narration of his escapades in the four different hospitals in the Klang Valley. He attributes his victory so far to good deeds that he must have done and God is slowly deducting them one by one. Looks like he has a lot of catching up to do to replenish his good records after this ordeal is all over!

Being a cardio-thoracic surgeon himself, he has had the first-hand experience of a sick patient in a very precarious position. The whole experience has been a very humbling one for him (and all of us as well). At least in his first month of his illness he was unconscious (to be worried about himself).

He actually was stricken by a mild febrile illness after a week of field-trip at the edge of the jungle with his medical students. It later progressed to a quite scary form of meningoencephalitis (infection of the brain and its covering).

I do not plan to be a spoilsport. FM plans to write his memoir on the events of his ailment after he has made of full recovery and we will all hear it from the horse's mouth. With his fighting spirit, that faithful day is quite imminent. One take home message; we whine, we cringe, we fret, we complain, we demand, we prosecute for our rights but at the end of the day, our lives are so vulnerable like a puppet on a string. Like the Malay proverb says, *'Telur di hujung tanduk'*!FG28.1.11.

I had a dream, then I grew up!

Pussycat Dolls (PCD) once sang... "When I grow up, I wanna be famous, I wanna be a star, I wanna be in movies! When I grow up, I wanna see the world, drive nice cars, I wanna have groupies!"

Martin Luther King Jr. had a dream that one day over the rose hills of Georgia, sons of former slaves and former slave owners will be able to sit together in the table of Brotherhood and that his four children would not be judged by the colour of their skin but by the content of their character!

Dream merchants like Walt Disney gave people a form of escapism through his Mickey Mouse, Goofy and Donald Duck characters. Soichiro Honda managed to pull his war torn bankrupt and defeated nation to be at par with its victors till of recent. From a humble bicycle repair shop, his company is now venturing into artificial intelligence and robotics!

I too had a dream... which remains a dream.

Growing up in the post May 13 era, what was fed on the mass media to us was pure propaganda and we were all made to accept it as the gospel truth. We were made to understand that everything was hunky dory and the Government was serious in their zest to eradicate poverty and foster muhibbah (interracial understanding) via their 5 year plans, paving the way to make this country a developed nation by 2020. Soaked in that kind of hope day in and day out, I actually envisaged Malaysia to be clean, mild weathered, modern, its courteous mild mannered smiling educated citizens in impeccable designer clothes talking to each other without malice and suspicion, with skyscrapers, shiny expensive vehicles streaming the seamless highway to everywhere. Then the bubble burst and there was a reality thud on my head!

Fast forward to the 21st century and a decade later... What do we have now?

Poverty eradicated? I think it is far from it. Over the years, a new set of obnoxiously nouveau riche have emerged. They have no qualms about throwing their orange peels out of their chauffeur driven imported cars. The poor are still aplenty in the form of some who were displaced off their homes in the name of development. There are also many illegal immigrants who either ran away from their legal employers to become illegals or came via trawler boats under cover of darkness of the night to occupy strips of land (settlements) in the edge of city where even police fear to enter. Thanks to the lax or non-existent enforcements, these settlements prosper. They may appear poor but they have loads of cash stashed away to be sent home. Just wait for a mishap to happen, either in the form of disease outbreak (the children do not complete the mandatory vaccinations) or violence to happen before heads will roll. But, will they?

Malaysians, generally have improved by giant strides from an economic stance but there will always be a small recalcitrant group who would forever indulge in self pity and escapism. There are still people wondering around town with no identification papers. Communication between Malaysians is still an issue as it was in the newly independent Malaya. Young adults, in spite of completing Malaysian education system still need interpreters when dealing with civil servants just like their grandparents did 50 years previously.

Skyscrapers we have but its maintenance leaves much to be desired. We employ security guards who are too old, too sick, too incompetent to hold any other job or foreigners.

Wearing short pants, singlet and Japanese slippers could get you anywhere in the 60s and 70s. Fashion sense has not changed much since.

Throngs of visitors to malls, clinics, offices are still dressed like this; just that the fashion police would say it is cool, trendy and metro-sexual. Anyway, their idols on Hollywood and Californians also dress like that and we are both in hot climates! Well, the 'holier-than-thou' Government offices have strict guidelines on dressing at their premises. They have set their air-conditioners way down low to be dressed down.

People are still suspicious of each other. In those days, it was whether you were a communist; now it is general stereotyping and that the other is going to cheat them blind. It is compounded by many foreign 'students' promising to convert white paper to green back (USD)! Just see how many Malaysians drug mule girls are counting bars caged in foreign gaols from Japan to Peru. Why is the word 'students' is in inverted commas? That is because these so called students do not act like students. They wear branded clothes smelling of expensive perfumes splashed all over the body liberally, sporting buff muscular physique, forever with their female company and drinking alcoholic beverage like a fish drinking water. They pay their bills from a stash of RM50 bills. These 'scholarly students' do not speak very good English for a start. Can you imagine students of English courses describing their predicament as, "My stomach is paining me, Doctor!"? And what is this with their frequent treatments for sexually related ailments? And have the local girls going hand and glove with them?FG24.2.11

Oh! When the brain goes down the drain!

So as usual, at this time of the year, the local newspapers will be plastered with news of how great the public examinations results were. They will give a breakdown of how the overall percentage of the result had improved. It is beginning to sound like a re-run of an old soap opera or broken gramophone record — just like me, too!

There would soon be pictures of handicapped students passing with flying colours and children of hawkers and seamstresses obtaining good results.

A few days after that the announcement would be out on the closing date of applications for scholarship and entrance to universities. Like clockwork, a few days after the results of acceptance of the above, flashed again on the newspapers, would be disgruntled parents who will be complaining about how his kids with such exemplary results failed to secure a place and how excellent his extra-curricular results were. Then Michael Chong (the Public Complaints bureau of Malaysian Chinese Association) would appear in the national daily posing with the result slip, rejection letter, forlorn parents and kids. Then there would be knee jerk responses from ruling and opposition political leaders.

All these would die a natural death when Singapore offers them scholarships on a carrot attached to a long string. And this disgruntled students will leave their motherland, vowing never to return, eternally grateful to their 'Newfoundland'. Little will they realise that even if they wanted to, they would be tied down with a long pay-back clause that by the time the tenure expires, they would be too cushy there with probably too big an extra baggage to come back home to Malaysia (which disappointed them, anyway)!FG24.2.11.

Centre of the universe

Hindu mythology has it that Lord Shiva's consort Parvati had a special fruit (*Gnana Pazham*) that she wanted to give to either of her sons, Ganesha and Murugan. It could not be divided half as its magical power would be lost. Hence, Parvati decreed that the first child to go across the universe would receive the booty. Murugan, using his peacock as his vehicle, flew across the universe in no time to claim his loot. When he returned, he was furious when Ganesha had already received the fruit as he circled his parents, claiming that his parents were his entire universe. That made Murugan raving mad and left home sulking in a self-exile in Palani Hills. The hill was named '*Pazham Nee*' (Palani, that he was the fruit of wisdom) by Shiva to cajole Murugan back but in vain.

Nicolaus Copernicus and Galileo Galilei had to retract their scientific discovery that the Earth was in fact not the centre of the universe. The church, I guess, wanted to be in the centre of things and have the final say!

Just like that, the children nowadays have the unshakeable notion that they are the centre of the universe and the sun actually sets for them and they deserve everything to be done for them. If you go to any mall or public place, you may encounter toddlers terrorising and their imbecile parents (mostly fathers) running around like jokers trying to keep up with their whims and fancies. This will also complemented by grandparents (if there are up to it) to feed them with the more sugary drinks to make them more a brat than they already are! Probably, these grandparents are trying to repair their dented image after being a tyrant with their children a generation previously. The sum of all these is a child with narcissistic tendency and delusion of grandiosity.FG25.2.11.

Winds of Change

One generation ago, parents insisted that children should get dressed on a Sunday morning for a family outing at the temple. Children obediently followed without raising any objections. Without fail, they would diligently follow the proceedings in the temple and partake in their activities.

The newer generation, however, being more vocal and assertive in their likes and dislikes, just stay from the temples as they find more interesting things to do outside the temple during the designated prayer times on Sunday mornings. As more and more youngsters of Generation-Y and beyond are not conversant in their mother tongues, they find the whole proceedings an exercise in futility as the lingua franca in most temple activities and sermons is neither English nor Malay!

To draw back these group of people to the path of righteousness and prevent them from going astray, one the temples I go to occasionally have started to have weekly 20-minute talk by non-religious figures (regular people with regular clothes minus the bodily applications of holy ashes or sandalwood paste) in English on topics related to Hinduism. This particular abode of worship have also started youth dance classes, language classes, social services (to help the needy, not guest relations, of course!) and have even included youngsters in their temple committee!

In another church, the music accompaniment during the services is by a band akin to a rock and roll band. The idea behind this move is to draw the young congregation back to the House of God. In most first world countries, studies have shown that people only go to church on their wedding or somebody's funeral (and theirs too, they are sent to, naturally).

Just like a snake charmer who convinces his spectators that his snakes (who are naturally deaf to sounds) are indeed dancing to their tune, modern day parents are dancing around with snake charmers' flute like madmen trying to get the children do what is good for them as so they perceive. They do not want their dear beloveds to live to regret missing it. But is it really good for them? Who knows? Only time will tell... At least the parents' conscious is clear!FG2.3.11

Tigers, cubs and cats...

Ever since Amy Chua's book, 'The battle hymn of Tiger mothers' started selling at book stands, it created such a brouhaha in most parts of developed (read Caucasian) world. For the rest the world, (because for the media and the US, they are the world and they are the children, just to quote MJ), the strict regimental upbringing is after the only way. Even just two generations ago, children use to hear the mantras-'Spare the rod and spoil the child', 'Children are to be seen and not heard' and even 'Wait till your father gets home!' Things have changed so much so fast before Superman can change into his super hero suit that children all over the world are fast becoming brats! They are now talking about their lives, their wishes, their freedom, their desires, their god-knows-what-else!

Anyway, for the Asians of Generation-X, ferocious mothers were the norm in our development into adolescence and beyond. Asians all our the world, especially if you are an immigrant population tend to try to blend into the society by what better way but through education and brain power, as due to their challenged physique, it seem humanly impossible to outwit their opponents in a face to face duel. Years of natural selection have taught them (their hostile motherland with constant battle with nature and amongst each other) to be *'kiasu'* and disciplined to achieve their ambitions. The proof of this constantly fed to the children by these Tiger mothers in the form story telling and bed time stories.

With evolution of time, with affluence and more exposure to the outside via the media (and Disney Channel), upbringing the Tiger mothers' way has taken a back seat all over the world. And this back seat driver has no say in the way the car is driven and its destination. Just wait and see where it lands up — the ditch or to the immigration checkpoint?

It used to be that these Tigers telling those children, "My way or no way!"; now it is the children telling the Tigers, "Like Frankie said, I did it my way, It's my life!*". The once growling incisors flashing Tigers without choice have now mellowed down to be omnivorous domesticated pussies!FG8.3.11

Holy crap

A few days ago, our newspapers were aghast with news of a *petai* tree in Kepala Batas showering its surroundings with droplets of water. People from near and far flogged to see for themselves and have a taste of the miraculous act of Nature. For a few days, people from many strata of society have given their devout opinion about this new unknown phenomenon which papers called it 'holy water'.

A former lecturer reiterated that it could be bodily secretions of mating cicadas whilst another entomologist claimed that these insects do not splay fluids from the body, at least in such massive quantity. Being entrepreneurial in their own way, some entrepreneurs decided to make a killing by charging RM5 per cup. For all you know, they may be selling pipe water!

Some people have tied 'holy' red cloth to give the tree its due recognition, to please the unknown and give it the divine feel that it needs. Punters predict '*Tua Pek Kong*' (holy spirit) has come to the vicinity and is predicting good fortune in the near future. And hopefully, He would also give them some lucky winning '4D' numbers on the side.

Meanwhile, the Islamic authorities have joined in the bandwagon almost like a knee-jerk reflex to warn Muslims that believing in holy water is 'unholy'. The Consumer Association of Penang, after warning people not to do this and that (from beancurd to *belacan* to ultrasound scanning etcetera), they warned people to be wary of contracting leptospirosis from consuming urine from some unknown animals. A writer to the editor got a brilliant input from his Indonesian domestic helper whose fellow villagers back home had seen many instances as this one. Her scientific brain suggested that that was how a tree expelled excessive water from its system. Her fellow villagers took it as a sign to denote that the vicinity was a fertile ground to dig a well. To disprove the maid's theory, the writer challenged the authorities to dig a well!

This reminds me of how holy ash used to materialise from a certain sage's photograph's feet for a short period of time all the world before the fad died a natural death as fast as it started. In fact, I had the golden opportunity of witnessing this miracle in my sister's abode. Even a few years before that (1995), the world was flabbergasted by the milking drinking antics of Lord Ganesha's statue. The mind boggling thing about the whole affairs was that it occurred simultaneously the world over to stone idols of Lord Ganesha and like clockwork it all stopped short all at once.

Some mumbo jumbo scientists that explained this occurrence by capillary action of the architectural makeup of granite stones of the idol as it did not happen in plastic or other crystal idols. They, however, could not explain why all these stopped just like that without recurrence.

Interestingly exactly 14 years after the milk drinking episode, there was milk vomiting episode which stirred many quarters for they feared that they may have upset or short-changed the Lord in their dealings with or during His birthday celebrations (*Vinayakar Chaturthi*).

Just like the unexplained events that have been happening around us, pretty soon these events will go into our annals of things beyond the comprehension of our simple minds. Maybe some smart paranoid individual may throw in a spanner into our mangled minds of conspiracy theories, alien visitations or even American biological warfare! — Just like the 2004 Boxing day tsunami. Think about it.... The chemical analysis from the floral secretions should be out in 2 weeks or so, In the mean time, let the newspapers start something wacky for us to ponder about.FG10.3.11.

Losing your marbles over the Big Blue Marble!

As far as I can see, the Earth Hour this year was a non-event! At the said time, I was finishing my meal at a Chinese Restaurant enjoying the chef's freshly cooked cuisines. Apparently, the owners were also enjoying brisk business and the last thing on their minds was to off all the lights and chase away all the customers or potentially hungry patrons to his shop. It was bad for business if someone were to choke on a fish bone!

Earlier, just before leaving the house to go off for dinner, my younger son was all excited about contributing to the Earth Hour by dimming all lights. Little did he realise that in the rush to rush off for dinner, he had left his room light and fan on. So, as a responsible parent, I had to educate him on bare facts about preserving Mother Nature. Just like buying expensive gifts on Mothers' Day does not proof your undying love to your mother, saving Mother Nature and reducing carbon footprint is an ongoing daily sacrifice. It is not about shutting down the lights for 1hour a year on Saturday in March and wasting energy 24/7 for the rest of the year. Our every activity hurts the environment in more than one way. Even rampant washing with oxidising detergents hurt her too; and the pesticides that ensure continuous supply of food to our tables; and the fertilisers that upset the nitrogen cycle; and the fossil fuel and so on and so forth.

During the hour of supposed darkness, I had to drive through town to pick my daughter from the other side of town. It seems to me as it was business as usual and there was not an inkling that Earth Hour was in progress.FG27.3.11

Priority! Priority!

The priorities of a society can be determined from its daily activities of its members. Jog through your memory of two telephone booths — one in KL and another in London. The one in KL would have been vandalised, the receiver would be missing or would be detached like a doll without an arm or you could be at the mercy of the machine which would be happy to gobble up all your money for nothing. But that is another story — you would also notice plastered all around the booth are numbers of generous people who are out there to finance your never ending financial woes that have plaguing you at this while at practically a cost of phone call.

In contrast, in a similar setting in London, the booth would be decorated with multi-coloured 'stick-em-on' papers advertising plethora of social services (escort, companionship of sexual nature, of different ethnicity, age, gender, techniques or anything you fancy!)

Now you know where each society's emphasis is. Asians, as all of us are aware, give importance to wealth to climb the strata of society. The rich are worshiped as one with lots of money can do no wrong and money can buy you love, health, sleep, friends, relatives and everything in between. As the Tamil proverb goes, 'At the sight of money, even a corpse would open its mouth!' I suppose in London, its citizens have reached a certain level of comfort in their lives that they can now look into finer things to enjoy life rather than be worried about their daily bread and butter issues as it is their Government of the day's job to do that!

Every now and then, our mainstream media is fluff with tear jerking stories of how families get torn apart and how victims succumb to the shame and the threat of the creditors and decide to take their own lives and spare everybody else of the torment!

Now, since the loan shark issue is a sticky one, what are the authorities doing about it? So far all their endeavours have been in vain. First, they said that all mobile phones (pre-paid and post-paid accounts) need to be registered so that loan sharks who normally display cell phone numbers can be traced. The menace continues, however.

Now, the powers that be are saying that the numbers go unanswered when the enforcement officers called them. I find this difficult to believe — advertisers not answering calls advertised? It is therefore status quo as it is. To add salt to injury, taxpayers now have to fork out money to clean up the mess of garbage contributed by the bills. From January 2011, the City Council of Johore Bahru removed over 31,000 sheets of loan shark advertisement bills there. In Penang, the contractors assigned to perform the same job has stopped doing so as the thousands of ringgit allocated from them is insufficient for the load of rubbish they have to gather!

In the mean time, the sharks are still swimming in a carefree manner in a sea filled with ill gotten stash of moolah...FG8.4.11

Short window of opportunity

The other day, an elderly friend of mine, aged close to being a septuage-narian was telling me about the financial turmoil that he was facing in his life. The last thing I would want to hear is the sob story of another never ending saga of self-pity and tear-evoking hopelessness. I guess I had enough of listening to these melancholic tales throughout childhood and my present vocation. Not having a choice, I offered a sympathetic ear. (Don't know what the Almighty has in store for me; cannot be so cocky!)

He had been under the weather with a debilitating ailment for almost half a year and had somehow made a miraculous recovery, albeit not a complete one. During his illness, he had used up all his savings as his wife's lone income was insufficient to manage his daily expenses and had been living on his brother's hand-outs. Hence, he had to desperately get back on his feet, get to work and bring the bacon home! Whilst listening through all this sad story, (No! he did not ask for money!), my inner heart was just itching to blurt out, "What the heck were you doing all this while, for heaven's sake you were already working when I was still in secondary school. Goodness gracious!" Of course I (being the chicken and non-confrontational person that I am) said nothing like that but instead reassured him that I would try to help in whatever way I can (how fake or what!). Perhaps, my conservative upbringing which en-grained upon me that the younger shall not be rude or the fear or uncer-tainty of what God has up his sleeves for me in the near future probably made me act the way I did.

Then I started thinking...

Life has given all of us opportunities, some more and some less. The window of opportunity is only ajar for a short moment in time. Then it slips away... Sometimes it is not easy to catch back the moment and bring back the glory.

As a child, you are given a decade and a half or so to absorb knowledge and develop all the characters needed to be an adult. After this period of knowledge acquisition, you are required to determine a career path for yourself to indulge for the rest of your life,unless you are a rolling stone which is now perceived to collect moss also (unlike a generation ago when it could not). Once you are settled in a vocation you decide to pur-sue, you only a short window period of about 10 years to prove yourself.

After this point of time, by this you would have reached 40 years of age, it is a matter of expansion and consolidation. It is quite difficult to start all over again. It is like a lady having a baby after 40 - it is difficult to conceive in the first place and if it happens, it is not going to be a stroll in the park but rather a soul-searching, hymns-chanting, frightening walk in the ghetto.FG13.4.11

Tête-à-tête with a Chinaman!

"Damn, these car batteries do not last!" I cursed as my car refused to start as the battery went kaput. Just one and half years and it had reached the end of its lifespan! Being a Sunday afternoon, as all the mechanics in the vicinity were closed, I had to send an SOS message to my good old mechanic, Ah Kwan. He obliged and asked me to pick up one of his workers for rescue.

So, I picked this late 40s worker of Ah Kwan. While driving him to my car, I engaged in a tête-à-tête with him, tea followed after his job was done.

Incidentally, I had just finished reading a small book on the Malaysian Chinese educationist, Mr Lim Lian Geok, who lost his teaching license and citizenship in 1961. It was changing times for Malayan education. After the Barnes' report (to abolish vernacular schools) and later the Rahman and Razak reports (which demanded Malay language as the premier language), there was increased pressure to change the curriculum of Malaysian Chinese education. His overzealous efforts to fight to put Mandarin as one of the official languages of the country and to maintain the status quo in Chinese schools landed him in hot soup with the ruling party. In fact, he started his job as a dedicated teacher and carried a lot of cloud during Tunku's days. He was one of the dignitaries at the 1955 Malacca Talk to draft the country's constitution. Political outplay and supporting the wrong faction landed him in his predicament. Along the way, we read about the infamous (by Dr M's standards, whom he called communist) Dong Jiao Zong which is an alliance between Chinese school teachers and directors of Chinese School committee. After reading the book, I realised that we as a country are still arguing about the same basic things like language and education like we did more than half a century ago.

So, what did I gather from my little Tête-à-tete with my Chinaman friend?

He seems very savvy about the current happenings in the country, probably you have to give credit to the Chinese media and the evening newspapers. Now you know why suddenly cars stop in the middle of nowhere in the evening traffic jam — it is either to buy papers, to buy 4D results chit or to watch any accident on the other side of the road, as if there is more to lighten up their mundane life!

Ah Keng, the worker, grew up with his rubber tapper family in Kuala Pilah, Negeri Sembilan. He was narrating in many words about his carefree childhood days and his experience in indulging in various exotic meats like snakes, wild boar, fox, frogs, dog and even monkeys! He simply cannot imagine how he managed to swallow the monkey meat then!

The conversation then went on to Botak Chin as we were passing Jalan Ipoh where Chin used to reside. As told by many, he too thinks that Botak Chin was 'Robin Hood' — robbing the rich to help the poor. Ah Keng had very strong views about his political stand and his distrust of others was quite apparent from his conversation. His son decided neither to follow his father's nor his grandfather's footsteps and have ventured into air conditioning maintenance business.

My conversation also reminded me how things have not changed. We were still talking in broken conversational pidgin Malay (bahasa pasar) in many syllables of 'L's instead of 'R's as did our grandfathers 50 years previously.FG20.4.11

Money CAN buy me love, memories and everything in between!

Heard it through the grapevine that our man who co-wrote the song *"Can't buy me love"* has found love again and is trying the matrimonial noose again! But why, I wonder *at 69* to an old girlfriend? Hopefully this time he would be lucky or at least would not be the *sentimental fool on the hill* again but wiser in separating money and love. Earlier, believing that the element of love would be tainted by having a prenuptial agreement, he found out the hard way after being bruised, battered, ridiculed and losing a million pounds that love won't do but *all that she wants* is your *money*. It is interesting to note our MBE has recovered and recouped from his just ended ugly smack down with his former beau who he was throwing dirt and washing dirty linen in public and is star-struck so soon. And decided to take the plunge again! *Obladi, Oblada, life goes on...*

Somebody told me recently that best things in life are indeed not free. Ask anybody about the best time they had in their life or about their best event that sticks on their minds. Invariably, it will be a trip to a far away hideaway, a joyous holiday, away from work, a family reunion of sorts-birthday, wedding etcetera, etcetera. Trying taking all your love ones to a paid holiday — they would worship you as a demigod and put you up on a pedestal. All these cost money. Money can indeed buy you love and the money that buys the pleasant memories will make anyone contended for a long time....

Love indeed must be an overrated virtue — uttered by everyone from parents to young lovers to pastors to women from the oldest profession to paedophiles!FG10.5.11

Pity Nasi Lemak!

Of late there is a wrangle brewing between the canteen operators and the education officials on limiting the number of days that *nasi lemak* can be served in the canteen. It all happened one day when the Honourable Education Minister was suddenly enlightened during a visit to a school when he made an astounding discovery that the school children were getting fatter. Then started the musical chair charade to pinpoint rather nail down the culprit (synonymous to fall guy or sacrificial lamb to the slaughter). Suddenly, all the relevant government officials in unison were rudely awakened from their blissful post *nasi lemak/nasi kandar* stuporous beauty sleep (which they will resume after the dust has settled on this one) to show everyone else that they are in control. The Minister categorically proclaimed that the root of obesity is the amount of nasi lemak that the children eat (which is way too much). He decreed that that all report cards must have the BMI (Body Mass Index: weight in kg/square of height in metres) written as if the kids would then miraculously shrivel up to Shia LaBeouf's physique with this gesture!Then he suggested nurses must be employed to educate parents on the significance and relevance of increased BMI and educate everyone on good eating habits. Somehow, time and again, the national food (*nasi lemak*) has been portrayed as the axis of all evils — that the number of days of their servings in canteen be reduced.

My humble opinion is that we are totally tangent from the real issue at hand. Most parents of the school children are in their 30s and 40s and have been generally well educated by our what has been a fairly comprehensive and extensive education system. Everyone knows what is raised BMI and its cause and effects as most would have spent at least 11 years in school. They are not retards as they are painted that the government has to tell them that their brads are darn fat!

Maybe he (Minister) should one day see how his subjects (citizens) spend a day at the picnic or what the kids eat during a long train journey on KTM - the children eat and eat gluttonously carbohydrate and oil laden, arteries choking fried processed food from port to port with an interval of snooze along the way. This type of routine will fatten even the thinnest of any famine-stricken kid.

Anyway, school recess is just maybe half a meal that school kids have in a day. The major meals (3 or 4) are consumed at home and parents are in control of that, I am sure. The minister is barking up the wrong tree.

If my instincts are right, all this brouhaha will just be a storm in the tea cup. It will be business as usual come next month when another issue will crop up (like the you tube depiction of bullying in school). The minister will say that the powers that be has the welfare of the ailing canteen operators at heart and would strive for a win-win situation. *Nasi lemak* will on the menu as usual. The canteen operators would be pleased as Punch with the decision. Maybe the minister would pose eating *nasi lemak* in the papers. What he means by win is win the elections, *lah*!

Yet another case wrapped like the *nasi lemak* packet....FG15.5.11

Sentimental fool on the hill!

Back in the 80s, my cousin RR, sister and I all bought similar combs of the same colour and make and promised to keep in forever as a sign of our bond. At that naïve carefree age, we made a pledge that we would keep till the end of time as a sign of our friendship.

During about the same time, over the same holiday period, RR and I used to go crazy over the rock band 'Cheap Trick'. Over and over again, we found intense joy in croaking in our untrained hoarse vocal cords to the song 'If you want my love, you got it' till it hurt and felt so good about it. The song used to be a regular feature on Radio RAAF Butterworth those days.

30 years after that eventful holiday, when I last met up with RR, I happened to mention about the comb and the song to him. And what do you know? RR had absolutely no recollection of the song that we used to sing. In fact, he asked; "Cheap who?" Do not even bother about the comb! And there I was keeping the blue plastic comb in pristine condition all this while. Well, somethings mean more to some than others. Or maybe I am just a sentimental sensitive fool! Different things mean differently to different people.FG20.5.11

Candyman coming to town!

Just the other day, in the midst of talking to one of my relatives, he quipped. "Oh! I have to call Japan. This is the best time to move into Japan."

He was not talking about uprooting his family and settling down in Japan. Neither was he planning on a mercy mission to give a helping hand to the unfortunate victims of double whammy victim of earthquake and tsunami of Sendai. (Believe me, it is the last thing on his mind!) He was, of course, talking of moving his investment and loose change to the Tokyo Stock Exchange as the indices were down at a bargain. As far as he is concerned, he is smart to earn for himself and his family as well as help to develop business and rebuild the damaged infrastructure and get the grieving Japanese economy back on its feet. He is actually doing them a favour.

On the other hand, the way I see it, it reminds me of predatory vultures and hyenas moving in, to prance on the remains of the lion kill in the Savannah of Africa or a scene from 'Snows of Kilimanjaro' where vultures wait patiently perched on the skeletal tree awaiting Gregory Peck's leg to rot so that they can feed on it! And in Clint Eastwood's western movie, a cowboy stranded in the desert bordering Mexico dying of dehydration.

Or the touts who hang around accident victims in a hospital to prance on them to make a kill either way. If the victims survive, he would introduce a lawyer for a cut to fight for compensation as a helpless innocent victim or a cut from the funeral parlour if otherwise! Or the businessmen who build private business entities called hospitals to thrive by making a sick person think that he is sicker than he is and to make him poorer as well. And the insurance people who would make you think of the worst accidents and diseases that may afflict you to cajole you to sign up and commit yourselves in their protection plans while they make it to the billion dollar boys' club.

But hey! Everyone is doing it and has been doing it from the time known to men.

Why do you think the noble Missionary Men and Women came over to the savage land to tame the lost savages? True, they changed the landscape of the under-privileged who were downtrodden and outcast by their own people in the case of lepers and Harijans and gave them dignity and reason to live. Father Damien undauntedly touched and cared for lepers in isolation. The Father Damien I am referring to is of course not the one in 'Friday the 13th' horror flick but the Flemish Saint in Hawaii. And the nuns and the La Salle brothers and who devoted their lives to the work of God and building convents and English schools to educate the unfortunate subjects all over the British Empire. The critics would reminisce the good old Islamic and Eastern civilisations of the yesteryear and how the Westerners destroyed it. But, hey! Whatever said and done English is the lingua franca of the modern world!

Acquiring brownie points and serving the fishes caught to the Lord were the fringe benefits of this exercise. Not everyone has an ulterior motive when performing a good deed.

What do think Father Damien and all these people do the things that they do? He lived amongst victims of Hanson's disease at a time when they were ostracised and sent off to live in exile. He subsequently contracted the disease and died amongst them to be beatified later by the Pope.

A few days after the conversation about Japan, I had the honour to chat up with an honourable individual who had dedicated her life to the work of the Lord. She had just come back after serving in Sudan for 2 years. She had a lot of stories to tell about the war torn and ethnic tension raged country which was in the verge of separation into 2 countries. Corruption and in-fighting has left this oil-rich country into a basket case.

People living where the Blue Nile originates were dying of, of all things, dehydration. There was recently a cooking gas shortage in a country which produces oil and natural gases. Again, in this 'poor' country many multinational companies have set up businesses to prosper themselves while the citizen still live in absolute poverty. It is mighty courageous for her to go around to spread the word of the Lord in this volatile Muslim nation. There is hope. There is hope...

In the end, everything can be compared to a scenario of the visit of a circus to a town. There is a lot of hype before the arrival. The circus will come to town. All activities will centre around the circus. Circus will have its show. Circus managers will collect their collection and leave. Town dwellers will be poorer by a bit but will be contended and richer with the memories. Everyone will be wiser in handling a function of such scale in future and perhaps better. And life will go on...FG24.5.11

Can the real Hussein please stand up!

If you drive around KL town, you may start to wonder what is the real spelling of Malaysia's third prime minister. Is it **Hussein** Onn (as we always knew) or **Hussien** Onn as depicted by many signboards around town? This, I discovered during my early morning run around Bukit Tunku area a few weeks ago. It got me thinking... Now, is Hussein Onn real name spelt **Hussein** or **Hussien**? Not that it really matters. Both sounds the same and we have other pressing things to think about in life than semantics! Talking about spellings, the place I work is also misspelt on signboards - *Connought* instead of *Connaught*. It is one of the legacies left by the British. Connaught (anglicised from the Irish term *Connacht*) is a piece of land in western Ireland with a rich history of sorcerers to talk about from the 6th century AD. Many towns in the British Commonwealth like New Delhi, Hong Kong, Sydney and others have buildings and districts named after Connaught. And our local authorities goofed it up on the signboard.

Is it that the people in charge of checking them did it one eye closed or left the supervision to illiterates? Is this the same lackadaisical attitude that got the 16 inmates of the illegal orphanage killed recently? As in any major mishaps in the country, if they cannot blame God, they would start blaming each other.

My point of contention is that the orphanage was there like a sitting duck for 10 years without the local authorities realising of its existence. Don't the workers or officer travel along the road? Don't they bother to go out their way to bring its existence to their superiors so that the efficiency of their department can be uplifted?

Just as I was wondering and wandering back, what did I see? A pickup van with the lettering boldly screaming 'UNLCE ALI CATERING'! I rubbed my eyes to see if my eyesight was failing. It was Unlce Ali Catering', not Uncle Ali Catering! Maybe it stands for '**U**npalatable **N**on-appetising **L**ow-Priority **C**leanliness **E**nterprise'? If Uncle Ali is so slip-short in things like signage on his van, I dread to imagine how he would be in his catering. I do not want to know it the hard way with the runs and drips. Thank you very much.FG27.5.11

Seeking Employment: Fly Swatting Specialist

I often come across people who complained that the work that they do is much too difficult to do and they need to take rest off work. Over the years I have been desensitised by these moans that I just tell myself, "You think my job is easy?" — talking to sluggards like you! When I was working in Klang, I encountered many plantation workers negotiating with the Medical Officers to squeeze out as many days of medical leave as possible. Initially, I thought that these people were plain lazy. I found later that it was not so straight forward. After working many long weary hours, they were paid 'peanuts'. A rainy day means no work and no pay. If they fell ill, they have to take a long bus trip to town — awake at 4am, preparing house chores to catch the 5.30am bus to reach town to collect a number to see a medical officer who starts work at 8am; they will depart from the hospital close to 12noon. By then, they could not go back to work and they lose a day's pay. If the worker managed to produce a Government Hospital Medical Leave Certificate, he would be entitled to a full day's pay which is better than nothing. A tough life but isn't everybody's? Even the skiver has to think hard to dodge from work. Ask anybody and everyone will say that his job is tough-the bricklayer — tough; waiter and those in the hospitality service-tough; the businessmen — tough-because he cannot get a car park when he gets to the bank; those in the medical services-tough because of increasingly litigious society and the list goes on. Even the illicit drug dealers find it tough to carry his work and he has almost ran out ideas to bring his merchandise in and out of the country as the people have 'wised up' that they are made mules by the drug cartel. The syndicates have used their charm to lure local gals to carry their 'hot items'. When we were growing up, Amma used to tell us that our ancestors in India were duped by the middlemen into thinking that work in the land of milk and honey called Malaya was darn easy. They would be paid lots of money and fringe benefits for just swatting flies in Malaya to ensure that the raw sugar that is laid to dry is not eaten by pests. In droves, they raced down to Malaya only to find themselves trapped in rubber estates, mosquitoes, pure manual hard work, ruthless *mandors* (stewards) and the same white colonial masters that they had in India.FG29.5.11

Shoo the shoes!

Just the other day, I found myself invited to an expatriate (Caucasian) friend's abode. After finishing their contract in Malaysia, they were heading home sweet home, their country of origin. They came in as a newlywed couple and they were returning with a newly born baby of a month old!

Now, why am I ranting about a baby's celebration?

After getting trapped in the maze of parking lot which had all exits (stairs and lifts) locked, needing authority card to swipe for its usage, I finally made it to the couple's condominium doorstep in one piece with the help of an apologetic foreign guard who could barely speak English. That's high-end condo living for you - trapped in a virtual prison at the mercy of grills and technology.

When I finally reached the unit on the 26th floor, I was surprised to find shoes all arranged outside the house. Hey! I thought it is an Asiatic practice to enter a home without one's shoes and barefoot. Well, they have a newborn and walking in with the shoes seem unhealthy with all the bugs that accompany our footwear. Malaysia is a tropical country making it a fertile ground for moulds, insects and protozoans to propagate the year round. Our footwear makes a perfect conduit for these pests to infiltrate into our homes. In template climates, toes may get too cold for comfort

and chill from the floor may literally seep to the bone, making it impera-
tive for one to wear their footwear.

Interestingly, I have attended many functions hosted by affluent
Malaysians that I know where the hosts insist that I walk into the house
with my shoes. Asians think that moving up the ladder means walking
with your shoes into your house.

At one time, when you run, you wear shoes. Research by footwear companies (?coincidental) made our feet well padded and cushioned to
make our runs comfortable and to prevent immediate and future injuries (so they said). It has now taken a full circle. Now runners are advocating barefoot running just like our cavemen ancestors did as it de-
velops all the intrinsic muscles of the foot and leg!FG31.5.11

Peter Platter, how is the weather?

Sometimes one wonders who is right and what is wrong anymore. Is
there a divine power up there righting the wrong and otherwise, anymore?

So much of bad publicity has been given about the biggest football governing body of late of scandals, corruption and manipulation. The elections still went on as usual. The incumbent clung on to throne even after
8 years, in spite of the alleged misdoings, the competitors to the throne
essentially put in cold storage and are outcast as a pariah. And it is business as usual. The victor, the 75 year old Sepp Blatter, promises of
putting the house in order whilst in the same breath denied any money
politics in the body's dealings of which he was the boss for 8 years. If the
house is already in order, then why bother to clean it up? Unless you
have OCD (Obsessive Compulsive Disorder), that is! Of course nobody
knows where the real truth lies. I guess it must be somewhere in between.

That reminds me of a somebody who denied having sexual intimacy but
admitted being gratified, well, orally which was not (in his books) sex!
And he survived that and had come out smelling of roses as a comeback
boy and a peacemaker in the international arena presently.

Maybe it is my distorted view of reality or unfulfilled childhood dreams,
I always taught that a leader is a model of whom his followers or subjects
will try to emulate and behave. He sets the gold standard how one

should act. The landowners' wives in ancient Egypt used to dress up like Cleopatra as she was their role model. When Madonna told the world that it was cool to flaunt your assets in a lace brassiere in the 80s, it caught like bush fire!

On the hand, there are people out there just to get you if you are rich and famous. Imagine an intern who decided to immortalise the special moment by preserving malodorous musky wild-oats sowed stained blue dress just in case she might need to use at the time of need for Deoxyribonucleic acid evidence. How convenient?

Hey, Big Guy, what are waiting for? Show me a sign! You already have and I don't see it, you say?FG3.6.10

Human sapien weaklingus vulgaris

The law of Nature as described by Charles Darwin is that the world is for the fittest. Over time, to allow the survival of the not-so-fit (the sick, handicapped and weak) and to allow them to share the wealth of Nature and co-habitat on Earth, man created the concept of God and putting the fear (of God) of a super Being watching your every move and deciphering your every thought with the promise of virgins in the after-world and possibilities of moving up the ladder of karma with every divine deed must have been introduced.

65 million years ago, the last the roaming dinosaur was wiped off the surface of Mother Earth probably due to adverse planet conditions or attack by giant meteors. Apparently certain die-hard never-say-die survivors survived this catastrophe and have managed to cling on to their style of living amongst us even as we speak. I am of course referring to our not so friendly home grown roaches (have been around for more than 300 million years) and members of the lizard family (200 million years). These two creatures may be the only beholden of the secrets of Mother Nature and how man can survive his own made increasingly hostile environment. It is said that the adaptive features of the cockroach is so good that they may withstand a nuclear holocaust! Of late, I have been thinking....of our offspring. Are they tough enough to face the challenges of the world amongst its citizens and the adverse environmental conditions?

The desire for continuity of species in the animal and plant kingdoms alike is so great that under severely extreme conditions, nature had resorted to self-pollination and parthenogenesis within the same generation for the continuation of species!

Many years ago, we, as children, played in the rain with the sand, soil and whatever which came. Worse things that happened were cuts and bruises which healed over time but not the memories. Fast forward to 2011. Send a teenager for National Service and the child comes back in a body bag - C.O.D. Leptospirosis due to drinking water tainted with squirrel's urine!

Are we becoming weak or what? Not to sound inconsiderate to the bereaved ones, our children are becoming weaklings, too guarded for their own good.

Are they tough enough to face the challenges in store in their future journey? Many things that are happening in our daily lives make me think otherwise.

From the time they are born, they are sheltered and guarded like the incarnate of the Dalai Lama! The bottles that they drink from are sterilised with sterilising tablets and water filtered through myriad of water filtration systems, BPA is painstakingly eradicated for safety, immunisations are given in mammoth proportions, a single drop of rain cannot befall on toddlers hair, maids running around to dampen their every fall, prepare their every favourite food and clean up their mess and chores that their parents used to do in their childhood. Whilst their ancestors had to sing (work) for their supper, these nouveau riche offsprings have TV to sing for them during all their meals.

As they grow older, they do not have to wrestle through the early morning rush to get to school but arrive neat with iron folds uncreased via their private school buses and roller school bags. They do not have to rough it out with the HSC/STPM examinations which are deemed as the toughest exam in the world but have it easy by enrolling in private colleges which pave a sure way to success!

With this type of mollycoddling and spoon feeding, will they be able to rough it out in the real world with real challenges? A point to ponder is the phenomena of peanut allergy. Whilst most Malaysian kids can easily enjoy the succulent satay with the peanut-rich gravy with no qualms whilst peanut allergy is a real clear and present danger which to be on the rise in the developed countries.

In Britain, Southampton University's Dr. John Warner issued a statement: "The increase in allergy generally may be explained by better hygiene. Foetuses used to respond to parasites present in the maternal blood. Now that these have been eliminated they are reacting to other things in the blood, such as antigens."

Surfers in Surfers' Paradise in Australia who were instrumental in the development of Billabong and its off shoots, used to say life is a beach — some days with good waves and other days with none. But FG used to say that living with a bitch is like living in midst of a tsunami every day!

Homo sapiens — the only surviving hominid; species to which modern man belongs; bipedal primate having language and ability to make and use complex tools; brain volume at least 1400 cc;

Weaklingus - pseudo-Latin sounding word for a weakling or wimp, milksop, doormat, 98 pound weakling;

Vulgaris - common, not referring to the vulgarities that culminates from their oral orifices that seem second nature to them to add 4-letter prefixes and suffixes to emphasise the gravidity of their messages. FG8.6.2011

I love animals too, but...

Just the other day, I visited a close friend. I was shocked to see his home in a topsy-turvy condition in total chaos like a hoarder's house would be. Besides the books and bags that my friend had to house in (besides his two adult kids), he was also a proud father to three dogs!

You see, his son had finished his undergraduate studies and returned home for good (or bad). Besides acquiring his credits for his coursework and a girlfriend along the way, being an animal lover that he is, he started rearing dogs. The 'headache' has now been passed over to my friend. (The feeding, cleaning and the irrational bark for no apparent reason — maybe it saw some apparition, must be his evil neighbour who died recently!)

There are amongst us who claim to be animal lovers. Just like vegans who choose to be so to minimise sufferings endured by a slaughtered but have no qualms about kicking a dog off his lawn, an animal lover who parades for equality and kindness for animals sometimes find it cumbersome to relate to a fellow being! They find it easier to relate to animals.

In fact, psychiatry has identified this trait as a pre-morbid personality disorder and a precursor to schizophrenia!

On one hand, we have people from PETA who lobby for total ban of hunting of all kinds of animals for fur and another group may find solace in propagating the number of Bengal tigers in the wilderness. I once had a roommate who had a fetish for tigers. He plastered the whole room wall with posters of tigers. I suppose he was just suppressing his inner tiger-like appetite for companionship. He later pranced on many potential mates but sadly is now living as a lonely but majestic narcissistic He-tiger!

These lobbyists should take a trip down to Sundarbans Plains in the Bay of Bengal. Almost every family from this area has a gruesome tale to tell about one of their family members being attacked or eaten alive by a so-called endangered species which need to be preserved for the next generation!

Who are we to tell them, 'Save the Tigers!'?

I too love animals. So much so that I decided never to be a vegetarian.

I love animals so much that I eat them....FG10.6.11

The Vultures are out again!

I just discovered a breed of humans who only manifest in the social circles when someone is dead or when death is imminent. Repeatedly, I have seen this happening with certain individuals amongst my relatives and I am sure it is not a pure coincidence. And he is not working in a funeral parlour and neither is he an undertaker!

More than once, when someone was at the tail-end of their life stricken with the big C, these people who were nowhere to be seen — all the get-togethers and simple socials visits were insignificant and never participated. Once the heart went into asystole, they spring into action like a bear up from hibernation or a hippopotamus re-surfacing after a long submerge underwater saying, "So much to do, so little time!"

Like a scene from the movie 'Snows of Kilimanjaro', the vultures who wait to feast on putrefying dead meat in the savanna of Africa. It takes all kinds to make the world go around. And they would disappear until somebody else kicks the bucket!FG11.6.11

Yet another amnesty!

...only this time it is mind boggling. Keeping with my predictions in my previous posts, the Immigration Department has decide to continue its perennial malaise and conduct its annual jumble-sales-amnesty programme (like the Mammoth Malaysian Sales-everything goes, including the kitchen sink, after being constipated for so long; the sales which we know is just an eyewash). Only this time it decided that, in good measure and the spirit of neighbourliness and the fasting month of Ramadan, to go one step further — to legalise the illegal immigrants rather than giving them a free ride home as they have doing all these years.

Somehow, every Malaysian who had his drop of blood on the soil of the nation, (*tanah tumpah darah ku*), knows without being prompted that it is all an election ploy which should be just around the slippery corner.

This topic was the subject of discussion among my family members during our last dinner meeting. Amongst us were two foreigners who married into the family. One had to be married for over 10 years and deliver two children before she obtained her permanent residency. The other, the more frustrated one, is in his 8th year of frustrating trips to and encounter with most not-so-forthcoming clueless Immigration reception officers who are contended with clocking in and out of office and enjoying their regular (too regular) tea and *nasi lemak* breaks.FG15.6.11

Vision is hardly 20/20

Just the other day, as usual, my younger son with his profound questions asked me, "Will our country be a very developed country in 9 years' time?" I, as usual, could not give a straight forward answer but take him on a long journey of circumlocution and make him more confused than he ever was!

To me, being a citizen of a developed nation mean all its citizen have a certain role to play. It is not just a matter of having lots of money to spend, mammoth buildings for others to awe, seamless cheap infrastructure for its entire citizens to use for free. With great powers come great responsibly. A citizen from a certain first world nation is expected to behave in a certain socially acceptable way, just like any professional body has a code of ethics for its member to emulate.

Certain current events do not speak well on our journey to be developed nation. The ruckus and free-for-all that occurred during the Energiser Run is one living example that I witnessed myself. And the worst part is there were Singaporeans amongst the participants. Guess they will now have something else to snigger or sneer about over their nocturnal chocolate drink or Chinese tea made with *New Water* (water recycled from sewage treatment plant). People throwing big plastic bags out of their half a million ringgit car are examples of why money cannot buy you good etiquette.

Being highly developed to me means include being cultured enough not to look down others who are not so fortunate.FG22.6.11

National aspirations turned apparitions?

During one of my channels surfing sessions, to avoid meaningless advertisements and melodramatic mind boggling Kollywood dance-around-the-park sequences, I stumbled upon the live coverage our female badminton players slugging it out with the Indonesian pair in the finals of the Sudirman Cup. It was not their game that fascinated me (they lost meekly) but rather their (the players and their coach) off court antics. Somehow, in that live coverage, the camera was precariously close to both teams. Every word of their conversation was crystal clear to the TV viewers. The Indonesian coach was ranting away in Indonesian language giving final points in playing. The Malaysian coach, on the other hand, was talking away in what sounded like Mandarin. I do not know whether the coach is Malaysian or Chinese but I would not be surprised if he is Malaysian as it is a common sight indeed to find Malaysians finding it more comfortable (some calling it preserving the dying mother tongue - it used to be a common thing amongst Indian (Tamil) students in varsity teeming with the *Anjaatha* fearless Dravidian spirit) to chat to one another in their respective mother tongues — as if they are dealing in some kind of secret society transactions even in the presence of other ethnic groups so much so that, like it or not, the languages seem to have seeped into others. Just that we do not use it. Just do not curse us in our face or behind our backs. It will alert our antennas and they would be trouble.FG23.6.11

Time after time

Life is a moment in space, so goes the lyrics in the song 'Woman in Love' by Barbara Streisand with the lyrics written by Barry and Robin Gibb. Cindy Lauper sang about how time after time she is there every time her friend needs a helping hand.

In my kind of work. (defusing time bombs), time is of essence! Sometimes masterly inactivity seems to be the wisest thing to do whilst in other instances I would be accused of sleeping on my job.

Good times, bad times and superstitions arise because of ignorance and the fear of the uncertainty of outcomes of some chain of events. Being apprehensive on possibly ominous outcome of certain important events in one's life, it had decreed by our animistic ancestors that certain astronomical positions of planets in relation to the moon, earth and sun may influence end results of events!

In the present time, it appears that this hullabaloo is confined to the Asiatic cultures only. Not wanting to rock the boat or being the direction to which accusing index fingers were to fall, most young Asians just follow suit. Furthermore, the elders are still the majority stakeholders in most family decision-making scenarios.

A good deal of holy men amongst the Indian and Chinese community thrive on this unshakable belief. Their abdominal girth and fleet of cars as well jewel chest is ever expanding.

In the South Indian community, time of delivery of a baby would determine his entire future. Hence, parents would go great lengths to prevent births of babies in some inauspicious months including preventing consummation of marriage and conjugal activities 40 weeks before these doomed days. In fact, in the Tamil tradition, sex on the first night is only allowed after astronomical nod! (Provided they remain unabated on the shelf prior to deflowering ceremony)

When I was due to be born some 48 years ago, Amma was flabbergasted as the bad month was approaching and there was no sign of labour. As she had a fresh stillbirth before me, anxiety was at all time high. Then came the intense prayer and plea bargains with the Gods (that a gratification prayers would be held afterwards — as if God is hard up for food that human will consume anyway). It was already the 31st day of the good month. By twist of fate or divine intervention, that auspicious month had 32 days and yours truly came sprawling out on the 32nd day!

Not being grateful on avoiding the bad month of *Aadi*, Amma was worried that the time of birth only corresponded to the second best of the birth stars, not the best! (Typical selfish Asian mum). Again, after recalculation and allowance for Malaysian timing (versus Indian timing and other errors like in physics experiments), the star turned out to be indeed the best, according to another astrologer-how convenient!

The Chinese have their own share of good times and bad. They also have many superstitions to accompany that — elements, number and a gamut of rationalisations under the heading of *feng shui*.

I know how a Chinese lady who planned her Caesarean Section so meticulously after consulting many mediums and changing the surgery time many times just to have her water bag bursting way before the scheduled date and undergoing an emergency procedure.FG24.6.11

L'histoire de l'origine des 'Nasi Lemak '

Translation: French: The history of the origin of 'Nasi Lemak'

Maka termaktub dalam Hikayat Melaka akan terjadinya satu jenis makanan kegemaran yang sememangnya berasal secara kebetulan dan tidak terduga-duga pada zaman pemerintahan Sultan Muzafar Shah yang teragung. Mak Leha yang menjadi balu akibat suami yang dipukau jin iblis. Terpaksalah dengan yang hati yang berat dan pilu menyara kehidupan sebagai tukang urut dalam Kesultanan Melaka yang agung menyuap dua mulut peninggalan arwah suami.

Anak perempuan Mak Leha, Timah namanya, menjaga dapur sepeninggalan ibunya. Maka terjadilah suatu trajedi semasa menanak nasi. Santan yang diperah untuk gulai jatuh tertumpah ke air jerangan nasi. Air mata Timah berlinangan mengenang nasibnya yang malang, sudah jatuh ditimpa tangga, sudah papa kedana pula. Beras secupak yang dipinjam Pak Ali ditumpahi santan. Kerana kesuntukan masa, tanpa cara lain, disidangkan makanan nasi dan gulai untuk ibu yang kepenatan dan kelaparan dengan hati kencang berdenyut bak lancang kapal Cina di selat Melaka pada hari bertaufan.

Maka dirasakan Mak Leha masakan anak belasan tahun. Nasinya terasa lain, dicakap manis tidak manis, dicakap basi tak basi, pegat pun tidak, lain tapi sedap pulak! Ditanyakan ibubanda akan anakandanya, "Hai Timah, nasi apa pulak ini?"

Seolah-olah tidak memahami soalan Mak Leha, Timahpun menjawab, "Nasi-lah, Mak! Nasi le, Nasi le Mak"

Ibunda menjawab, "Sedap juga nasi lemak ini!"

Maka tersebar luas akan kehikmahan dan kenikmatan juadah ini sehingga tersebar luas harum namanya hingga perantauan... Nasi lemak menjadi makanan ruji penduduk kebanyakan.

Demikian termaktub kisah hikayat Melaka.....tentang asal-usul nasi lemak! FG1.7.11

Imp in the making? Or just a transition?

Again, I have become a listening ear and a shoulder to cry on for one of my old friends who had to deal with his rebellious teenage daughter. She thinks that he is a worthless piece of sh*t. At least this is how he perceives her to think about him and the impression he gets. I know the worse thing that anyone can do is to take sides in a family feud. I had had enough of melancholic tales in my lifetime, but he seems to jump into talking about his sad tale every time I make a courtesy call to him. Maybe I look like a sucker and sponge for everyone's woes. So, I punctuated my replies with the occasional 'Oh?', Oh!', "Is it?'.

There are always two sides of the story and I am listening to one side of it. He was telling about how his teenage daughter does not know the value of money and how friends take precedence over everything else in her life. She is forever on her mobile phone, either texting, e-mailing or speaking as if her dad is a telecommunication magnate whose telco charges are free or just petty cash. My friend, growing up in a humble background and saving every penny to get an overseas education, is thrifty with his wallet. Being a cancer survivor himself, I am sure he means well for her. All for a reason, imparting his lessons in life to her to guide her into adulthood.

His other half also sees eye to eye to his ideology and gives her two cents worth of advice to her daughter in a harsh way. Somehow, he is painted as a bad guy, leaving him to feel unwanted and redundant, just a cash cow, nothing else.

What can a seemingly understanding friend like me can tell him? That it is what every modern father with a teenage daughter living in a big city who believes in giving equal opportunities to their children and exposing them to modern thinking and American TV goes through. And that things could be worse and unthinkable... or that it is alright!FG2.7.11

Whose dough is it anyway?

People get into in the intricacies of life, they fall sick, they get hit by natural calamities, living becomes unbearable. They persevere in their daily dealings in spite of adverse turn of events with the undying faith that the Almighty would pave a way for them to live in their place in the sun. This, they did, by the way, they knew best. They frequented the house of abode of the Lord, made here on Earth by men who claim to possess divine wisdom or spiritual connexions. They, in a way, bribed the Gods with worldly possessions like money, gold, precious stones and various alms in the hope that the Divine Powers be pleased with their subservience. By the twist of fate or divine intervention, things actually improved. Serenity was returned. Forget about the occasional tragedies - God knows best, look at the bigger picture, it is the Butterfly effect, bla, bla...

These halls of worship become too small for its congregations. Peasants and even rich zaminders follow suit in this way of herd mentality and mass hypnotism. It became the coolest place to be hanging around. It became the meeting place to procure new business clients and ventures. This status symbol had to depict the greatness of the village to keep up with the Joneses. The rich contributed to the grandiosity in the understanding that they and their family members would be the leaders for generations.

Time trickled on.... Invaders came...Emperors reigned...Empires crumbled with self-destruction...but the temple hanged on. This seemingly low profile temple somehow escaped the fancy of fortune seekers and invaders (divine protection or otherwise) but continued as business as usual. Upheaval and uncertainties were fertile grounds for theological assistance. Hive of activities in the temple (now a golden shrine) go on.... Fast forward to the next few millennia....

Due to the curse of the Gods or a case of 'too small the cake for too big a crowd to lick', the general poverty and infrastructure around the temple have hardly improved over time. The new socialist-minded committee were reminded of the temple's secret vaults and their bottomless pit of wealth which could be used for betterment on the needy. That started the snowball of events.

Suddenly, the shark-suited black draped men of the law manifest out of thin air. The superior protector of law and order have decreed that the vaults be shut and the temple wealth be frozen till further notice. Then the debate began! Whose wealth is it anyway?

Does it belong to the temple committee who were given the enviable task of custodians of the temple wealth who would decide the destiny of the treasure? Or should it be nationalised and the wealth utilised for the good of masses? Yeah, right!

How about the temple forming a trust to improve living conditions and future of those living in that vicinity? If only humans can agree or are they waiting for a divine intervention for common sense to prevail? FG8.7.11

Aaah! I already know that!

Sometimes when you tell something which is good cum advice to people, it is often taken in the wrong sense even if the teller does it with a pure heart and pure of intentions. In fact, it may be construed as meddling, being jealous or being just simply irritating. You will soon make it to their list of people who they dislike or just be blocked on Facebook!

Only when someone draped in a saffron robe tells them the same thing in a different tone and laced with pseudo-religious words do they do see the light. Or if a shrink, who blames your deprived inner childhood sexual desires for everything from short stature to inability to prosper in your life, dittos your advice.

Take home message is just keep your mouth shut. Everybody already knows everything. It is all stacked up inside their memory bank. It needs someone of authority or commands respect to open their inner eye or knock some sense into them. Being the good friend or human being that you want to be, you just do not have the heart to see the person rot into oblivion without giving your two sen worth of sense. But then, it is karma, it is karma... I'm just sitting here watching the wheels go round and round...♪♫♪►FG9.7.11

Of wallpapers, wallflowers and flavour of the month!

While meeting up with a friend's father, a mid-septuagenarian, who was recuperating from a major illness, his mobile phone rang. After he had completed his conversation, everyone noticed his romanticism from his mobile wallpaper. He had placed a snap of husband and wife studio pose!

Suddenly, everybody was looking at each others' gizmo. Everybody had their accusing eyes cast on my el cheapo G-less cell phone when they saw what they saw. Instead of immortalising the picture of my love of my life or the product of thereof, there was a nocturnal snapshot of Sultan Sulaiman building with its clock tower which I took during my last run! Being a good sport, I just laughed it off.

Hey, my phone wallpaper is like the restaurant's flavour of the month. I change it when I get bored with the picture. Before this, it was a picture of a comb, preceded by Tasmania pics, etcetera, etcetera...It is not indicative of a degree of passion or lack of. I am not a PDA type of a guy (PDA = public display of affection). No one knows what goes in the mind. Everything is a mirage.

Remember, for umpteenth times, suspected gruesome murderers and child molesters have appeared in courts in full view draped in conservatively religious tunics and head gears to highlight their docile predisposition just to be sentenced guilty on all accounts. And the numerous politicians who claim to be servants of the masses just to serve their own coffers. Here I stand alone like a wall flower...—FG13.7.11

A for apple; P for pokai!

Of late, I have been contributing to the coffers of a multinational company whose brand is so famous its name need not be mentioned (like Lord Voldemort), its logo itself suffice, whose interior decoration experts believe in minimalist outlook, the logo of a partially eaten fruit (the first fruit that we learnt in alphabet class in pre-school) — or is the logo a constant reminder of our exodus from the paradise of Garden of Eden for our original sin? In the modern world, nobody gives a damn about inner beauty and endurance but of the external package and presentation, this telecommunications and computer whiz of a company has managed make that precisely its selling point.

It all started one day when good old el cheapo cell phone, due to melancholia, decided to take the plunge inadvertently (or on purpose?) into the monsoon drain as I was coming down the car carrying more than I should. Good old faithful must have been feeling pretty withdrawn and small after seeing all the PYT (pretty young things) strutting their stuff while her overused and abused body had seen better days. And the things the newbies could do with their bodies and the way they flaunt their assets would make any man salivate and go gaga!

I tried to resuscitate the old one via modified surgery of dismantling its parts and heat drying it thoroughly. It survived for a couple of days but stopped short never to go again when the LCD panel went berserk. So ended the life of cell phone which served me for more than 3 years and was a hand-me-down from wifey when my previous RM1 cell phone (after buying a TV set) died suddenly.

About that time, wifey's mobile started giving problems. And my daughter suddenly became obsessed and thought that she could not see another living daylight without possessing a particular brand of laptop with a logo of a fruit from the same brand of company of indisputable reputation and nothing doing! There was no talk of Sony or Lenovo or Asus! Everybody is having it, so it must be good and I want it not now but yesterday!

That started my love affair with the forbidden fruit. I soon realised that the moment you attain the impossible, you realise that it is nothing sacrosanct about it after all. On the other hand, with greater powers come great responsibility and greater hole in the pants and thinner the wallet becomes....

Pokai — colloquial Malay term for being broke (financially). Correct term would be muflis, patah kandar or bangkrap. Must have been popularised by P. Ramlee's movies. In fact, P. Ramlee is credited for introducing many new Malay words into its treasure. Some of the words include pawagam (movie theatre)-shortened from panggong wayang gambar; kugiran (band) — from kugiran gitar rancak! How about bedikari (berdiri atas kaki sendiri) — independent?FG29.7.11

Minimum wage, minimalist life?

My heart bleeds every time I see security guards waiting meekly at the malls, looking at the passers-by at the mall he is guarding. I wonder if, with his measly pay and long hours, he could ever think of spending time and money with his children and loved ones at the malls just like the passers-by. I wonder if, when his kids stand drooling at the sight of mouth-watering buns and steeply priced roasted chicken pieces, would he just blame it on his fate or live happily without a care in the world on credit and then blame the whole world for his dire straits?

RRB and his siblings had all been in similar predicament before. Peeking through the railings of our balcony into the opposite neighbour's living room into the brand new colour TV and admiring the spanking colourful eye-catching hues that scintillate from it; waiting anxiously for Appa to come back with a packet of Craven 'A' *Meehoon Singapura* at the end of the month and enjoying the once a month 'A Block' *Char Koay Teow*. We have been there!

As all of us can see around us, the gap between the haves and have-nots have leaped by leaps and bounds over the years, no thanks to all the capitalistic minded policies.

This is what the socialists, with the helplessness of the workers' community at heart (since workers' rights movement died before *Merdeka*), have been advocating all these while — minimum wage and an earning capacity to alleviate them off the poverty line. But how can you go and for how long can you sustain it? Humans have that insatiable appetite that cannot be easily satisfied.FG6.8.11

Socially emphatizing capitalism!

Give a man a fish, he will stay full for a day. Teach him to fish and he will not be hungry in his lifetime. So says an ancient Chinese saying which we are all well aware.

Amma used to say, "Your thumb can only swell to the size of your thumb". A man can only earn this much. Don't get your fingers burnt with greed, some say. These are all naysayers and negative vibes according to giant megalomaniac unabashedly capitalistic minded enterprising moguls.

"Aim for the moon! At least you do not make it, you would be among the stars," does not sound quite so right, as the moon is 240,000 miles away but the stars, many light years away. That seem to be the mantra of most greedy CEOs who are basically the product and creation of the capitalistic system whose productivity (interpreted as profit) can only go one way, i.e., up and up only! The last thing they are bothered is the suffering workers who toil the sweat and hours to realise the dream of the bosses. The lip service that is given through community services and handing of big mockery of a mock cheque is nothing more but just tax write offs!

On the other hand, if the society believes in ensuring that everyone is taken care of by hook or crook by the state, things will surely be hunky dory when the going gets good. This alms receiving citizens will swear that there is no state as good as theirs, the state is caring and they would worship the hands that hand them the handouts. Over time this would be expected of the state and eventually will transform into their birth right. When the tide goes down, when the going gets tough, when the coffers for the handouts dwindle, then it gets tough. The state induced paralysis of able bodies need massive Faradic stimulation and physiotherapy to incite axionic action potential to trigger the sodium pumps to generate work all over again. In the interim, there is bound to be chaos and instigators who would promise their own way to blissful paradise... (with something up their sleeves too)!FG7.8.11

We all live on the assumption of...

Today is Assumption Day, the day Mother Mary (no, not the one that comes to you in times of trouble in 'Let it be', but the real one) is assumed to have ascended to heaven. How do I know this? Well, a mother who was in active labour was hoping against hope to postpone her delivery to today for obvious reasons!

Talking about heaven, the hell gates are open now, according to the Chinese folklore and the ghosts are out to play. Hence, throughout the 'Hungry Ghost Month' (Phor Thor), many distractions are given to these ghosts so that they would be sitting down watching the Chinese opera, the scantily clad singing girls and feeding on the food stuff left at the roadside during prayers. The distractions are meant to divert their attention from their daytime duty of haunting the living!

Talking about that month of the year, the middle of July to mid-August is the inauspicious month for the Hindus. Most important events in life are postponed if possible. Agreements, moving into a new premises, births (by prohibiting intimacies 9 months previously), buying of properties, marriage and engagement ceremonies are postponed till after the *Aadi* month is over. The temples used to be void of activities and the time was used to spruce the temples and conduct repairs and what not. That was in those days, when I was growing up. Now, many activities (even religious ones) are happening. *Aadi Puram* which seem to be a low-key fare then is a celebration of sorts lasting many days with chariot procession to follow. The snake goddess also has joined in the foray. Guess, the temple had to fatten its coffers.

Talking about hell, heaven and spiritualism, an icon of songs he used to lip-sync to and I had to bear the brunt of listening to it day and night when I was desperately trying to cramp my facts in RRF kicked the bucket recently. The Bollywood film fraternity moan and wail that his death is an irreplaceable loss even though he has out of acting for decades! Nah, I do not think they miss him. They are just telling that as they know that the media people are out with their memo pads! Shammi Kapoor, the chubby crazy sometimes monkey-like dance-moving star of the 60s passed on at 79 due to renal failure. All the songs from Andaz, Junglee, Love in Tokyo which were the background score of me studying for SPM still reverberates in my ear drums... Ironically, India celebrates its Independence on 15th August in the month of Aadi. I wonder why?

Did not any learned holy men try to postpone the handing of self-rule from the British? Guess they could not wait! Perhaps then, they could be less mayhem than there is now, and I wonder...FG16.8.11

Scurrying over spicy curry

Of late, the mainstream media seem to be bragging of how in two instances, two multilingual cops saved the day. One helped a senior citizen to write a police report (conversing in Hockkein dialect) whilst the other helped to negotiate 2 warring factions who were at logger-heads via his skill in Hockkein. Big deal, kudos to the police for being community friendly, bullocks!

It might work in the 50s and 60s, but in 2011, 54 years after independence? Two bona fide Blue I/C holders and Malaysian citizens communicating like a chicken talking to a toad? You cannot blame the education system as Malaysia boasts of 98% literacy rate.

I remember a friend of mine relating the following true story in the 1960s in the interior of Kelantan (Kuala Krai) where and when literacy was low and many births were recorded by policemen for birth certificate notification purpose as home delivery was norm. This old farmer went to the police station proudly to register his first born son. Being illiterate that he was, he engaged the policemen to do the paperwork...

Cop: Pakcik, nah bagi nama gapa? (What name would you like to give?)

Farmer: Bagilah nama mudah-mudah. (Give a simple name! -in Kelantanese dialect)

And so the newborn was registered as '*Mudah Mudah bin Awang*' to his horror but a comic relief to friends and teachers who called his name with full of glee for the rest of his life.

And in the late 80s when an elderly Malaysian Chinese lady complained to the attending doctor that they are many dogs in the tummy, nobody laughed. Everybody knew that she meant to say '*angin*' (wind) when she said '*anjing*' (dog)!

It was okay years ago but now after 40 years of introduction of National Education Policy, which single-handedly murdered the mastery of the English Language in this country, there is little reason to substantiate the lack of competence in the National Language.

The reason of this discord is the non-amalgamation, jealousy and distrust that occur between the various communities propagated by the self-centred politicians in the country.

Maybe, when the living becomes more difficult, when the pie becomes smaller, when they have a common enemy, various ethnic communities may congregate to fight together the common offender like in the case of Singaporeans who are up in arms against mainland Chinese immigrants who find the pungent odour of fellow Singaporeans' (who were there since the inception of Singapore in 1965) curry offensive. The internet is also rife with photos of mainland Chinese acting in an unacceptable fashion — bathing by the road-side, urinating in the park, drying laundry in the children's playground and even adults defecating in public drains! In years to come, I envisage, if things do not change for better, in Malaysia, there would be a further divide between the haves and have-nots as well as by racial divide. This demarcation would be made more precarious when the newly immigrated foreigners easily get assimilated as citizens and the rest is best left to each other's imaginations!FG25.8.11

Bizarre thoughts at a bazaar

So there I was, on a Saturday afternoon loitering around in an up-market bazaar on Petaling Jaya because my daughter just decided that she simply had to be at this place, like this place was the greatest innovation since sliced bread! The bazaar was a collection of canopy covered stalls selling various items that one can just do without, predominantly of dresses (which were made from not much of material, quantity and amount wise) and cute handicraft souvenir items.

Even one of the attendees was dressed like she was strolling along in Oxford Street for New Year sales in a crimson red suede long coat in the tropical environment of Jaya One! It was as if the patrons were loitering with blinkers oblivious to the reality of our climate and third world status!

The site was actually an avenue for small time on-line entrepreneurs to exhibit their merchandise. I was just wondering how many of these clothes were recycled hand-me-downs clothes or from somebody house's backyard clothes line! The thought just sparked in my brain when a pungent odour emanated from one of these canopy stalls as we passed them. It was definitely not a figment of my warped imagination. I distinctly overheard someone in the crowd mention the same (about the odour but theorised about a leak in the container carrying the garment, hence the mouldy musky odour).

Amidst this entire bourgeois capitalistic ambiance, tucked neatly in the corner were a few nurses and student nurses (working class?) trying to highlight the importance of self breast examination and (by the way) to support the victims of the dreaded malignancy by selling some over-priced t-shirts for that cause. Proceeds of the sales were supposedly going to the victims (yeah, right!).

The intentions of the youngsters may be noble — educating and propagating the news for a good reason. Whether the money actually reaches the intended recipient, that is anybody's guess. Like the tsunami area of Banda Aceh which is still undeveloped despite the outpouring of funds from the world over, and the Singapore NKF chief was found guilty of using the NGO's funds to fly first class and how the UN casual workers are only good at filling up claim forms in USD and on and on......

Just the other day, I found out that my sister had been contributing RM30 monthly for the past 10years through direct debit of a credit card to WWF. I know that she is an animal lover and all but 30X12X10 = RM3600.00 for beastly animals?

Yeah! I love animals too, so much that I eat them regularly, cooked and nicely garnished, of course.FG27.8.11

Eat to live or live to eat?

Malaysian's favourite pastime, besides sitting down at the Mamak's over a cuppa complaining about injustices in the country and doing nothing about it, is eating. This is evident from the ever mushrooming of stalls here and there as well as the existence of 24hr shops serving death-calling unhealthy food at each corner of the city. Hence, it is only logical that the 24hr cable TV be filled with cook shows. Besides the usual variety of food show depicting cuisine from the four corners of the world, of late they are cooking reality shows. The famous show run by the Scottish chef with a razor sharp tongue, infamous temper and fussy temperament (otherwise referred to perfectionist) seem to be a current favourite amongst my kids. I do not think they particularly plan to take a career in culinary field or plan a cuisine for their parents to appreciate their efforts in feeding them! I think they are more fascinated with the dialogue (or rather lack of!). It is filled with so many beeped out sentences that there is hardly a decent conversation as it is filled with profanity but one does not need much imagination to figure it out!

Gordon Ramsey behaves as if the errors made by the contestants are life threatening as if they are driving a 100-tonne lorry or performing life and death precision-required brain surgery! For God's sake it is just food. From I learnt in Form 1 commerce studies, food is one of the basic items to live, period. We need food to live. We eat to live, not live to eat and life is not all about eating tasty food. There are other things in life than eating. The meat is slightly rare to your liking. So what, you should be grateful that you are able to eat at all! Even Manoj Kumar said the same message in '*Roti Kapaada aur Makaan*' (Bread, clothing and abode).FG2.9.11

Nature vs. Nurture

You can only motivate someone so much. After that, it is left to nature or genes as one may call it. The more you push him to the brim, the higher the chances are that he may just flip. Everyone has his own capability to achieve his place in space and time at his own pace or bar of achievement. We cannot set our target and expect everybody else to follow. And just because the other person does not reach our expectation, it does not mean that he is a failure. At his own leisurely pace and perhaps longer duration, he may actually attain enviable dizzying heights. The ability to explore and try out one's varied, sometimes eccentric ideas, not following blindly to preset norm is the cornerstone of innovation that started the Industrial Revolution at the end of the 19th century which categorically ended the greatness of the feudalistic empires of the world to be replaced by republics and people's rule of law by consensus. Let it be....FG8.9.11

What makes them tick on and on (like a Duracell bunny)?

We are all used to hear of employees in Malaysia who have no qualms of calling in sick for the flimsiest of reason that one can think of — great grandmother sick, grandfather died at the age of 100 or the dog in ICU! Sometimes the same relative die repeatedly and conveniently so as to ease their absence from work. Sometimes 3 days of national holiday in the middle of the week means a whole week of holiday! For example, recently *Aidilfitri* and *Merdeka* holidays were from Tuesday to Thursday. Most employees took it for granted that holidays start from the Saturday before all the way to the Sunday following *Merdeka* (a good 9 days of rest if Monday and Friday is sick leave!)

On the other end of the spectrum, believe you me, we have people who persevere through thick and thin with only one thing on their mind — to achieve their One Vision against all odds, what may come! Life goes on...

It comes to mind how two recent British Prime Ministers came to the height of their respective careers in spite of happenings at their domestic (meant their own homes) front. Gordon Brown (2007-2010) had his first (2001) born prematurely and succumb to cerebral haemorrhage. In 2006, his son (third born) was diagnosed to have cystic fibrosis(CF), which in the UK, has a life expectancy of 31 years. David Cameron (PM from 2011) recently lost his beautiful 'special child' Ivan (b. 2002 with cerebral palsy and seizures) in 2009 aged 6. In spite of having a child who needs constant round-the-clock supervision, he managed to climb his ambitious ladder to reach his present stature. Do you call that apathy, being self-centred or being practical — life has to go on? Do their wives nag them for not being a helping hand around the house, that do they (the wives) have to do all the job around the house, that charity begins at home or to take care their own flesh and blood before jumping to help others to garner votes? I was just wondering.... Perhaps politicians have thick skins, thicker than the toughest crocodile hide!

Whatever said and done, hats off to these gentlemen for persevering in their ambition in spite of the adversities in life and ticking on and on like a Duracell bunny!FG13.9.11

Are we mature enough?

Are we, Malaysians as a nation, mature enough to discuss so-called sensitive issues without being all sensitive and sentimental about it? The answer is an emphatic NO! It is even more difficult to 'discuss' as a big chunk of so called Malaysian citizens cannot converse and communicate with each other due to inability to converse in a common language and deep rooted suspicion of each other. Eating and enjoying other's delicious cuisines and slurping till the last drop is where national integration stops for some!

This is evident by the recent two happenings in the country. Ruling coalition leaders are crying foul with crocodile tears asking for the scalp of opposition leaders who suggested the possibility of a) the communist warriors/terrorists (depends which side of the fence you are on) as freedom fighters and the policemen who defended the British fort in Bukit Kepong as British stooge; and b) the national flag, *Jalur Gemilang*, looking like a carbon copy of the Star Spangled Banner, be re-designed to reflect our own identity!

In this country, everything that is taught in History lessons is expected to be accepted as the gospel and divine decree. There are always two sides of the coin, sometimes three if the coin stands on its side! History has also shown that the churches have been wrong on numerous occasions, starting from Nicholas Copernicus onwards. At least, they changed their stand as time went on when they realised that their belief does not hold water any longer!

Now, the conquerors ruled their conquests through appointed agents and proxies. From the Romans to the various Emperors, they ruled their subjects with their own (meaning the conquered) people so as to maintain peace, order and fear whilst the victors can enrich their own race. As to ease administration, they introduced systems of education, policing and cultures which were naturally perceived as 'modern and cultured' by the ones defeated. Does that make the agents traitors? Or the people who fought for self rule trouble makers? These are the points to ponder in a civil debate! Not making police reports and whining like a toddler whose toy had been snatched away by the bigger child.

Everyone knows the uncanny resemblance of our flag to the US even though the majority of Malaysians hate the gut of the American and their hegemony of world policing. At the time of the birth of our nation was at period of Cold War and Iron Curtain, hence to showcase to the world that we are indeed not a tool of the communists but in cahoots with the capitalistic and democratic league of the world. What better to show this than to have a flag which is almost identical to the Big brother's?

Malaysians may boast of having 98% literacy rate but are we really learned or educated in the real sense?FG27.9.11

The Eye in the Sky will get you!

Just the other day, I visited my long-lost schoolmate for Raya. There he was in his bungalow with 2 Porsche parked majestically in his posh porch (Cayenne and a 911) with a 24 hour security guard stationed in front of his house which was already sitting in a guarded community housing estate. Understandably, his sensitive position as a high-flying executive in his line of work warrants such an arrangement.

After living and working in the US for more than 10 years as well as living flamboyantly in the fast lane, he returned home to settle down. And here he was sitting down with me and other old schoolmates.

I noticed that he had become quite private in his outlook. He does not have many friends. He does not have a Facebook account for fear of intrusion of his daily activities! Eh, does he has more that he needs to hide? Maybe...

Later, we were discussing his toys — his Porsches and their performance! He had apparently hit 240 km/h on the highway! When asked about speeding tickets, he answered to the affirmative. The worse part, however, was when a summons was sent to his house with an ensuing digitalised 'mugshot' photoshoot depicting him and another temptress who was not his wife driving along as a passenger in his SUV. And he was supposed to be in a meeting, not *en route* to Port Dickson where the shot was taken. Now we understood the privacy and secrecy!

With the advent of the internet, Google and the World Wide Web, nothing seem to be sacred or secret anymore. The tentacles of the web will spread its stuff like what spiders do into all nooks and corners to expose everyone's secret lives. Just like how MCA's feeble attempt to draw youngster into its wing fell flat on its face. Everyone went agog when a bevy of beauties claiming to be party members paraded shamelessly to the assembly to entice the roving eyes to join the party something like how the mice followed the Piped Piper of Hamelin.

Leave it to the Netizens, a few days later, the full expose of the said members were out in the open, complete with pictures to match. As predicted, these beauties ranged from lingerie models to pit stop babes! Go ahead, try to make out who is who. They are look alike to me! All straight hair and manga inspired heroine's eyes!FG12.10.11

Have you found it?

I remember a time circa 1972 when the streets around my primary school were plastered with billboards bearing the words 'I found it!' — with the letter 'O' written in at heart shaped manner. Nothing else was written on these billboards, stirring the curiosity of everyone in town and a few cats died with their curiosity! A couple of weeks later, the rendezvous was flashed across billboards without indicating the purpose of the meeting except with messages like "I found it, have you?"

That got more people more curious and the dead cat twitched too! And the curiosity mounted to a climax as time went on. People started asking each other what that was all about. Was it a new wonder medicine which was the panacea to all human woes? Or a new shopping mall? Whatever it was, they knew that it was all a business strategy.

Never in their wildest dream did they expect to see what they saw when they saw it anyway. It was a mass congregation of souls in a field to listen the gospel word of the Lord by a world famous Man of God who had worked wonders with his brand of evangelism with his congregation back in his hometown where he preached.

That is the beginning of the realisation of the power of advertising.FG14.10.11

Poverty: A prerequisite to succeed in life?

After the recent passing of Steve Jobs, his touching meaningful speech at Stanford had been making its rounds again on the radio, social media and blogs. And everybody now knows about his unwed mother giving him up for adoption and how she reluctantly signed the adoption papers after months after she discovered that the intended adopted parents were not university graduates, as, in her mind, only graduates become successful in life. And how he had to travel 7 miles to have free Hare Krsna food! We have also heard of the story of Lincoln Murthi in previous blogs about his roller-coaster escapades from the clutches of poverty to succeed in life. And the list just keeps on going, from AJ Kalam all the way to God knows who!

Just the other day, my buddy and I were discussing whether Steve Jobs would have still done what he did for the computer world and Apple if he indeed had been adopted by a lawyer or a doctor. Would he still have brought in changes in the IT world if he had grown up in the luxury of American life?

Recently I managed to catch the concluding episode of a *realimentary* (reality documentary) series on History Channel named IRT: Deadliest Roads where truckers were sent on assignments to transport sensitive cargoes along the scary roads in the Himalayas amidst the harassment of the horn blaring happy, irritating, courtesy-challenged Indian drivers. Surprisingly, a rose (a petite 28-year-old) emerged victor among the thorns (big beer bellied moustachioed bald tattoo displaying monster truckers) after the final tasks. She braved the icy mountain roads to supply aviation fuel for helicopters in a God forsaken place in the Himalayas!

In her last departing prophetic dialogue in that episode, Lisa Kelly, 28, the only North American trucker to have driven the amount of miles in that part of the world had to say, "We have to be stretched in order to grow!"FG16.10.11

Melatah.tah.tah...

The Malay diaspora can stand tall in the eyes of the international arena for at least two distinctly unique behaviours - Amok and Latah.

The act of warriors going on a killing rampage for pride and honour (amok, meaning frenzied Malay in older dictionaries) was recorded as early as 1670 by European seafarers. Even James Cook, the 'discoverer' of Australia noted in his journals of these occurrences in the Malay Archipelago. In modern times, it has been described as a mental defence mechanism or a suicide attempt in a society where suicide is frowned upon, knowing well amok results in loss of life of the sufferer.

Over time, amok has been made aware to the international community and had made it to the Oxford dictionary many years ago. It is also said that the warring psyched Viking would also go into a trance-like rage before a duel.

Another phenomenon which is unique to the Malay people is the act of 'latah'. Apparently a small obscure tribe in Hokkaido also has sufferers of latah. Typically it is seen in middle-aged peri-menopausal ladies who upon simple prodding would start singing, dancing and talking in incoherent language. The trigger factors for this could a simple slipping of a tray or slight pulling of the garments, much to the amusement of people around her. People of other cultures may not see the joke surrounding the action of the sufferer, but it tickles them so much that they do it repeatedly. The person who *latahs* acts almost at an unconscious level and has no recollection of it afterwards.

Intermingling and close proximity at work of races in this country over time has 'latah' a kind of contagious infliction. It is a common sight to see Malaysian Indian civil servants going '*Pecot,cot,cot......*' at a little startle. This, I think is self-inflicted *latah*, in an attempt to blend with fellow working colleagues. And my Cambodian maid also *latahs* when startled!

"Latah is a condition where, triggered by the startle reflex, victims fall into a trance in which he or she engages in repetitive speech or movements. Often these take the form of echopraxic and/or echolaliac automatisms. Latah is found only in certain world cultures and is therefore commonly considered a culture-specific syndrome. Wikipedia"FG20.10.11

Jung Punks - Psychoanalyzing psychotic deviant teenagers

I have come across many teenagers who rationalise their inertia in life and their inability to attain their full potential by going under the cover of psychological rationalisations. They suddenly become junior Jungs and Freuds to pass the blame to (thank you very much) their parents who did what they thought were best they could do in their best of ability, knowledge and resources.

These young loafers have no qualms in blaming the absence of paternal love, dearth of fatherly bonding, peer pressure of their dog eat dog world, regimental upbringing, systemic humiliation by parents, yearning for brotherly or maternal touch, sibling rivalry or everything else under the sun except themselves for the reason for their ill-fated situation — everyone and everything else except themselves.

They call it the stress of modern living and their role models are none other than the Kardashians - yeah, the dysfunctional family with quirky and warped sense of values but the teenagers all over the world use them as yardstick of how life should be lived!FG24.10.11

Angered by Angry Birds

It looks like in a cycle of every 10 years, someone from some corner of the world would come up with some droll character which will be personified with human characters, cute with aesthetically pleasing features and take the world by storm. At the end of the day, it would be aimed at reaping financial benefits out of it. That is always the bottom-line, is it not — $, £, ¥ and €?

In the 1980s, it was the irritating pink female feline kitten which ruled the world. Suddenly, it was Hello Kitty everywhere! There were even shops selling only Hello Kitty merchandise — dresses, slippers, makeup, nightgowns, accessories, you name it. I suppose even before that people used to have a fetish for domesticated hairy bears fondly named Teddy after Theodore Roosevelt! And the China Dolls, of course now it means something else...or Japanese porcelain dolls ala Chucky!

Just for information, as of 2003, Sanrio, the Japanese company who designed this Kitty, was earning USD 1billion annually.

Then in the 1990s, it was the reign of the violent Pikachu characters of the digital Pocket Monsters (Pokemon). Maybe, because they were Eastern in origin and came out at the correct time when computer games were at an embryonic state and had the world by storm, many sore losers hurled many brickbats against them. The Christians, Jews and Moslems discouraged people of their faith to embrace its cult-like practices of violence, albeit being just a mirage! If that is not enough to add to their list of problems, some children started having seizures after watching one of their stroboscopic red and blue lighted episodes on TV and it had to be discontinued. 2 kids in Japan filed a legal suit blaming Pokemon for making them compulsive gamblers.

Not to be left out in the race for cute animal craze of the world which had been dominated by the Japanese all this while, a Finnish company managed to capture the hearts of the pet-figure deprived population of the world with their computer game called Angry Birds. Suddenly you see people wearing T-shirts bearing the grouchy irritated faces of these avian species and carrying balloons with their caricature! The whole aim of the Angry Birds' game is for the birds to destroy the hiding place of the pigs to retrieve their eggs which were stolen from them, hence their anger!

So, download the application on your *i*-phones (intelligent phones) and degenerate your brain cells in the process and kill your precious time in this time deprived fast world as if you have too much of them. Hurt your joints, dim your vision, have a headache, be a recluse, be addicted and basically use your skills to hurl things at pigs like a bird-brained loonies! Enjoy...FG29.10.11

My house, My home, My kingdom

Growing up in RRF, we yearn to have regular addresses, not an address with block number, floor number and unit number. We were quite fed-up explaining to our schoolmates why there were so many dashes, hyphens and digits on our address instead of just the house number and road name. I suppose the stigma of living in a low-cost high rise slump-like flats in the 70s was more the reason of the above. Even though living in the 21st century means condominium resort type of living is the norm, we from RRF still find contentment living with our feet on the ground in landed properties!

If you have access to people's addresses like I do, then you would have noticed that some addresses leave no place for imagination on their social economic strata. Home addresses like '*Projek Perumahaan Rakyat*', '*Projek Rumah Murah*', *Taman Bukit Mewah*' will tell you how their home would look like.

Someone told me that many years ago, the mental facility in Kuching, Sarawak used to be called '*Rumah Sakit Orang Gila*'! And Tampoi Psychiatric Hospital had been known as wad '*Orang Sakit Otak*'. When we grew up in Penang, anyone originating from Tanjong Rambutan was mental unless proven otherwise as the premier northern region Psychiatric Hospital was stationed there.

There is a place in Sabah called 'Menggatal'. Are the people ridiculed to be promiscuous, I wonder?

One cannot help it but over time certain names are acceptable by the public may one day become hurtful or politically incorrect. Many years ago, children with Trisomy 21 (Down's Syndrome) used to called Mongols without batting anybody's eyelids. Ever since, Mongolia started being heard on CNN and started producing models, nobody called them Mongols anymore. Down's baby and special child they are!FG31.10.11

Toloooong..! Ah Long!

Just the other day I saw two mean bad looking (not the opposite of good looking — like the lyrics of The Beatles' Come together — "*Got to be good looking 'cause he's so hard to see*" but rather the one referred to in Jim Croce's Bad, Bad Leroy Brown-"*The baddest man in the whole damned town, Badder than old King Kong, And meaner than a junkyard dog"!)*- late teenager young men with a skeletal-like physique with matching drainpipe slim jeans and tight ebony black t-shirts to attenuate their appearance, blondish streaks on their otherwise straight Oriental hair pasting away A5 sized stickers to their heart's content of their services on the road signage and road side pillars! Their services? Answer to you financial woes, call mobile ##! Or rather the start of your woes!

Now, what should a law abiding country loving who loves himself more, do when public property is being defaced? Just pass through looking the other way whistling to your favourite tune oblivious to what is happening around you, that is what! Even the long arm of the law in the country cannot do anything about it, what can a lowly ordinary citizen like me do?FG2.11.11

Just where do you draw the line?

Dr Steven Shafer, the Columbia University Anaesthesiology Professor, at Michael "Whacko" Jackson's trial on using propofol as a sleeping aid....
"'Yes' is not what a doctor says to a patient request that is not in their best interest."
"We are in pharmacological never-never land here, something that was done to Michael Jackson and no one else in history to my knowledge," he told the jury.
"...Dr Conrad Murray had acted like the pop star's obedient "employee" and not his doctor, who should have refused the star's requests for propofol."

FG was once told by his part-time casual employer not to return to do locum work as the patients were unhappy with FG's refusal to administer a narcotic analgesic injection as outpatient to someone for something trivial (a headache) when an oral medication should suffice. The joke was on FG as the employer went on to prosper to become a local leader and was bestowed numerous suffices to go behind his name for services rendered to society. He was also honoured with honorary prefixes to his name while FG still ploughs along, living from hand to mouth, with a clear conscious hoping to have garnered plus brownie points when he is judged at the Pearly Gates and St Peters as well as when he has to continue the karma and cycle of life in his after life!

The honourable physician's excuse of justifying administration of a narcotic injection with his ensuing danger of haemodynamic collapse and secondary injury as result thereof is that the patient will still get it elsewhere if you do not oblige!

This incident resurfaced in my mind when Michael Jackson's trial came to fore. This guy just loves pomp and publicity. When he was alive, he created a blast and he went off with a blast as well! When everybody else can go to sleep by tiring themselves or with beer or even counting sheep. No! When some of the recalcitrants sleep like a baby sucking their thumbs with Dormicum or Xanax, no, MJ needs general anaesthesia! And The King of Pop became a statistic in the Doctor's file.

Why did the good doctor do it? To anaesthetise someone for sleeping disorder? Whatever we discuss is pure speculation, as he is not giving any press statement for fear of retribution.

Imagine what being a personal physician to MJ would have done to his serendipity of a career. Dr Conrad's asking rates would have skyrocketed and he would be confiding in his friend just to say that if he does not the take the ridiculous offer from this fool, some other clown would have taken a killing and at least he would give superior care as a cardiologist!

It is just like a state physician whom I used to know whom used to be called '*dei*' in a derogatory way for attention by the not so intelligent state monarch for the flimsiest discomfort. This friend of mine used to oblige as that was his nature and he was happy that he was serving the King and country!

Money clouds everybody's sane judgement and in the race to make a killing in the financial sense (sorry for the pun) where the margin of moral and finances is blurred, anything goes. We can go on talking and talking till cows come home and go grazing till our time on earth is up and we would have not come to a reasonable agreement!FG5.11.11

Faux Pas

We all have our foot in the mouth moments in our lives. One that comes to mind is an incident that happened some 20 years ago at a time when spaghetti was a carbohydrate filled meal (not an outdoor outfit) and visible bra-strap was dented modesty (not a fashion statement). And values were values... And this is after the time when subtle remarks like "Your Monday is longer than Sunday" were passed between girlfriends when their petticoat was visible.

One Monday morning, the operating theatre staff was excited to welcome the newest addition to their army of married women, with their heckling and giggling. It was common knowledge that a colleague got married recently and had just returned from her widely publicised honeymoon. So, there I was, after finishing with my work, bumped into newly appointed Mrs X. She was sitting in a corner feeling distraught and retching away. Being the joker that I am, I joked, "Wow, just came back from honeymoon and you are having morning sickness! Fast worker".

To my dismay, she sheepishly answered, "Actually, you are right. I am 2 months pregnant!"

Suddenly I felt the flushing of blood to the back of the neck and occipital region with a tingling sensation at my toes and a lump at the back of my palate and uvula!" I shrivelled up into a ball and disappeared from the scene with my tail behind my back after expressing, "Congratulations!"

Religious Renaissance?

At one time in my early life, I was drawn into the Bhajan group (Hindu religious group) which introduced me to the likes of saintly figures and the basic teachings of Hinduism. At a time when achieving academic excellence was the only agenda in our lives to uproot ourselves from the perpetual sorrows of our household, he were hoping for divine guidance and assistance to peel open our third Eye of Wisdom. In our simpleton minds, we assumed that education which would lead us to easy wealth accumulation which in turn would be the panacea of all our worries in life. If only life was that simple!

In a world filled with deceit and forgery, one sometimes wonders why when it comes to matters pertaining to God, humans always transform to exhibit the best of their inborn excellent primitive virtues. This was evident from photos from Banda Acheh after the tsunami — only the mosque stood up tall amidst ruins of homes and other infrastructure. Probably, the contractors did not short change the mosque when it came to using the correct ratio of mix of cement to soil during construction!

Quite a number of times during my not so frequent visits to a place of worship, I find the same group of people blissfully returning with full of joy savouring the moment they are there, doing the things they do there. I wonder why?

Is it that the parties involved have ulterior motives or they have found people of same frequency and mindset to do the same things i.e. serve humanity? Have they done some much sins that no amount of divine forgiveness can rectify? Or is it a place to find solace for the wounded souls? Or birds of the same feather flock together, hoping that well thinking people will only augur pleasant thoughts and healthy activities? My recent observations revealed a few revelling discoveries. It is by no means exhaustive. It is only to satisfy myself and bloat my own ego.

I noticed a guy who found sheer joy in cleaning the soiled plates after the worshipers had eaten their temple food. He was there faithfully, without fail, come rain or shine, on Sundays doing his thing humming his hymns. I later discovered that he was a physician and a vegetarian who had a bitter experience at matrimony — the bride did not turn up at the wedding — sounds more dramatic but actually the bride-to-be decided to call of the wedding a few days before the big day. The grieving groom never tried to get another's hand but decided to find solace in the Way of the Lord.

Then there is a family who commemorates all functions in the temple. Can you imagine a 21year old young chap announcing to the world his freedom key by having a sombre bash in the temple? Of course you do not clap and you do not blow the fire on the candle (*Agni*), you chant when the fire is lit (*Jyothi*). You are supposed to rejoice when there is light (hope), not when the flame is blown away! Mmmm.... But then cutting cake is not Indian, you should cut *kesari* or *halwa*!

And you also have obviously oversized grandiosely wealthy grouchy grandmas with their accompanying helpers trotting along... If religion advocates moderation in all your activities, how did you get so fat? — could not control the temptations of the taste buds, despite being a vegan, eh?

And there are people like me who hope to cleanse his soul and mind by being in the house of God but keep thinking with devilish recurring ill deviant thoughts of people and things around him just for the kick of it. What's the point? I am back to square one!FG26.11.11

Alien Nation?

The more knowledge a person has, the more confused he would be. The more a person knows, the more a person cannot give a straight answer to any question. A typical answer to a question would be an exercise in circumvention, circumlocution, circumflexion, circumspection, evasion and dodging. Ignorance is bliss, they say. And the more you learn, the more there is of subject matter remains unanswered.

Armed with the knowledge of Erich von Daniken's Unsolved Mysteries of the Past in the 'Chariots of the Gods?', I attended one of my good friend's daughter's engagement ceremony in a temple. Yeah, my friends are getting older just like me!

Even though this was not the first time I was seeing the things I saw but I was seeing things from a different light, not only due to my recent exposure but due to the boredom that hit me even before the ceremony commenced. Remember the saying about the idle mind and devil's workshop.

With Lord Ganesha (the deity with an elephantine head, trunk and belly) in the heart of the *Gopuram* of the temple, it just looks like a driver in the drivers' seat. The elephantine head with crown and trunk goes well with a head geared space suit and breathing apparatus connected to the oxygen cylinder (?belly). About 10 metres ahead was a tall flag-like structure which could pass off as a steer and the mouse (his mascot) could be a navigation probe (mouse in computer!). You just have let your imaginations go wild — you will see what your mind wants you to see. And do not forget the fire and the smoke from glowing incense (*sambraani* — benzoin resin) may just complement the aura of a lift off a space ship. And the climax of the prayers occur at the time the priest parades a multi-tiered tray of burning camphor and the loud chiming of giant bells......... Symbolic or what?....FG2.12.11

This is it? Look, See, Visualize...

Life is a continuum that Man is trying to make sense of. Ignorance and the zest to acquire the hidden secrets of the universe and space, which he perceives as 'an awful waste of lots of space' lingers on and will linger on till 'Thy kingdom come'. From time immemorial, Man tried to figure out various mind boggling natural events like natural calamities, disease and emotions. The eldest amongst the pack, the most powerful, the most domineering, the bravest or the furthest travelled will take charge and dictate how 'life' should go on. And life went on with a few hitches here and there. The magnificent forces of Nature still could not have answered all their questions. The question of angering the 'forces' above came to mind. The leaders decided that certain manoeuvres be done to appease them.

Much to everybody's dismay, the misery just kept on rolling. Variations to ways doing things were introduced by disgruntled individuals. Alternative explanations were given to occurrences of events. Later, science was introduced to negate the word God from the equation. The questions just got more and more numerous to be enumerated than there were answers. Everybody gave their own explanation and it got more complicated. They went to the elders who gave their own interpretation of how it used to done in the good old days but failing memory due to senility, diseases and apoplexy gave less credibility to the fact. Anyway, some of the answers were given in riddles and were lost in translation. Consummate believers made their own interpretations and rules as they went on and called it progression of religion (to satisfy themselves that the answer is indeed out there).

We can go on and on but believe you me, it will get more perplexing. And frightening when everyone start thumping their chest emphatically and dancing to their war dance tune trying to prove their point at all cost, having no qualms in dying a martyr proving it.

At least we can console ourselves in knowing that there is a common good and orchestrated system that these teachings give to the down-trodden and weaklings in the society by threatening its believers that somebody is watching their every move and taking points and would be judged at an unspecified date in the future or after-life! At least it gives some law and order to homo sapiens who would otherwise happily regress to their ancestral Neanderthal ways of the survival of the fittest with no remorse. And the grip of religion gives a purpose and grip to life when the going gets tough and all hopes seem forlorn! And pacify themselves that He knows best and it is all a trial and tribulation before things gets better, something akin to a tuft of grass to grasp on to avoid jumping off the cliff or going berserk, walking aimlessly in life losing all zest and purpose to live. In other words to persevere, like in a **scene** from P. Ramlee's *Pendekar Bujang Lapok* where the trio goes to the grave-yard at midnight to chant for 4D numbers and brushing off the funny eerie noises that they hear by sayings "*Cubaaa..n!*" and carrying on the task at hand!

Of course, there is an alternative theory to all these. Predecessors of homo sapiens (hominids and Neanderthals) were walking (crawling, trotting, galloping) along when they were visited by alien visitors with advanced civilisation and know-how. They infused their DNA to correct certain deficiencies and imparted their technologically advanced knowl-edge to them. They taught them how life should be lived after living in the universe way longer than their 'young' inferior friends. The Earth-lings, awed by their culture and machinery idolised their visitors (men-tors) by moulding structures after them and worshipping their great-ness. Follow their teaching about your environment, daily routine of life,

interpersonal relationship, etcetera and your life will be paved with least resistance because they have been there and they have seen that. He is omnipotent and omnipresent. May the force be with you!
FG20.12.11

Joy to the World

The spirit of Christmas is already in the air. It started when I was ushered in to join my dear friend's church's musical presentation called 'This Little Child - The King of Kings' — a musical extravaganza showcasing the true meaning of Yuletide minus the commercial tags associated with it. His church members decided to put up a choir plus narration presentation.

I only managed to sit through two-third of the show as I had to entertain some foreign guests. What was sorely missing in most other religious organisations in Malaysia was nicely cultivated here in this hall! Youths were literally undergoing training to survive in the real world by improving their event management and many other skills — human interaction, stage decoration, music recital, band performance, sound system engineering skills, allaying stage fright, developing public speaking skills and many many more.

It may be a little preachy but, hey, good deeds and good values are universal to the betterment of mankind in general. In my opinion, the highlight of the show was the short film presentation symbolically depicting the gripping tale of a father who sacrificed his son for the safety of 400 over passengers aboard a speeding train. It was supposed to be a true story of a John Griffin in 1937 who became a rail bridge operator after losing all his money in the 1930 stock market — symbolically depicting the sacrifice of God in giving his only Son to die on the cross to wash the sins of mankind!

That my friend, is the true meaning of Christmas - the celebration of the birth of a Son of God to the world to save Man, not the clinking of wine glasses, countdown to stroke of midnight on Christmas Eve, the Santarinas and Santa and his elves!... Watch and learn....FG22.12.11

2 ways of dying?

Over the weekend, I met up with a friend who had moved into a spanking new house in the up-market part of town. After the usual cursory formalities and niceties, I had a chat with her father who had been diagnosed to have serious heart ailment.

He is a 77 year old man who, after the recent passing of his wife of almost 50 years, is living between her 3 daughters' houses at his own leisure. After striving hard to bring the bacon as a policeman through the hard times of the nation fighting bandits' intelligentsia in the country, he is glad that his 3 children are self sufficient and independent. He feels that his life and duties on earth is done and he is living on borrowed time! (Especially after being a chronic smoker of 50 sticks a day for 50 years till one fine day when he developed distaste to cigarettes upon completing pilgrimage to Holy Land.) Perhaps, he should have made the trip much earlier in life.

So, when his doctors investigated him for neck pain and found that, through a morbidly terrorising angiogram experience (for him, at least) there were 5 blocks in his coronary vessels, his decision was pretty easy to make. "No, sire! No intervention for me," he said despite all the well meaning persuasions from doctors and nurses. "For all you know I may have had these blocks for years before. Thank you very much!"

Well, there is no right or wrong decision in these situations. After all it is his life. We may have heard of complications during and after surgery.

I was just reading the other day of a doctor who had devised ingenious surgical procedures to treat a particular type of pancreatic cancer which itself had a poor prognosis, by prolonging life by 3 to 5 years, albeit with its poor quality. But sadly when he was afflicted with the very same disease that he had been treating patients for years, what he did was mind boggling to his peers. He called it quits. He closed his practice and decided to spend of his remaining days with his family. Sure, he did spend a lot of quality time for the next two years before leaving the company of his family.

That brings us to the two ways of how people deal with sickness — one quietly without pomp and splendour whilst the other in an almost fiesta like atmosphere. In the former, he would decide to deal with his trying time alone or with immediate family in secrecy. The latter would enjoy the attention, gifts, sympathy and self pity conveyed by equally extroverted family members and friends from near and far who would have no bearing on the outcome of the disease! The only thing missing would be confetti!

Perpetrators of the latter would vouch that kind support, gentle touch and sympathetic attention goes a long way in the organisation of fibrous tissue and resolution. Call me weird but how is answering the same question on the discovery or detection of the disease, mode of treatment and the constant reminder that everything is going to be okay is going to make you feel rejuvenated, get up, acquire Kryptonic supernatural powers and run?FG26.12.11

Help, I am married to the mob!

There goes my Newton New Year 25 km bash over the hills of Puchong and Bukit Jalil. As part of my extended family is dismantling from the country (lock, stock and barrel) early next year, I was literally arm-twisted to join in a family excursion up north with convoy of 20 in 4 cars. I would like to call it *'Jalan-Jalan Cari Makan'*. We would be stopping at big towns for meals to continue the journey and finally eat and sleep in the hotel for a real unwinding before marching into the challenges of the new year-2012. The year which is the last year in the Mayan calendar and the year where rumour mongers, naysayers and people who are good at creating a mountain out of a molehill predict to be the end of civilisation as we know it! Yeah! I have heard that many times before. Like the end of 1999 as in the TV show 'Space 1999' where the Moon loses its gravitational pull from the Earth to go out into space aimlessly and the news of San Francisco and Venice being underwater like Atlantis due to melting of polar caps and ......

...but like Elton John says, "I am still standing!"...however!

On top of the uprooting story, there is another reason to party as in previous years. 2 family members celebrate their birthday on 1st of January - My mother-in-law by default both husband and wife were given 1st January as their birth dates. The last thing on their minds of her parents in the difficult hunger and misery filled times endured in the trying times of colonial India was to remember their child's birthday, what more to celebrate it! Surviving another new day was indeed a birth day.

My brother-in-law, however, was genuinely born on the first day of the first month as a first born child. Just like in any traditional Sicilian family, we would all gather on new year eve to mark attendance, pay respect and usher the new year in unison! So this year was no exception. The following quote from Mafia move make more sense than to anybody else! Man who does not spend time with his family is no man.FG1.1.12

Different meaning to different people!

The reason horoscope (?horror-scope) columns in newspapers have stood the test of time and remained relevant to its readers is because of the way it is worded. It is so vague and can be interpreted differently by different individuals. An individual reading the daily report will perceive it as if it was written for them. And at the end of the day, in retrospect, they would swear that what was written was actually true to the last alphabet!

Well, the truth is so malleable that you can bend it whichever way you want to satisfy your personal agenda.

I suppose in the same vein, a guru would appeal to his congregation in the same manner. The sermons that he preaches about good human value would pierce into the very heart he is trying to arrow via Delphyan type of double talk which can construed by his listeners as if He is communicating directly with him, about him, to him oblivious to the hundreds or thousands in the crowd!

*Pearls of wisdom from FG: Just accept rituals that are not detrimental but has a positive message in it, do not ridicule them!*FG7.1.12

Masterpiece from the unheard decibels of a scream of a lunatic!

During my visit to the Louvre, I had arrived just at opening time. In spite of all the fantastic artwork and relics around, people were not interested. They were all zooming in to view the highlight of the revered museum-The Mona Lisa! — only to be disappointed be its miniature size dwarfed by all the surrounding mammoth work of art.

Ask anyone which is the second most painting in the world, chances are that they would probably only about Mona Lisa, Da Vinci and the mystery surrounding the identity, the masala and the uncertainty of the gender of the subject. The second, No!

Just to prove my point, I asked my two sons. Just like throwing a pie on my face, they matter-of-factly told me even without looking at me, The Scream. On probing, I found that they knew it from watching 'Sponge Bob Square Pants'. Yeah, the show which is accused of shortening attention span! They are more knowledgeable than I thought they were.

Just like all works of art, 'The Scream' has its own story.

I first saw it in primary school (painted by a student) decorating the hall without me knowing what it was. And it appeared again in secondary school as somebody's linograph printing in art and craft class. When the posters of 'Home Alone' started staring all over the world, little did I know that it was mirrored after the famous painting.

'The Scream' was painted by Edvard Munch, a Norwegian painter in 1893 in a street in Oslo.

This street housed a mental asylum in a country with the highest rate of suicide in the world. Walking along the street, one could hear screams of its inmate. Hence, the painting and the scream.

In 'Home Alone', the posture of the boy is meant to accentuate the scream of a boy forgotten by his family and is left to fend for himself on an otherwise innate piece of paper!

"I was walking along a path with two friends — the sun was setting — suddenly the sky turned blood red – I paused, feeling exhausted, and leaned on the fence — there was blood and tongues of fire above the blue-black fjord and the city — my friends walked on, and I stood there trembling with anxiety — and I sensed an infinite scream passing through nature." **Edvard Munch, 1893** *FG8.2.11*

To reach your destination in comfort or reach there anyway?

I have put down in words these two occurrences that happened this week over a short span of time. One of it happened in my scope of work and the other to someone I know.

The first person was a lady who was having menstrual problems for years altogether. Her GP, whom she saw last year, hurried her to have her problems sorted out ASAP as she appeared like an apparition to her, paler that a clean sheet in a deathly shade of pale that would make Casper the Friendly Ghost appear tanned! She, however, morbidly fearful of the people who use stethoscope as their trade tools, decided to procrastinate. Eight months later she presented at my workplace to be told of large growth in the cervix that need to be removed via a simple surgery but after treating her severe anaemia. Her haemoglobin level was 2.9 g/dl! *(Normal female range: 11.0 - 14 g/dl)* The last time I heard she was trying to get admitted at a medical facility near her house. Good for her....

My friend who has been suffering in agony for the past 25 years had finally thrown in the towel. He has decided to lose some of his wisdom by putting a final stop to his recurring problem of exacerbations and remissions of an impacted wisdom tooth. After having a painfully bad experience with a similar problem in the past during surgery on the contralateral side, he decided to procrastinate. Come Valentines' Day, he would lose his wisdom under general anaesthesia. Oh, no! If you indeed have certain memories erased from your brain as an effect of anaesthesia and you lose 2 of your total 4 of wisdom teeth, are you less than half smart? Anyway it cannot be that bad as 35% of the population do not develop wisdom teeth at all, but still wise all the same! FG11.2.12

It is all about money, honey!

Over the past few days Malaysian netizens have gone aghast with the YouTube clip that went viral over cyberspace of a scene of a staff of a KFC outlet having a tiff with a his disgruntled customer when the chicken ran out (the supply, that is, not literally).

From the customer's perspective:

After waiting in hunger in queue for more than an hour for a piece of the now easily the world's most famous poultry flesh, I was told right on my face that their prized merchandise had finished just when my turn was up. That is it! At least they could have forewarned that their supply was low.

When I stated my case, what I got was a rude reply which screamed of need for training in social etiquette and emphasis in customer service 101. After all I have my rights, I was a paying customer. KFC being a multinational company with standard operating procedure manuals should know how to handle such situations amicably. Shameful!

From the workers' point of view:

Here I am working day in day out for a measly RM4 per hour whilst the cost of living escalates exponentially. And the demands and the volume of the customers just keep on climbing. Just because they are paying me and are financially superior to us, they think we are their maids or slaves. It is vulgar how they buy chicken like nothing. Their individual purchase is more than what I make in a week but that is my problem. I should have studied harder and paid more attention in class. What will happen in my future, 20 years from now? On top of that my girlfriend is pregnant and I am not financially stable to marry her yet. The number of staff to man the counter and kitchen hardly increased since its inception. Two of our regular guys have called in sick and the hay that broke the proverbial camel's back is when this guy abused me for informing him that our chicken stock is finished, so I flipped!

And the wise man says....(in the comfort of his meditative posture and air-conditioned ambience)

Everybody was born on this world to perform their godly duties and they must do it well whether it is menial or earth shattering. It is clearly mentioned in all our scriptures. This case is the classic manifestation of anger of a member of the economically challenged side of an otherwise successful capitalistic economy. The victims at the lower rung of the ladder have bottled up much anger directed at the contentedly flaunting opponents. History has shown again and again that this can trigger of great human experiments that result in major change in man's history and economy. Disgruntled starving peasants barged into the Bastille in 1789 and guillotined royalties and noblemen. The Russians persecuted the Czar's family and Rasputin. In present time, a frustrated Libyan graduate self immolated to ignite the Arab Springs to ouster a seemingly indestructible tyrant. So beware! Capitalism is not perfect but it is here to stay to satisfy the unsatisfiable satiety of man of wealth and power. Changes have to made to ensure that those who are marginalised are taken care of as well.FG12.2.12

Funerals are too emotional

When I was small (even now), I just could not understand why Amma made it her divine duty to attend funeral ceremonies of her relatives, near and distant ones alike. When I asked her why she did so, she would reply that nobody would come for hers if she does not do so. I would retort that when one is dead, he would not know who came for his funeral, anyway.

So when my dear best friend's father was terminally ill recently, I made it a point to visit him when he was still alive and able to converse and say his peace to all friends and relatives. We all had a good chat reminiscing his younger days as a soldier serving in Congo back in 1962.

He took leave soon afterwards.

Attending funerals are a strain to the attendees and recipients alike. There is too much emotion involved. I rather be at the scene after all the dust has settled down. There are always people who take offence on this type of attitude!

P.S. I have seen too many times long lost relatives who never bother to keep in touch, just turning up miraculously at funerals to show their talent in theatrics and ability of self-expression that would evoke a tear or two from bystanders.FG16.2.12

All shook up!

There is a reason why games traditionally started and ended with a handshake. The two 'warring' factions who are out for each other's jugular during the games but will be having drinks again afterwards. This is known as gentlemanly conduct. What happens on the pitch is left on the pitch!

Times changed. People came out of the conquest of war mode and natives gained independence. Man's unquenchable inner desire to kill and dominate each other is steered towards games which promise equal footing of action and gore. Suddenly, games especially football became too big for its own good.

Along came creatures likes publicity and public relations managers who plucked out promises of the sky and the moon out of thin air moon to take the game to dizzying heights. And 'poof' came the vultures in the form telecommunications whiz to bring the players to everybody's living room. And the hyenas of lawyers sauntered in their circumlocutory lecture about ensuring justice and fair play to players, clubs, everything and everyone involved in this entity. They had started a pastime for the rich and famous, who had the luxury to flaunt the affluence to the scavengers who were out looking for crumbs in the royal courtyard!

Any news is good news for the development of the game. So when a racial outburst occurred during a multi-million bookie deciding match of the two most famous football teams of the world, it got people interested. With the average modern man's attention span on the decline, misadventures like these were played again and again to arouse interest in the game going on and on.

When a veteran suggested that they should just kiss and make up (not literally but with a handshake), his idea was shot down with the fastest ammunition. The powers that be decided that sports must be a beacon of hope to eradicate the fire of racism at its flint. The perpetrator was punished and when he returned to play the same opponent, he was expected to be dandy with him obliging with a handshake.

Now, for all the publicity yearning game had hoped for, the issue remains unsettled and people are still talking about it. Good for the game, any news is good news!!!FG17.2.12

Love will keep us together!

Fate has a warped and cruel sense of humour! In my limited exposure to turn of events and people in my lifetime, I have come to realise that people may have misunderstanding between and amongst each other for the most trivial of reasons — over pride, ego, worldly material, (lack of) show of respect, he said she said, etcetera. All it takes is a tragedy, in a form of accident, death or loss of love, all will be forgotten and everyone will cry together!

Paradoxically as love and money may be the root of all evil, they can also draw warring factions to the table and at the same time waiting to do a quick draw as and when the necessity arises! Love will keep us together, or whatever! FG20.2.12

One man's wastage is another man's economic stimulus!

Of late, they have been talk of unspeakable wastage of stream of milk filling the drains of Batu Caves all through the days surrounding *Thaipusam*. Money that otherwise can be used for the upliftment of the Indian Malaysian community is said to be literally down the drain.

Milk, as described by Datuk Zainal Alam, a fellow Penangite, comedian, entertainer extraordinaire, described it as the first and last thing consumed by human and would not have commanded so much stature and reverence in life in not for its pristine white hue. Imagine a purple liquid called 'milk'! I digress....

Much have also been griped about the humongous garland donned upon 'The First Lady' and her consort, which would have taken half an acre's yield, going to waste.

Ever since my language teacher in Form 1 (AA), told the class that we could not say the space expedition is a waste of money in our essay as money just changes hands, I took upon the idea. These acts of pouring gallons of milk, breaking grosses of coconuts, deflowering of plants to glorify idols are not usually a waste of resources. In fact, it stimulates economic activity. Dairy farmers, small plantation holders, florists, middlemen, transportation companies and small men all benefit tremendously from this sudden surge of demand. In turn, the need to improve production and distribution becomes necessary. Philanthropic act is still done but people have to work for it — no handouts!

It is just like the Chettiars in early history of our country. They were big landowners but were contented in keeping them idle for cows to graze and keep trespassers at bay. When the Chinese bought over the land when the British gave away independence and the Chettiars returned to their motherland, they started building supermarkets, factories, restaurants etcetera there. This had a snowball effect on related businesses and eventually these small and medium industries have now become the lynchpin of Malaysia's economy. But then, these activities are still going to leave our carbon foot prints of which our descendants will be cursing and trying to clean up. May all the worshipping now would help them then!FG22.2.12

Migration makes the world go round!

Yet another meal from another relative to mark their departure to the 'Land of the plenty'. With so many dinners in their honour, it looks like they simply cannot reverse their decision now to migrate lock, stock and barrel to Land of Vegemite Sandwich.

K's ancestry saga began at beginning of the 20th century when K's grandparents made their own boat to escape unliveable living conditions of the jewel in the crown of the British Empire. They, with a couple of friends, set sail on a thug boat to Maldives. The captain, obviously a captain of circumstances who got all his bearings crossed, found himself and all the passengers stranded in the wide open ocean at the mercy of the elements of nature, clinging on to whatever bits and pieces of their dear lives in no time. Rescued by a passing steamer, left with Hobson's choice, they landed in their next port of calling, Pearl of the Orient, Penang. Seeing many of their fellow countrymen (and women) in a harmonious symbiotic life with other immigrants and locals, they decided to set home there, as if they had much of a choice. In that situation, I suppose, everywhere you lay hat, that would be home!

They built home in a vacant plot of land in Parit Buntar, started cultivating and pretty soon were prosperous enough to be known as the place for a square meal where the kitchen never sleeps. After scaling through life in the rough seas to the edge of life and back, they took it upon themselves to be guardian angels to fellow travelling men. They had no qualms of helping others and appreciating inter and intra-personal relationship. Their home was home to anyone who would walk through their front door and never returns hungry!

The blessing uttered by the contended hearts of a full stomach must have gone a long way in ensuring the longevity of its inmates and prospering lives of its descendants. The next generation of the clan saw its members educated, responsible and holding respectable vocations. K's father became a top ranking police officer feared by villains of the day.

He posed majestically in the dailies after foiling yet another attempt by the bandits in creating mayhem! With his wife, a Kirby-trained educator, he travelled the country over, their motherland, educating the natives and ensuring peace in the newly independent nation called Malaysia. With the continuity of showers of blessings, like the falling petals of lotus flower off Goddess Laxmi, -gratitude of the satiety of a sage, perhaps, ensured life to be smooth sailing with succession of offsprings all well mannered and well educated.

Looking at the direction of the country with its uncertain gutter politics and communal upheavals, the 4th generation of the Malayan's own Quakers (who migrated to American fearing persecution only to prosper their *Newfoundland*) suddenly felt they had to migrate for the well being of their downlines just as their ancestors had fled adverse living environment a century earlier . They have decided that Australia would be their new found home. We all wish them the best! Bon Voyage! Over time, perhaps living conditions in Australia may decline and the need to migrate again may arise in generations to come. The whole cycle may be complete when migration to India may be the 'in thing' and the way India and China are holding the helm of economic prowl, its pull factor may not be an illusion but indeed could be imminent!

I just cannot help but remember the little caption from Indy Nadarajah and Alan Pereira's stage show (Man-O-pause) a few years ago where they were cross-dressed as Devi and Myrtle respectively. Devi, a happily living-in-Malaysia contended gossipy housewife meets up with her old neighbour, Myrtle, who had earlier migrated to Australia for 'better life'. Being inquisitive and busybody as most Malaysians are, Devi asks how Myrtle's children were performing as they were the main reason for her immigration. "Oh, my first son has got a skating scholarship to teach children at the beach, my second has become gay and my daughter is living in with a married man and have 2 children from two different men. And they are all very happy!"

*[*My English master(KSG) would be very crossed. Even though now migration and immigration used interchangeably, he strongly believed that migration is strictly for movement of animals whereas for humans the word is immigration!] FG24.2.12*

Obligation to remain sick!

A quarter of a century ago, when I was still in training, there was a patient who used to stay in the wards for weeks on end for asthma. Even though he may be moving around the ward, chit-chatting and carrying tales from patient to patient to create territorial animosity between chronic long-staying patients, when it comes to morning rounds, he would be wrapped in blanket sweating like a pig creating wheezy noisy breathing insisting that he was still unwell to return home. It went on for some time until the senior officer of the ward, aware of chronic asthmatics' ability to feign a wheezing sound of an asthmatic attack, managed to coax him to return to his worldly duties like working for a living! I can swear by the look that he had on his face, he was screaming *ala* Arnold Schwarzenegger avenging to be back-"Hasta La vista baby!"

In our daily lives too, we see many able bodies running their lives as if theirs is the most tragedy-stricken, ailment filled torturous life that is a burden living. Yet, they failed to see how so many physically, mentally and economically challenged individuals carry on life making do with what they have and are capable of and utilising it to its fullest potential. Yet, there remains an obligation to remain sick as an outlet to garner sympathy to avoid the stresses of getting up early in the morning and facing the obstacles of the real world.FG28.2.12

Some people thrive on hatred?

Look around the world! There is much so of hatred and division around us. Even amongst apparently homogeneous-appearing societies, there is suspicion and desire to dominate over the other. There is the West and East, North and South, Muslim and Christians, the fair skinned and the dark skinned, Sunnis and Shiites, indigenous people and immigrants, moderates and conservatives, between differing political ideologies and the list goes on.

Left in desperation with the will to survive against a common enemy, people will flock together and put their resources together. This is evident from scenes after major catastrophe like earthquakes and tsunamis. Even then, there would be people with economic reaping on their minds rather than helping the downtrodden. Maybe, we are waiting for Armageddon or attack from an alien civilisation to take over Earth like in 'War of the World' by H.G.Wells.

After the dust has settled from the tumult, leaders will instigate fear by dousing suspicion against fellow beings to garner support and loyalty to usurp power and stay there.FG15.3.12

Another chicken and egg story!

So you think you had it bad. You got a bad deal. You were born at a time when the stars were aligned at the worst constellations. Think again! Others who appear happy may have endured worse.

Yet another success story to share...

He hated it when people referred to him as 'the *pasar malam (night market)* egg seller lady's son even though it was on a positive note, usually awed by his excellent results in school. Being a small town, everybody knew each other and each other's children. He often wondered why his parents could not be like other regular parents with regular 9 to 5 jobs. Why has it got to be chicken, eggs and all the barn and feather? He also hated it when he had to give up his precious revision time to set up stall at *pasar malam* as early as 3pm so as to ensure their usual business area is not hijacked by others. This squabble amongst the small men was a common daily occurrence.

The increasingly raging teenage hormones propelled with desire to 'be somebody in life' were reasons for his oft common argument with his hardworking old man and woman. The atmosphere reached a critical point that he had to leave the household to stay with his grandparents. And away he went on his mission to be somebody....

Poverty is often said to be a driving point to kindle the inner spirits to succeed. And somebody he did become, self sufficient and role model for his family.

Fast forward to the future....The fences have been mended with his parents and relationship is cordial. The friction board (i.e., money) is out of the equation, everybody has more than enough money to spread around - Parents' egg business has blossomed like Sakura on cherry blossom season and they are more than self-sufficient.

Yet another happy story from the land of aplenty!

It still baffles me why different people deal with adversities of life with different ways - Some decide to indulge in self defeating negative ways, others fight the fight with tooth and claw and give fate a run for its money. Why is this so? Is it because of karma, fate, the company he keeps with, his DNA or just that inner eye of self righteousness (third eye) opens early in life before it is too late?FG29.3.12

Happy New Year to Fools?

After the PR disaster of handling of Copernicus and Galileo Galleili's assertion of the law of nature, the Vatican wised up. The new Pope invested their new earned contributions from the masses into books, library and scientific research. One of the new investment was a sundial monument to observe the movement of the sun.

New discoveries showed that the Church and the rest of the civilised world have been getting it all wrong. The radical minded Pope decreed that, to synchronise the season and to give leeway for the errors of the counting of the calendar all this while, modern world should fast forward the year by more than 10 days. He also set the New Year to start on 1st January every year from that year onwards. News spread like wildfire across the European continent.

Their transatlantic cousins who never really fancied the Vatican control (and in absence of global news network) continued ushering their new year at the end of March. The high nosed aristocratic Europeans used to sneer down their buffoonery and named their New Year All Fools' Day!

Interesting to note that the original new year used to be celebrated from March 25th all the way to April 1st, which coincided with the *Holi* celebration of fun and pranks as well as Persian new year, vernal equinox and springtime!

Rather than rejoicing to the pagan festivity of the position of the Sun in relation to the equator (even though the Sun is the elixir of life as we know it) in the Julian calendar, Pope Gregory decided that the beginning of the year should coincide with the biggest relevant to mankind — the birth of a child through Immaculate Conception of the Son of God. Even though, science have shown this event did not happen on 25th December 0 BCE but rather 15th October 3 BCE (through the back calculation of the bright star that the three wise men from the East followed- and named it the Gregorian calendar.FG1.4.12

Who decides what?
Who decided that Nicol David should be a world class squash star and not, say a chess master? Is it the parents' strict drilling and tireless pestering which Nicol took willingly at her stride that helped? Is it the neighbourhood that she grew in? Is it that an unexplained power from above that gave her and her parents this vision? Did a wise man who appeared from nowhere who suggested to them this path to follow? Did she or people around her realise that she had this special talent that made her where she is today? Is it the alignment of stars at her time of birth, if so I am sure there must be someone born exactly at the same time as she was but has not held a racquet in her life? Who gives the inner strength for an individuals to excel in something whilst someone else with almost the DNA make-up fails miserably. Who decides that the adequately prepared marathon runner should have a bust up midway through his race? Is it karma?

If so who decides who is born with a heart defect, with congenital blindness or congenital syphilis for which the child suffers for no fault of his? Is God so cruel that He should decree that they were born to suffer? Is there really a pot of gold waiting for them at the end of their life (or afterlife)? If it is really a punishment, how come the body has no recollection of their sins so that they can regret and repent? How is the soul going to 'feel' the wrath of the Creator for disobedience of Law of Nature?

These are the unanswered questions that boggle a mind of a half centurion as he slips into his second and final half of time on earth. The questions keep on piling up and accumulates as the body slowly immerses itself into the loss of inhibitory effect of C_2H_5OH.

There are questions, but answers to my quandary? Maybe my nimble mind is too shallow!FG12.4.12

Politics of gardening!

A simple noble intention of beautifying a garden can upset many quarters. When some soul initiated the idea of beautifying a portion of the Taman, everyone agreed that it was a good idea. Then when the hat was passed around for kind contributions, the same people started telling about law and rights. The land belongs to the local county and they do not see the rationale of parting with their moolah for somebody else's land. Some query why they others (so and so) are not paying. Some try the delay tactic and so forth. At the end of the day, the plan remained a plan until somebody started the ball rolling through his own pocket and getting his hands dirty with a few other helping hands. The controversy did not end there.

A Roman statue, discarded from somebody's garden, depicting a topless maiden cleaning her mane, proved too provocative for some, probably giving vivid sleepless nights. Maybe, it was rejected from the well-wisher's house for the same reason - Lady of the house did not want to share the head of the house's undivided attention! Early one Sunday morning, the stony torso was seen draped in a worn out t-shirt I guess some Prince Charming would have manifested in the drape of the dark of the night to salvage the modesty of the damsel by covering her cleavage. Mama Mia!

It is always difficult to get people to agree collectively on anything. Any decision by the majority will definitely upset the minority, they would rebel, start a rival faction, start a mutiny or even a revolution! To go around it, the concept of gazing into the crystal ball was initiated. A third person (in the form of an omnipotent alien force overlooking our every move and turning the tide to hurt the non conformer was suggested) appealed for a short time but then even amongst the same minded people, disagreement occurred and voila another off-shoot of the same movement manifested. Both parties think that they themselves are doing better! And the debate continues......FG5.5.12

The tongue has no bones!

This is a blatant bastardisation of a Malay proverb which goes like this, *'Lidah tidak bertulang'*. Essentially it means that talk is easy and words can be malleable to suit a particular scenario. In other words, it shows the insincerity of man who would sway to the tide. Well, this colossal trait of the glossus (tongue) is a particularly useful tool of the trade of some professionals in the upholding the law (whichever side) business as well as politicians who have to make statements and modify them periodically.

Why this talk about tongue, bones and insincerity?

On 9th May, Wednesday, at 6 pm, a 51-year-old seasoned trekker went into the jungle to trek out a path for his fellow climbing junkies and never came back. By the following day, a search party had been organised by police, family and friends to track him down. Just as soon the newspapers announced the news by Friday, that is when the stories began to roll on...

Everybody started giving their worthless opinion on the possibilities of what could have happened even without their shoes soiled but with the comfort of an ice-chilled beer.

' *"He could have had a fall in the stream and could have been swept to the sea with our present unpredictable weather!' ' said one.*

' *"You know, there was a similar case a few years ago. Another trekker went missing and was never found. After a span of 10 years, a distant relative found him in America assuming a totally different look and identity. He had to run away from his overwhelming problems. You can never say..." '.*

' *"Maybe it was robbery and murder, with our appalling crime rate now..." '*

And the spin doctors kept on yarning their yards of stories whilst the family continued their search and prayers. Came Sunday, the trekker was finally found weak, dehydrated after injuring himself after a fall. Kudos to the diligence of the search party. *Waheguru!*

*The grateful wife said, "Every single one of them is a hero and they haves made today a Happy Mothers' Day for me. I thank them all,".*FG15.5.12

Listen, do you want to know a secret?

Tariq Ramadan, a liberal Islamist, once asked the Dalai Lama, "Why do you recite your chants at 4 o'clock in the morning?". The wise one replied, "It is for my own self-discipline!"

That, I think, my dear friend, lies the secret of mankind. The secret of all secrets is now out in the open. The rationale for people to do what they do as somewhat ritualistic, obsessive and compulsive-like is actually to instil self-discipline in oneself. The purpose of prayer is not to request the Creator for wealth, health, happiness and protection for a pain free life and after-life but rather to instil this human value so that he can think out rationally his next course of action so as to ensure he leads the path of least resistance. The quiet ambience in which one partakes his meditation and prayers must be the cornerstone for him to rationally think out his actions and act accordingly without rash.

The ritual of allocating one day in a week for spiritual work, faithfully doing seemingly repetitive actions several times a day, sitting in a literally in a spine and leg breaking postures are all for the sole purpose of self-discipline.

"Self-discipline for what?" you may ask....

Self-discipline to do what you are supposed to do on earth — a butcher, baker or tin-can man. Whatever you may do to maintain that equilibrium on the big jigsaw puzzle that is a fragment of events of the butterfly effect of life.

But remember, too much of self-discipline can also be self-detrimental. As Buddha (before Enlightenment) was finding for the ultimate truth to relieve Man of the tortuous repetitive cycle of life, he discovered that meditation was the way to go. He dwelled into high level spiritual form of meditation where one can control autonomic nervous system of body where one can go into a vegetative state without food and water for days. If not for a young girl who fed him forcibly, he would have been history without leaving a mark!

N.B. Did you know that the trace of Buddha had disappeared from face of India, no thanks to the attacking Hindu and Muslim kingdoms? It took archaeologists of the colonial masters from 1860 to 1890 to locate his birthplace as Lumbini and Kapilavastu where his father's Shakya kingdom palace used to be. They pinpointed it to be located in Nepal.FG24.5.12

Satyagraha and Thaipusam penance

Reading through the excellent parallel biographies of Winston Churchill and Mahatma Gandhi, one can imagine what went through his mind when Gandhi proposed 'passive resistance' as a mean for Swaraj (self-rule). Devoid of artillery superiority, reliance to economic and financial might, leaders of that era could only manipulate their subjects' mind through past glory of ancient civilisation and nature!

They said that Indian civilisation had a much longer past than their invaders. So, the event of the intrusion of foreigners like the Mughals and the British were just but a drop in the ocean of India's very long civilisation.

Having able to boost their own self-image, the next step was not to go on a head long collision with the invaders but to win psychologically — by gaining sympathy through pity through self-torture or passive resistance. You can hit a person once or twice. How do you keep on slapping the person who turns the other cheek repeatedly? When the aggressor stops, you win.

This type of soul force has penetrated deep into the Indian psyche. I think it had been there even before Gandhi proposed his satyagraha. From time immemorial, Hindus have been doing penance either through self imposed starvation, self-flagellation, self-piercing during temple ceremonies, fire walking and many other extra human feats to garner sympathy from the powers that be for private intents. At a society level, suicide and self-immolation had been and is fairly rampant amongst the society to prove one's innocence and clarify the truth. A great Hindu sage once said, "To bear injury and bear insult is the highest *sadhana* (achievement)".FG27.5.12

Loss of Art of Medical Sciences

Two recent events made me think of the good old days, yet again.

Early in my training, I was awestruck by the excellent clinical acumen that some of the surgeons manifested in their day to day work. A surgeon or even a registrar in training would just roll the hand gently over the abdomen whilst looking into the patient's eyes and stirring up a conversation just to make an accurate diagnosis of acute appendicitis even when the clinical manifestations would be far from that described in most medical textbooks. Believe you me, most of the time, they would get full marks for their diagnoses without the need for sophisticated imaging techniques. Registrars went as far as to say to his trainees that the mark of a good surgeon is the ability to correctly diagnose acute appendicitis clinically.

Two recent events queried the competence of surgeons these days.

#1. An anaesthesiologist friend of mine was fretting about his ever increasing workload of working early morning (starting late nights) just to stare at surgeries of 'white appendix'!

#2. A friend's 11year old son with painful abdomen was almost operated upon for appendicitis. Second opinion suggested that it was probably musculoskeletal related and the young boy escaped the knife.

Now, what is happening?

Is it that doctors nowadays have lost their clinical acumen? Or the drive for financial remunerations superseded their earlier oath to serve mankind etcetera etcetera? Or is that he is worried that somebody else would make a killing and steal his rice bowl? Or somebody else will diagnose correctly their patient? Remember the patient who shopped around 4 doctors in 3 days to sing praises of the last doctor after she was correctly diagnosed her to have dengue fever after a blood test?

Are the doctors' succumbing to client's express lane attitude in remedies to maladies in life? Has the plans of leaving market forces to decide on medical need led to doctors taking short cuts? Now that medical education is now is now a multi-million industry, the good doctor may still be paying for his education! Maybe it is the system where doctors are not gatekeepers to the health system but are just pawns in a system controlled by businessmen and insurance companies. FG29.5.12

Bridge the gap?

Affluent societies' kids take things for granted. No matter how much stories of life experiences are impressed upon the younger ones, it just cannot penetrate their skulls. It may just appear like bedtime stories or Aesop's fables!

Asian mentality is do things fast and complete studies in the shortest time possible without flunking any papers, getting as many paper qualifications as early as possible and start earning and to pray eternally to the Money God! Who cares whether the kids earn enough life experience or enough professional qualifications with enough emotional maturity to match. Once the qualifications and money start rolling in, they believe everything will fall in place.

Now, Asians themselves are questioning this type of approach to life. Quite a vast of them are considering gap year in their year of studies, especially in the late teenage years. No, I am talking of people being hospitalised or incarcerated for delinquencies! I am talking about teenagers who go students' exchange programmes, to join the workforce for a year or even go traveling to appreciate the splendour of God's creations.

By this way, children who have spoon fed or even Ryles' tube feeding throughout their growing years may find this exercise an eye opener to the reality of life. Only then would they realise that in order to be able to withdraw from the ATM some hard slogging joker has to deposit it and the supply is not infinite. Behind every transaction, there is always someone flogging his butt out to pulp trying to garnish the bacon that he brings home.

Being exposed to mix unguarded with regular people, break some sweat, learn from mistakes and bad judgements, hopefully, the Facebook generation will come off their cyber dream and live the real analogue world!

But then, parents being parents would probably pamper the kids again to bend the rules here and there to ensure that their haplessly helpless ducklings are shunned from miseries of 'real life'. It would all go through a full 360 degrees circle and come back to square one. They would never be allowed to blossom to the majestic swan that they always want to be.FG9.6.12

Life's a beach!

Gone are the days when people will do anything to stay away from medical facilities for fear that some unpleasant news on their future would befall on their ears. From a therapeutic and corrective role, the medical industry or rather business has metamorphosed to a preventive one. So, from the position of righting the wrong, it has started looking the wrongs in a complete pink of health person to give him the pallor of ill health — that is, after so many further expensive tests and dead ends of inconclusive results.

Paranoia (to the level of hypochondriassm), hunger to perform their daily duties of acquiring wealth, fear of death and fear of litigation on the part of the providers have skyrocketed to need to have a comprehensive exhaustive full (fool) proof way of detecting disease even before its genesis. Like mushrooms after a rain, health sanctuaries with resort like set-up have mushroomed offering membership to exclusive (richly gullible) members to guarantee peace of mind if there willing to part with a large chunk of their dough to undergo multiple annual dubious screening procedures to detect sign of early diseases. Tests like full body imaging and respiratory function tests in an otherwise healthy individual have not shown to yield conclusive information but if someone else is paying, anything can be arranged. The minuscule but real risk of idiosyncratic reaction to contrast is always overlooked. As they say there is no such thing as a free lunch — something got to give.

On the other hand, these unnecessary interventions and business ventures have a snowball effect on others. It opens job opportunities for the menial workers, cleaners, sanitation companies, caterers, undertakers and not to mention the clinicians who are bored of looking at sick and terminal patients. The mundane mood can be replaced with rich blabbing executives rather than the depressingly poor malnourished real patients who need medical attention in the first place.

Meanwhile, the sharks with robes will saunter in with their hawk eyes looking for loopholes and malpractices. And the capitalistic businessmen will stomp on their cigar and laugh all the way to bank with their stash of moolah carrying their portly paunches, a mark of their prosperity.

And the clients of the sanctuary carry on with daily activities with a certain boost of confidence that they would survive until the next appointment. In spite of listening to lectures on healthy living, they continue entertaining their guests with unhealthy diet of nicotine, ethanol filled spirits with different hues and flavours, bodily pleasures that involve two to tango and the list of goes on....Life is a beach so stop bitching...
FG11.6.12

Culture is dynamic

We are always told that we must preserve our culture and the values of our ancestors are slowly but surely eroding as we speak. What is culture anyway? It is something agreed by the majority of people in a particular location to carry out things in life in a particular fashion. The diaspora of individuals from this community/ethnicity/same language is supposed to act in the same way if their geographic location differs.

I remember getting an earful of tongue waggling 'advice' from Amma for not being able to buy a comb of bananas for a particular *Ponggal* prayer as she had requested for. It was not my fault as in that particular year in mid-70s, everybody became pious and bought up all the bananas from the shops. There was also another Chinese festival at that time. Maybe at that time, the economy was also not doing so well and divine intervention was badly needed. I tried to 'educate' her that it was all right to substitute it with other fruits just like our fellow Hindus in America and UK who would not be able to lay their hands of banana and that it is the thought that counts. And came to mind, the Hindu epic story of how Lord Shiva accepted the humble offering of an aboriginal hunter, Velan's, slaughtered meat and lighted lantern with pork lard. Even the Brahmin priest who had laboriously and ceremoniously set the whole ceremonial offering with the regatta of prayers and purity by society's standards but with a not-so-clean but judgemental superiority complexed heart did not get Lord Shiva's nod! Of course, Amma was not amused and Appa had to take his bike and buy a comb of banana from town to meet religious/cultural requirements!

We can see how culture had permeated into our religious beliefs.

A wedding is the epitome of the showcase of one's culture. Steps have been laid down step by step, by word of mouth, from the step of seeking potential bride/groom/victim to the ceremonious deflowering of the maiden, all done in what is considered as the auspicious times based on the positions of Saturn, Uranus, Sun and others. In the pre-Revolution Age era, a wedding was indeed an occasion looked forward by friends and relatives alike for some fellowship, merry-making and setting up of other potential wedding candidates. It would go on for weeks altogether with the bride's party coughing out the expenses for good measure (or curse for bearing a weaker sex).-But then, everything powerful on earth is associated with women, e.g., Mother Earth for compensation!

In modern times, of course, all these are not possible. People now live in different structured lives. They do not share the luxury of their predecessors but work in boxed offices almost daily. The exposure via telecommunication modalities and movies to the outside world would have fascinated them with other cultures that have slowly crept into theirs and have been accepted as the norm.

A point of interest is the wine toasting ceremony that has become part and parcel of most Indian wedding receptions. Sceptics will fret that indulging in intoxicants is a deviant practice alien to our civilisation. If that is the case, then even the loads of tomatoes in our favourite Indian cooking and tomato purée rice cannot be claimed to be Indian in origin. Tomato, a native of the Mediterranean land, made its way to Bharat land via Arab traders even before the British and had claimed their place in Indian heartland.

Why bother by all these? Just savour the moment and enjoy it. At the end of the day, one is just left with distant memories of youth and how we were before senility sets in and its backbreaking problems starts.

A wine toasting ceremony with the masters of ceremony suggesting a toast for a blissful married life, joined by family and friends on stage at a dinner I was invited to. While looking at the world go by with my hawkish eyes, my devilish mind starts wondering and looking at perspective at things as if I were an alien looking at the antics of human!

The presentation at this reception was excellent with a magnificent video montage of the wedding edited and choreographed to the standards of Kollywood with proper use of relevant music track.

P/S: People of Indian diaspora are quite comfortable with hugging these days. A generation ago, eye contact and salutations with folding of hands in front of the chest would signify greetings from the heart with no physical touch necessary. Culture has evolved to include an embrace to cement the bond. It is now accepted as culture.FG13.6.12

Too much knowledge is a bad thing?

The unquenchable thirst of mankind for knowledge seem insatiable. From the time of cavemen, people had always wanted to know what is on the other side — of the river, of the horizon, of the hill, of the rainbow, of the sky and so on...

There are a lot of things that man is learning every day. Some are pure theories but seem to make sense so everybody accepts it as the gospel truth — like the Theory of Evolution for example. It makes sense and man cannot dispute it, hence he accepts it, putting two and two together. Now, people in power in certain countries think they should withhold some information away from public knowledge in the name of national security and government secret. Others will cry that this abuse of power and that the public should be made available to this important information for their scrutiny.

Information is power they say, hence, people will little knowledge would think they know everything. However, if they dwell further and further into the sea of knowledge, only then would they realise that there is always an answer to a question which raises yet another question and another till there is no infinity.

In some cultures, things related to the birds and the bees are best unspoken and left in the confines of each others' imagination. Secrets of bodily pleasures and the forbidden apple is left to be discovered after a laborious ceremony with the nod of the moons and the stars with a pledge of public declaration of intent! With time, these restrictions have succumbed to liberation and 'self-expression'.

The truth about the beginning of time and man as well as the future is a constant curiosity to mankind. They have brought in God into the equation to answer some of them. Although it pacifies some believers, it does not convince other naysayers. They demand proofs for this and that. The believers say that some things are better not known nor questioned. Herein also lies the dilemma whose God is the truthful One and his respective believers claim superiority.

Now, psychiatrists argue that the constant over-bombardment of information confuses the young mind and stunts their mental maturity. A 26-year-old man today is equivalent to a 21-year-old man one generation previously, due to stunting of his mental maturation!

Now I am more confused....FG28.6.12

Whatever happened to gentleman's golden handshake?

Someone just told me the other day that in case of an accident, even if it is due to your own fault, never admit it when making a report afterwards. Keep your fingers crossed, arrange for a confession later or whatever you do, tell that there was a motorcyclist or pedestrian you had to avoid but was not in a correct state of mind to jot the vehicle number. Failing to do so will find yourself in an embarrassing situation of having your insurance claims rejected. So much for standing for the truth and the truth will prevail against all odds or that God protects the side of the truth. Now money talks.

A generation ago, a mark of a true gentleman is one who sticks by his words. A simple handshake or smoking of a peace pipe would seal an agreement. The word of a person from a civilised society is held in highest esteem as compared to someone who is a loafer, a blue collared or a native from the colonies.

Gone are those days. Words are just that, words, a jumble of alphabets to express one's wishes. The intent, however, can be different or differ according to circumstances. Things become more complex when the long arm of the law comes into the picture. A case that came to mind is the mix-up at a prominent fertility centre. The error was discovered by the clinicians and was duly informed to the affected parties who did not want to hear any of their explanation. The next thing the centre heard was a lawyer's notice, suspension of their practising licence and a fat fine.

Even at world level football scenario, a handshake at the end of a game which used to end all disagreements and anger at heights of the passion of game has no value anymore. Thanks to the press who like to create a mountain out of a molehill to spruce up their sales and have no material to write on, the flame of discontent is fanned almost after any small incident on the field and in the dressing room!FG2.7.12

Look Ma, no hands!

My last trip to perform filial duties to the people who contributed to my DNA was sort of kick in the butt of sorts.

Suddenly I realised that the lady was not as agile as she used to be. Giving an occasional cough recovering from the common flu, she moved slowly to dutifully complete her duties as the half contributor to the built up of her offspring who manifests occasionally for a peek. The duty that she had performed all her life for him until he was strong enough to fly off the nest. I thought she appeared fragile with a slight stoop and restricted right shoulder movement.

Recovering from recent repeated bouts of ill health, he, on the other hand, looked haggard further exaggerated by the three days' unshaven stubble. Gone are the full-bodied arms and shoulder muscle mass, he walked slowly yearning for coordination affected by failing eyesight and sluggish blood flow.

Man, it hit me! They have now gracefully slipped into the geriatric population.

Hey, I am no spring chicken myself. With thinning greying hairline with a near visible scalp and soon to hit the half century mark, I hope to be level headed and rational. The world changes around us. We do not have to change with them. We have to just to accept their change and play their tune. You cannot change the world. Insisting on doing so will only cast a label on yourself as a loony, a grumpy old man, living in the past, suspended in time, etcetera.

I gazed deep into their eyes, reminiscing and thanking silently for all the good times, hoping that the gaze will transfer my soulful gratitude for lending their supporting hands during the falls from my baby steps. Being inadequate in public extroverted display of affection, I was hoping that my deep gaze would transfer my inner unexpressed desires. Suddenly all the good times just flashed before my eyes. In those memories, they appear so youthful and gay. Secretly (but cursing myself for thinking so), I was hoping that that was not the last long gaze.

After all their guidance either directly or indirectly all those years, now I can say, "Look Ma, No hands!"FG10.7.12

National integration in temple

In Rome, do what the Romans do.

When the English brought indented labourers from India, they brought with them their culture, religion and way of life. To keep them contended, the colonial master built arrack shops and let them build their own place of worship. Over the generations, the Indians who migrated to this land for better lives have blended well into the society. They contributed their sweat, life and blood to transform this backwater malarial infested land into a near developed country with the help of other citizens. Well, malaria has been replaced by dengue, that's another story!

National integration, at least from the food perspective has infiltrated into Hindu temples. This, I discovered today. Generally, the *Aadi* month (the fourth month of the Tamil calendar) as I knew when I was growing up, was inauspicious for many life altering events like weddings, consummation for newlyweds, moving into a new house or childbirth. Now, I have come to understand that it is actually a good month for Goddesses and unmarried ladies to pray for a good husband! And now over the years, the temples have started becoming hive with activities in *Aadi*, thus generating business again for themselves and its off-shoots that benefit from it (i.e.florists, caterers, textiles etcetera).

Historically, *Aadi* may have been a busy month for the farming community to work on their next crop cycle, hence a bad month for business. Couples who slept in *Aadi* run a risk of delivering their offspring in May, the hottest month in Tamil Nadu, perhaps when the highest rate of puerperal sepsis was!

So, I attended one of these prayers honouring Goddess Amman. After the long symbolic ceremony, again signifying the greatness of a weary space-traveller with her various paraphernalia exhibited during the course of the elaborate prayers, we were treated to a vegetarian meal in the temple premises.

Adding Malaysian flavour to the menu was our good old nasi lemak, one of Malaysians' all-time favourite dish. Of course, in keeping with the sensitivities of the host and the premises, it was a strictly vegetarian fare. Off the list of ingredients were eggs, anchovies and shrimp paste (*belacan*). In its place were fake anchovies, peanuts and hot red spicy sauce. The taste may not satisfy the taste buds of die hard nasi lemak enthusiast but it tasted more than 80% as good.

And I was thinking to myself, "You can't force national integration. Given time, it would evolve by itself sooner or later!".FG21.7.12

Whoever said that life is a beach...

¶♫♫♪There is a house in New Orleans..They call the Rising Sun...And it's been the ruin of many a poor boy...And God I know I'm one.... ¶♫♫♪
(House of the rising sun, The Animals,1964)

It is called the Beach but no sea was around... They say it is this is the holy month but it is business as always. Another day another crowd whose thirst need to be quenched. Thirst of being on holiday and letting their hair down and needing to have a memorable time of their life. Exciting memories eased with the aura of being a millionaire in a third world country where goods and services are dirt cheap and are at your disposal at a whistle or a snap of the finger. Thirst of desire to savour all pleasures before the final call, octogenarians flock here.

Like a scene from the opening scene of 'Manchurian Candidate (1962)' or 'Good Morning Vietnam', the club was a *shangri-la* with flowing golden intoxicating juices, music to soothe the ears and to reenact the lost years with retro music and a smorgasbord of pretty maids (who are everything but maiden) all in a row to dance to your tunes and fancies as long as they are handsomely greased with moolah. In fact there were more pretty maids that the patrons themselves. It was like a display of participants of the Third World Olympics where the poor were sufficiently represented - Philippines, Indonesia, Cambodia, Vietnam, Myanmar, and the crumbs of the now defunct Soviet Union! The providers all had a sad story to tell to justify their sadly demanding profession — money thirsty shark agents breathing down their neck for daily payments, the sob story of family in some kind of calamity, useless lazy husbands who fathered their children at a young and impressionable age, the relatives near and far who are always in some kind of financial difficulty and coincidentally the head of the family feels compelled that she should help and the list goes on and on. Devoutly religious back home, they justify their actions by proclaiming that they were drawn into the profession by sheer desperation and they purify their actions by carrying a rosary at all times.

The bosses of the premises are putting up a happy face. (Hey, people come here to have a good time. They do not want to hear my sob story). Boy, they must have a few especially the patrons and their companions in the club who missed a heart beat when a patrol car with its revolving blue light passed by. It must have been a subtle reminder by the men in blue that the regular dues are due! — further adding their blues...

Then the bartenders in the midst of making their clients happy must have their own tale to tell, just like in Billy Joel's hit 'Piano man'. Trying to stay sober and sane despite all the intoxicated incoherent regulars, there is another place he rather be but then it pays the bills in this trying times.

In midst of all these negativities, the joint helps to line the pockets of the little men. Scores of cabs are patiently awaiting potential picks who are probably too tipsy to drive or yearn for a more private environment for private activities. And the row of stalls nearby are ever ready to cook up a sizzling meal to feed those ethanol induced hunger pangs.

The club has put the capital on the world map and Discovery channel — as a fine example of congregation of citizens of the world, the third world playing dance monkey to the affluent first world due to lack of financial prowess and lack of distribution of national resources.FG11.8.12

So you think you know everything?

In our everyday life, we see many who walk around with an aura around them exuding confidence as though they know all the answers to all of Mankind's age old secret of the universe. Unfortunately, things in life are not so black or white, they always come in various shades of grey to complicate things.

If you think you have covered all angles in dealing with a problem, then you would receive a knock on the head on a yet another angle that missed your scrutiny. If you think you have to move with the times and embrace modernity, then again you will be disappointed with equally dismal outcomes. Then you would tell yourself, 'Old is Gold'!

The dichotomy of choices is driving everyone nuts. If only you could turn back time... Then you would stumble upon new sets of hurdles to cross.

At least, the people who go with their noses and shoulders up in the air showed confidence to the masses and hopefully provide yet another path to tread upon for those who are lost for direction after hitting a brick wall.FG17.8.12

An afternoon at the barber's

They say a doctor and a barber knows more secrets about their clients than any other professionals. Sometimes, politicians and policeman hang around the tonsorial artists' outlets to gauge their popularity or hear about the latest gossip around town! The barbers, by just starting a conversation with their customers and keeping their eyes and ears open will pick up so many cues. Just like a scene from the sitcom 'Cheers', their customers keep on coming to continue their banter and small chats.

On my last visit to my barber, who is very Indian in his outlook after being educated in Tamil medium school and only has Tamil magazines in his shop, our conversation which is usually in as much as possible in pristine unadulterated Tamil (avoiding English words) went on to the topic of P. Ramlee movies!

His assistant, an Indian immigrant on work contract joined in the fun. I was pleasantly surprised that both of them were also fans of P. Ramlee films. They had viewed his movies for umpteen times and still laugh at his antics. Off hand, they narrated their memorable moments in Ramlee's films — scenes from *Madu Tiga, Labu Labi* etcetera.

It is amazing how the old Malay movies transcended all barriers and had infiltrated all levels of society!FG22.8.12

It is all about the bacon!

Dream job, job satisfaction or a job to satisfy the worldly needs?

A few years ago, someone I know decided to sell off his private medical practice. He had it up to his neck with all his daily dealings with people who were clueless in the 21st century about pathogenesis of disease and were adamant that illness were mystic in nature and imbalances in cold, heat and wind in the body tipped us over to ailment. And that their grandmother concoction made them immune to sexually transmitted diseases! He fought the fight and surrendered the war of mass education of his patients and their guardians. Anyway, his clients/customers/patients hold the custodian to his practice — they would decide his success or failure! He thought he was sent to Earth for higher callings. He left his practice and he is now happy rubbing shoulders with people who speak his language, with corporate figures in a medical centre. But is he really happy, I wonder! Even though they speak the same *lingua franca* with romanised alphabets, the businessmen's minds —are plastered with many numerals and currency signs. Latin, unlike in the medical literature, to them is a dead language, just like humanity.

Another chap left his multinational company post as it was leading him nowhere — he had reached his maximum achievable level the conundrum of having to think of the future of his young expanding family. So, he took the bold step of venturing into private practice.

After dealing with intellectuals from the local scene and abroad, he was in for a culture shock having to deal with hillbillies. He felt that he was overqualified to deal with his dimwit clients who had money but neither the culture nor the brains! He thought he had made a blunder by putting one foot into the quicksand. As he was almost swaying to the swirling pit of the black dog, he received a timely metaphorical smack on his head by the veterans in the business. "This is the life you chose for your family, now you either swim with the tide or drown - the choice is yours!"

Ten years down the line, he had come to terms with the demand of his job. He is happy, brings home the bacon and occasionally there is extra meat to 'throw some shrimp on the barbie'!

The perfect job is a myth. We have to make do with what we have. If we do not grasp what is available, we will be forever be waiting and waiting. Just like some jobless people who blame everything and everyone else except themselves for their woes. Regular prayers and soul cleansing manoeuvres proved fruitless and they are still waiting for that lucky break and that lucky lottery ticket win!

Have I told you about the man in the recycling business driving past in a spanking Mercedes?FG11.9.12

Some characters أحرف อักษระ **символов** გმირები

No, I am not referring to the character in Roman alphabets or in any other language. Neither am I referring to characters in a play or caricature nor to certain traits of human, physical, chemical or biological object. I am humbly referring to some characters with whom you have to make small chats in a party!

As we get further and further away from the only day that our mothers smile to see us cry (to quote AKJ Kalam), as did as our forefathers before us, we fret about the generation next who would take over the helm of leadership of the nation and world arena after this. Everything they do seem to be counter productive and heading to doom. Like that, a conversation came forth... Generation Y and their antics.

This guy was telling about his newbies who are forever trying to cut corners with their designated duties; how they are last to come and first to leave irrespective if he (the boss) is still around. He was narrating how in his younger days used to be early to rise, beat the morning traffic jam, grabbing a quick bite near the office, be immersed in work long before the bosses saunter in and later idle around fiddling with things appearing busy to wait for the boss to leave to call it a day, just to give a good impression to the paymasters!

Then the conversation went on to the gargantuan number of medical schools in the country superseding even that of the UK and hospital bashing reports in papers of late. For good measure, he volunteered his bad experience with the medical fraternity.

A gloomy day, he was feeling under the weather. Even his wife told him he looked run down with his face all puffed up and his jaw ached. Even before the sentence ended, he was zooming all the way to the city's premier private medical concern.

After a laborious discussion, outpouring of symptoms, the extensive battery of investigations and further discussions, a definitive diagnosis was not put forth by the front line medical personnel. Admission was advised in view of a myriad of mind boggling symptoms. After further haggling, the sufferer left the scene unhappily as further discussions met dead ends.

A few calls here and there through country club contacts placed him on top of a top notch doctors' appointment list.

Review notes of the earlier meeting of the day before by the 'top notch' consultant revealed a disturbing diagnosis-hypochondriasis! All hell broke loose. A few calls here and there ensured the parties involved be reprimanded. A diagnosis like that would have bearings in his future dealings with the insurance company, with his fraternity and at any time when his character assassination is attempted! He was happy he managed to nip it the bud before bigger damage control needed to be mobilised!

How is this related to Generation Y and their work ethics, you may ask? Yes, I wonder too. The people in the front line were younger than him. But what I know for sure, is God is not so unkind sending so many sicknesses all at one go.

By the way, a simple course of analgesics and antibiotics did spare him of his miseries, all at one time eventually. Perhaps giving a name to his predicament and having confidence in the paternalistic man with the stethoscope went a long way to exorcise the dwelling demon in the body!

Just some characters who appear high and mighty as well as condescending and we have to put up with so as not offend the host.FG21.9.12

Generation Next!

I probably will let my imagination go berserk on this one. It may stink of stereotyping, generalisation and gross assumption. I may be wrong but what the heck. It is the only way to keep the neurons firing away and keeping senility at bay. Talking about senility and selective amnesia at will, we have seen many around us guilty by the first degree on this charge!

Just the other day, I saw a lassy pushing a deep pram-like contraption with three thoroughbred puppies sticking their heads looking at passersby. The lassy, in her mid 20s, in a well confident poise, brimming with self-confidence with her equal well sculptured gymnasium time spent thighs and legs and hot pants, stiletto to accentuate her bragging rights and tops leaving little imagination of the modesty that it was meant to cover which was nothing to feel outraged about anyway, was trying to get her 'babies' into her car with her partner. The partner, probably not witnessed by fire, tea ceremony, cross or people sanctioned ceremony but by mutual consent, was finding great pleasure in gently making the animals feel comfortable in the car. Partner? Yeah, they look too cosy, touchy and civilised to be married!

Welcome to Generation Next! The generation who believe that they make the centre of the universe. Living, for them by their way and terms is their right. They would do it any which way they choose but loose! Societal and theological regulations are good movie scripts and Aesop's toddler bedtime stories. It is their life and they choose the way they want to live it.

Children? Nah, they have bigger things on their plates than things that bog them down, like career advancements and seeing the whole world before they die.

Carnal indulgence? Please! Don't ask the obvious. There is a reason why they call it carnival (carnal festival?) and that they have discovered contraception and sex education to empower women. Anyway, sex education is not wasted on them. Whenever they are afflicted with a sexually transmitted infection, they make it their God sent decree to impose upon themselves to contact their exes which ever corner of the world they may be so that all those in their wide web of sexual footprint are treated. That much they owe it upon themselves as social responsibility.

Role models? Kim Kardashian (who wants to elope with Kanye West) and socialite Paris Hilton who uses her giant sized handbag and puny sized lap dog chihuahua as an ornamental accessory to complete her appearance!

Of course my sweeping statements above may be utterly out of context and wrong on all accounts. After all it is just an observational study that does not hold any water...FG12.10.12

Human Sacrifice!

Call me spoilsport. Call me weird. Because folks, the historical white Taj Mahal, sadly does not excite me. If you tell me, it denotes the love of Shah Jehan to his wife, I say bullshit! You say it is a marvel of architecture, I say, at what expense?

It is a symbol of cruelty, of despotism, of one man's crazy dream to build the finest marble mausoleum for a lady succumbing to complications of postpartum haemorrhage after delivering her 14th heir to the throne.

The lineage to the throne is nothing to shout about anyway. We have all heard how the offspring without skipping a generation have imprisoned their elders, their parents and fought amongst themselves for greed of power.

The mausoleum is a reminder of all the devilish offspring borne by the mother's uteri to be born on Mother Earth for this eternal mother to carry the weight of the sin of their atrocities. It also reminds us of the worker force, skilled and otherwise, who lost their dignity, times spent with family, their sight, their limbs (for fear by the king of craftsmen repeating such a feat elsewhere).

I suppose the same can be said of other 'Wonders of the World' - Angkor Wat, Pyramids, Great Wall of China, Mayan Temples, Machu Picchu... But then again, some of these mammoth structures may not have been men made but rather ancient alien technology infused / imparted, human slaves toiled, self (alien) serving monuments... Food for thought!
FG1.11.12

As you like it*

Man is an animal who interprets facts how he wants to interpret them in keeping with the environment he is keeping with or maybe with his vested interest on his mind.

Many years ago, I attended a birthday party within a religious function. After the singing of hymns, came time to commemorate the moment of the birth of the guest of honour. In rolled an eggless vegetarian cake (it was announced). The leader of the pack started telling the rest of the crowd on so and so's birthday and extended his felicitations. The crowd started singing the song as the birthday girl lit the candles on the cake. The climax of the event was when all candles were lit. That is it. No clapping (it is not our culture) but instead hail the greatness of the Lord instead though it was all right when they clapped when they sang the hymns! You see, their rationale, as the 'MC' later said that was we should rejoice at the lighting of brightness, not rejoice at the extinguishing of the greatest invention of God - light (*Agni*), which is the pillar of all civilisations)! I decided to be a gracious guest by not being a wise guy and asking, "... but celebrating a birthday is not our culture and we are celebrating the birthday based on a non-Hindu calendar!".

21st December 2012 came and went, but we are still standing pretty. The world, though, is still as chaotic as before. Days before the D-day (End of Days) came a hoax prophesying that Nostradamus had indeed predicted, in not so direct ways, that from *the land of blooming flowers, when the man on a prancing horse hit nine zeros, the end will come* (something like that). Smart alecs rationalised the land of blooming flowers as referring to Korea (why? Because of picturesque Korean drama like Winter Sonata?), man on prancing horse is *Psy* doing his *Gangnam* style and nine zeros is referring to his YouTube hits reaching 1billion (1,000,000,000)! What the ....

In his effort to entice his congregation back to their path of righteousness, the priest rattled on. "Now people are more interested in their 3G and Internet connections then coming to temple. Well, I got news for you. We also have wireless 3G service in this temple. The first G is *Gita* (Bhagavad Gita), the second G being *GanggaJal* (the purest of water given by God to Man and the third G is the *Govinda Bhajans* (divine songs) which would guarantee uninterrupted Internet connections to God!".

He went on to say, "If you say you want 4G facility, there is always *Ghai* (Krishna's companion - the cow)!".

A Shakespearean comedy with the famous and oft-quoted phrase, "All the world's a stage" and the origin of phrase "too much of a good thing".FG24.12.12

Put on your seatbelts, it may be a bumpy ride!

Travelling through the journey of life, devoid of manual to navigate, we all depend on seasoned seamen who had the opportunity to scale the high seas and returned unscathed for guidance...

I met a friend's mother over dinner . She had recently lost her husband of 53 years and 5 successful children to complement the years of wedded bliss.

She was telling how everyone angle of their home has a bit of memory of their union attached to it, the furniture, the mementos from his various place of work and visit. The plethora of flashbacks still keeps on flooding her mind even after a year after his departure. What can you say, he is the only man she knew almost her entire life! (even before marriage)

They had their good times and trying times as all good marriages would. Her advice is to sail the rough seas with practising 'give-and-take' attitude and not being self-centred. It went on to topics of present day marriages and its inability to stand the test of times. From where she stood, the flimsiest of reason seem to justify as an excuse to wreck the divine institution.

I suppose what we see today is just an evolution of society. From a society which lived with no rules and regulations and no one taking responsibility of their weak, man drafted guidelines for his fellow men to follow, using the fear of God in it. It worked well for some time. From the beginning of time, man has been restless. Restless to explore new frontiers, ever willing to think against the grain of the majority and as he becomes more philosophical, critical, demanding logic and physical proof, he will continue rocking the boat even if the sea is not choppy....FG1.1.13

Globalization and paradox

Some things in the evolution of mankind cannot be altered. The need to communicate and travel has made the world indeed a smaller place. With the advent of communication technologies like the internet, this need just got a further gigantic push forward. If those days, man needed horsemen and the pony express to relay messages, now with a fragment of the time needed to wink, information travels further than the mind can imagine.

Man, however, instead blending with the rest of the people to live as one, choose to subdivide themselves to groups of same intentions, ideology or ethnicity. People use the technology to rekindle old sentimentality to revive old languages, old mega plans forgotten by history, instigate animosity and further subdivide people who have been finally united under a same flag after so many years of tribal fighting and bloodshed. Is it the fate of man to head for self-destruction? Is it in our DNA?FG5.1.13

Statistics are statistics

And they were always meant to be so... Unfortunately, we have always used statistics to generalise. Cancer of the lung had always been associated with male smokers. Of late, young non-smoking ladies have also been struck by an aggressive form of this dreaded neoplasia.

The last thing that you would expect to be stricken by this malignancy is a young mid 20 fit non-smoking male who does not indulge in unhealthy activities. - A pious individual with his whole future paved right in front of him with a new job and a soon-to-be bride awaiting to dream of matrimonial bliss and all the dreamy memories that come with it. It makes it worse when you have seen the boy grow right in front of your very eyes is stricken by this infamously deadly crab. Armed with a chest full of hope and passionate divine mercy the family is throttling along, praying for a miracle with diligent medical advice.

About twenty years ago, through the course of my work, I came in contact with a family who never really got over the fact that the fittest youngest member of their big closely knit family went for a football game with his friend and returned home as a corpse. The family could not fathom why a 22-year-old active athletic male could die from pulmonary embolism (clots in veins of the lung, commonly seen in obese, sedentary or pregnant individuals). The explanation of the Divine forces had bigger plans that we, mere mortals would not comprehend, was unacceptable. They stopped visiting the House of God and observing certain religious practices that they religiously held close to their hearts. One thing that they never failed to do was to place a memorial reminder in the papers annually on his death anniversary.

There are three kinds of lies: lies, damned lies and statistics as quoted by Twain.FG20.1.13

Banality of evil or devil at work?

Sailing through the tumultuous undulating wavy ocean of destiny and trying to make sense of this entity called life, I ventured deep into the crevices of my non-dominant right brain trying to find an explanation to the many bizarre every day happenings. I am only left more confused than I ever was.

Why do we do the things that we do?

In fact, this concept has been argued by modern man for aeons. People do evil stuff which seem unthinkable to others. Instances like the Holocaust, Khmer Rouge genocide and of late the Indian brutal rape-murder incident fit the bill perfectly.

Hannah Arendt, a critical thinker of a generation ago, sitting through the Israeli trial of Adolf Ikemann and his role in the holocaust, argued that, people who push the button in these heinous crimes are just like you and me. They do not have the personification of the evil of you and I have in mind. They are fastidious law abiding citizens leading mundane lives dedicated to do the task assigned to them.

On the other hand, opponents of this theory suggest that these people have certain traits which only surface in the correct environment and people of the same frequency.

The purist of theological minds would confidently negate this dilemma as a non-issue. The scriptures have provided us sufficient guidance on how life should be lived. Our forefathers and the Word of God have paved us the time-tested Path of Enlightenment which would unquestionably lead to peace on earth and eternal bliss. But then, I find that difficult to stomach as most of Man's raising of arms have been in the name of proving that their religion is superior over their brothers'. Is the human race doomed to annihilation right from the start?FG25.1.13

Meet me halfway!

We have heard again and again of two parties complaining about each other, each trying to justify their actions over the other. Each party would tell their version what they perceive as the truth and their actions should be the only natural thing to do. We, the listeners, would be roped in to be a yes-man so just to legitimise their actions. We would be left in a conundrum as to where the real truth lies. Both parties seem to be telling the truth and seem to have act on the best of interest of both parties. At the end of the day, if the action was carried with no malice intended, there would be in no feud in the first place. The easy way out of this wrangle would be to implement the no-fault or the Act of God clause. It seems that Man is always quick to blame God on everything and is an easy punching bag for fallacies of Man.

The truth is always in the middle, perhaps the party involved would meet each other midway before they reach a point of no return.FG29.1.13

When doves cry

A friend's 20 something years old son who has his bright future laid in front of his eyes and a female companion dying to share his life with, was bogged down by what was thought to be a minor ailment. It turned out to be not a minor disturbance at all. Beneath the triviality of its symptoms, lay the possibility of crab like tentacles of the big 'C'!
The mood around my friend's household understandably turned sombre overnight. 'Sombre' may be an understatement. Tears seem to be flowing freely, irrespective of age and gender. It is indeed disheartening to see a grown man of any age crying.
Why the crying you may ask?
Is it the fear of the imminent demise of the love one, the baby with whom many a precious moment was spent arguing? The arguing was well intended, though. The older wiser one, with his weather-beaten bags full of experiences trying to impart what he had acquired after getting lost in the maze of life. The cry, is it because of the inability to ever, ever to connect, to touch, to grow old together is lost altogether?
After the initial denial, devastation, soul searching and final acceptance, the family, after rejecting mumbo-jumbo kind of shaman advised by well-meaning relatives, has decided to go on full throttle crusade against the proliferating intruder with the strongest armamentarium known to mankind - Modern Medicine.FG1.2.13

It is a jungle out there

There she was, a mid 50s disciplined runner who is the envy of ladies of her age in the housing estate who would die to have a physique like hers, waiting outside the emergency room with her right hand all dressed up to see an orthopaedic doctor who would later assess the extent of her injuries and probably stitch up her hand which had been mauled by a stray dog. She, a dog owner herself, of many Rottweilers and Alsatians, as her husband trained guard dogs for a living could not believe her predicament.

Having lived a time just after a time when typhoid and tuberculosis were treated with eggs and fresh air, she believed in the outdoors. Equipped with earphones and iPod, she would just go for her evening runs without disturbing a soul but with her sole intention to complete her bodily duties.

In fact, a few minutes before the said event, she had patted the stray dog. On her way back, out of the blues, as if like possessed, it went for her hand. A Good Samaritan who came to her rescue was also injured!

The outdoors is becoming more hostile to us as time goes by. Forget about fresh air! The moment we step outside the comfort of our homes, we are greeted with fumes of automobiles and the ever deteriorating quality of air. If that is not enough, we have the ever-expanding horsepower capacity cars manned (and 'woman'ed) by mindless drivers with ever shrinking thoughts for pedestrians. Then we have to brace ourselves against the tyranny of knife yielding small time petty thieves. So it looks the outdoors is only for animals - it is a jungle out there!FG3.2.13

An exercise in desensitisation?

"... But you just killed a soldier," I tell my sons and nephew who naturally find fine bonding by staying glued to the TV monitor and go on a shooting spree in their computer game named 'Call of Duty'.

"But they are baddies, German soldiers!" they reply. I retorted, "...they are also somebody's son, husband, brother and father. Somebody is going to grow up without a father and is going to be a psychological wreck!"

Before the time when games were on hand-held devices, in the late 80s (1989), my housemate who was performing the unenviable lonely but essential anaesthetic service in a district hospital, was a lone wolf in a small town where the siren of the ambulance was the only excitement. To maintain his own sanity, he used to periodically visit a gaming shop to have his daily dose of radiation from the consoles of Sega panels. After killing loads of baddies and aliens, he would return rejuvenated, like having a shot in the arm, like back from a vacation, ready to face what may come in his next call of duty. He is still doing it now, after all these years. The only difference now is that, with Samsung Galaxy Note II, he can play his Temple Runs and Subway Surfer anywhere anytime.

The proponents of advancement of the gaming industry will boast that it is bigger than Hollywood and that it improves hand-eye coordination and so on. Some even promote it to improve surgical skills in keyhole surgery!

But then, the stories of able bodies being transformed to unshaven, unkempt, social outcast, immersed into the stroboscopic lights of the Internet games depending on fast food and pampers to answer biological needs does not augur well to promote it as technology next! Loss in social interactions and desensitisation to gore, blood, violence as well to death makes it a real possibility that this addiction may indeed turn us out to be zombies, just like the zombies they intended to kill! Are we heading towards a world where empathy and feeling others' pain like feeling the pain endured by The Lord who sent his only Son to die on the cross to wash the sins of Man is lost? Is the recent apathy towards an accident victim toddler in China testimony to this end?FG13.2.13

Life in the fast lane

In this time and age, where everyone lives in the fast lane where speed dial rules — nobody remembers numbers anymore; immigration is through the green lane; express lane to squeeze toll in a wink; dressed down to work and so forth, everything can be arranged for your convenience.

And I thought it only applies to our daily living!

Even preparations for penance can fast trekked. Just the other day, my son who is generally cynically and sarcastic about age old traditional rituals and ethnoreligious practices, blurted out that he was taking a 'paal kodam' (milk containers) on our Thaipusam outing. I guess the stress of wanting to excel in his recently concluded public examinations lured him to publicly display his private cajoling of divine interventions.

From my understanding of carrying out penance, one has to purify the body and soul by sacrificing simple pleasures of life over a protracted period of time to focus the mind with their ultimate task of surrendering their offerings at the lotus feet of the speared Lord of Destroyer of All Evils. Even a day before the said event, they (my daughter joined in the foray a day earlier) were seen enjoying the pleasures of cooked meat and comforting snooze on high-quality rubber mattress!

Hey, I guess it is the thought that counts, not the execution of the task....FG17.2.13

I come from the land of plenty

Yet another meaningless record was broken in the Malaysian Book of Records, this time for the longest ensemble of *Yee Sang*. It beat last year's record of 888 m by 111 m to 999 m. And what happened to the effort of 99 chefs and kilograms of fish, vegetables and the accompaniments? Well, 80% of the dish was dumped into the dustbins.

It is ironic that the concept of *yee sang* originated amongst the poor Teochew fishermen who did not want to waste the leftovers from Chinese Lunar New York and decided to throw in their fish strips, turnips, carrots, vinegar etcetera and toss it high in spirit of festivity. (and eat it, of course)

Some smart alec suggested that perhaps the leftover *yee sang* from the Malaysian Records endeavour should have been put to good use, like feeding the orphans and the underprivileged. Perhaps, the armchair critic is out of touch of the practicality of things around here. *Yee sang*, being a relatively uncooked mixed delicacy in the open air by the dirty streets would not last longer than half a day in our humid warm weather. And do they know just how difficult it is to get orphans to partake in a charity event? Their itinerary is so full that they would just turn down your offer. There goes your charity events without recipients! Some caretakers of these charity concerns, who themselves may have BMI >40, would not be too keen on food tossed around for fun and frolic and strewn by the roadside!FG20.2.13

Soon men will be wiped out?

There was a time when members of the fairer sex were expected to stay that way — stay fair skinned, at least for the high -heeled, away from the melanocytic activity enhancing UV light and powdering themselves smoothly pretty. They confined to the spectator pen to add splendour to the event but not as contestants. Their participation in international sporting events was only sanctioned by the governing bodies as late as early 20th century.

From then on, female contestants competed amongst themselves till some of them actually perform better than their average male counterpart. In 2012, the number of female contestants equals that of the male in the Olympic Games.

Fast forward to the 21st century...

A new breed of reality based competitions has emerged. A competition where men and women can compete as equals without any handicap given. One competition that I had the chance of viewing was 'Wipeout'. It is a very outdoors physical intensive kind of competition which involves hard knocks, thumping falls and slippery poles. Despite all this hurdles, the ladies still come up tops standing tall above the men!

But of course, we all know that reality TV is anything but real. After all the game show fiasco to improve rating and advertisements, it is hardly surprising that the TV would stoop low to anything and everything to sex up their shows!FG24.2.13

Speak in riddles, Parseltongue!

It is interesting to see men who had been in the limelight of late for deeds not deemed moralistic by an average simple minded plebeian, a simpleton, is invoking the quiet sleeping giants, i.e., the Gods. One was seen religiously performing religious rights and seen regularly in the temple. Whilst the other, thanked the Divine one and the spirits of the unceremoniously departed for saving him from the clutches of The Reaper and the Man on the Bull recently.

I always thought, which shows how naive I am, that a Man should say what he means and mean what he says, as succinct and precise as that - a mark of a true gentleman. There was a time when man would hold by their word to the grave. But then, that was a time which seem so distant, almost eons away. Now, words are just words - a mean to impart orders but not intentions. Only the wrongdoers, the conniving mavericks and lawyers were allowed to play with their words and bend the truth by introducing elements of doubt and technicalities.

The Gods must be taking a step backward and smiling to the antics of man invoking His name in all their deeds and misdeeds, oblivious to Master plan that He has planned......Hee..hee..hee...

When the going was too good, nobody complained and God or The Force was nowhere near the equation. Fast forward when the churning was in disharmony, people dissociate themselves from the union and start blackmailing with piecemeal information to spend most time grabbing the microphone and hoarding the rostrum!

And I always thought, one good deed deserves another.

In the Tamil language, they have a saying.... It is no use performing sun-worshiping rituals when the floods have risen your neck level. Go figure!

FG15.3.13

Cows, BS and mule!

Now that the news of the imminent 13th general elections is on every body's mind, it is only appropriate to mention something on Malaysian politics.

Some people talk passionately about politics. Now, with the dissolution of the Parliament, politics is at the tip of every body's tongue. People of all ethnicity and social class, as it appears to me, seem more courteous to each other as though have teamed together to fight for the betterment of the country at large.

One particularly peculiar observation that I realised is that whenever you are embroiled in heated political discussion, say in a social function — birthday, wedding reception, dinner etcetera, the person who leads the discussion with much passion, offering intricate inside information would invariably not be registered as a voter with the Election Council!

Of course, you have to ask him point blank on the face to skewer this information. And you have to indulge in a lot of face-reading to authenticate the truth of his statement. Be prepared too for lashing if the story-teller is the easily offended type or is a bona fide voter!

9/10 you would get a sheepish smile with the reply he had not registered for the flimsiest of reasons and justifications. At the end of the day, he would emphasise that he only feeds on the crumbs of the droppings of the present day leaders, whosoever holds the helm. One devil would not be more righteous than the other. He may add "Cows may come and cows may go, but this bull here (obviously referring to himself as a muscular alpha male type and not referring to his words that fall from his mouth like droppings, i.e., BS!) stays forever! But lest he forgot that cows are sensitive words in Malaysian politics that can lead him to trouble.

Come 5th of May 2013, these big talkers cannot complain much if the rest of the voting community decides to elect a mule as their leaders! These whiners just have to pick up their crumbs or droppings and move on....bray, bray, bray...FG11.4.13

Sour to the grave

As far as I can remember, it has been the practice of people to respect the dead. No matter how bad a person had been in his or her lifetime, they are generally forgiven. Only the nicest things are highlighted and the not so pleasant one are conveniently forgotten or omitted in the eulogy.

It is accepted that the person in question would be adequately dealt with in the afterlife by the powers above and the aid of The Book.

As a deviant from the norm, people from the working class of Britain, mainly miners, have been keeping their grudge of discontent all these years and have no qualms displaying it now. Even amongst the vast majority of the 'others', there are those who feel that the world now is a worse place than before she came to the picture. With the combo of Thatcherism-Reaganism, where greed was good, we are now left with a messy world of living in credit and mortgage.

I suppose the changes in the world are inevitable with or without Thatcher. Desperate situations demand desperate measures! Caught between the devil and the deep blue sea, when the economy was not resuscitable, the majority thought the grocer's daughter with her degree had the right chemistry to spark to the *laissez faire* British economy. And she sure did it — her way!

For that matter, the electorates are to be blamed for collectively deciding on such a leader in desperation to come out of their economic doldrums. Just like the Germans for choosing a certain dropout from Art School as their leader......FG12.4.13

Feel free to be free...

Another pastime that I occasionally indulge in is T-shirt watching. Some of the things written on them can be quite entertaining. Of course, some of them could be construed as sexual harassment if uttered by an individual. As it is only written and not uttered, nobody gives a second look. Actually it is meant to be looked again and again! T-shirts with messages like 'Wish these were brains', 'Hammer says, "You can't touch these"' would fit this bill. My favourite must be 'My girlfriend went to Vegas and all she got me is this lousy T-shirt'. Not to forget the abbreviations of the word '*F*ornication *U*nder *C*onsent of the *K*ing' purposefully spelt as the abbreviations of '*F*rench *C*onnection *U*nited *K*ingdom' to give a false sense of grandiosity to its wearer. Grandiose feeling by its wearer who is awed by his the fact that he is not wearing a garment but a statement. A statement that he dares to be different and fight against the self-imposed worldly prejudices against him!

Just the other day, I saw this man who from his appearance, a vagabond with his disheveled hair, unshaven 1 week's stubble, more of a beard, worn out Japanese rubber slippers which had seen much better days, walking aimlessly with his gaze far into the horizon donning an equally worn out T-shirt screaming with red clenched fist and the fiery red words 'Walk for Freedom' emblazoned on it.

My curious mind wondered....

What kind of freedom is he looking for? Is he not free to wonder where he fancied — unlike a time not so distant in the past, where signboards like 'Dogs and so and so not allowed' were placed outside reputable restaurants? Is he not free to be restricted to dress in a particular way or manner (lack of) of grooming? Is he free to speak as he pleases? Is he not free to pursue his dreams if he had any?

Even the epitome of freedom, the bird, is not totally free. He is not free from his daily obligations to look for food. He is definitely not free from predators and pranking kids.

Maybe our homo sapien friend wants to be free from the curse of the cycle of karma!

For all you know, the T-shirt could be a discard from a formerly radical thinking individual who had turned his back from socialism to the dark side of capitalism because it is more self-gratifying...FG14.4.13

Various shades of grey

Like my father who carries on his whole life with blinkers, minding his own work and not wanting to know other people's problems, I seem to have fallen into the same trap (or is a blessing?). Feeling that I have enough on my plate, the last thing I want to be dragged into is other people's melancholy.

However, every now and then, I do get sucked into this quicksand. The best I can do is walk around the quicksand and maintaining my foot rooted on solid ground. And believe you me, it is an art.

Two individuals had things going on fine in their business venture. After umpteen years of smooth sailing, their yacht hit a rough patch. Their term of the deal appears unsavoury to both parties.

The justification in supporting their side of the bargain is the typical textbook description of mirror image conflict. I am no skilled negotiator or arbitrator. So, the most I can do is lent them my ears and utter the occasional nods, 'umm', 'oh!', 'is it so?' and the occasional smile.

The last time I heard, equilibrium had been reached. They met somewhere in the middle and life goes on.

Lesson of day - Partnership is tricky. We have to anticipate eventualities and make periodic changes to satisfy all parties involved.FG18.4.13

The Secret of Life

Our body is very smart. After all these years, from the time we roamed about the Garden of Eden or were swept ashore as a unicellular being, one thing never changed — the life giving proteins of DNA and RNA. The basic tenet of carbon based life on earth as we know it becomes varied with varying infinite ways of sequences and numbers to produce so many species and variants. The main blueprint of DNA, over the years, with exposure to various offending agents propelled the master implant to self-regulate and auto correct the sequence to ensure the continuation of species. Only the fittest survives, hence the change is inevitable. When a body is deprived of food, the master control would initiate the sequence for starvation mode. Metabolism would be reduced and lipogenesis is initiated. And the next time we consume food, nutrients would be pushed into the body silo for a rainy day. And if you usually regularly indulge in strenuous calories losing activities, do not expect to lose much weight as the body tries to maintain the homeostasis and equilibrium.

And that is the reason, my friend, why you are not losing any weight despite your faithful early morning visits to the gymnasium and the vigorous 2000kCal losing routines almost daily. Your body is much too smart. Your gut wrenching diet and calories counting is not going to fool him. You need to outsmart him by varying your exercise routine so as to confuse it into maintaining internal equilibrium.

The DNA holds some of the secrets involving Man, a vast of it is unknown to him. Imagine a template for its progeny where it is constantly checked and improved with each generation to combat an increasingly hostile environment. Sometimes it gets too comfortable that the bored cells starts attacking their own kind or show an exaggerated response to something trivial and familiar like peanuts and wheat!FG20.4.13

I paid my dues!

Sand in my face, no bed of roses, no stroll in the park, no pleasure cruise...

Now that the general elections are imminent, all the political parties have engaged into turbo gear to bulldoze their respective opponents. I managed to catch one such political lecture recently. Then organisers, in the pretext of ushering in the new Tamil year, thought they should rather usher in a new dawn by inviting candidates from the opposition camps to ventilate their views and promises for the upcoming elections. Even though the function was a predominantly Tamil event with Tamil issues on the limelight and Tamil language was used by the master of ceremony, the mixed crowd had no issue staying till the end. Certain leaders from an overtly religious based political party had no qualms in partaking and wishing the organisers well wishes. Are we becoming more tolerant or is it a ploy?

As expected, corruption and wastage issues were the mainstays of the series of lectures. One particular part that struck me was how life is becoming harder by the day. He went on to say how, after all the years after toiling through rain and heat of the tropical sun, life is still no pleasure cruise. Their forefathers came as labourers and the descendants are still labouring through life laboriously. They say that predicament is caused by the ruling party and a new dawn awaits them through a new government.

I am sorry that these people are going to pretty disappointed come 6th May. It is going to be a new day, a new dawn but the sun is still going to rise from the East. They still have to get up and get down to the same job that they had been doing. They still have to break their sweat and break their backs!

It is not that they suddenly find themselves in Utopia or in Garden of Eden or transform into mythical monarch with slaves at their disposal at the snap of the fingers.

Get real! The leaders can only show you where to fish, maybe give you a net. Do not expect them to provide the drinks, lullaby and entertainment! FG25.4.13

The go-getter and the waiter?

I have been in the company of many grown men. That does not sound right, does it? The main agenda of the union may vary from group to group. Some try to relive their loss of youth, other of the same testosterone driven deprived males may instead pursue their dream to compensate their losing prowess either in the athletic and conjugal fields.

An interesting discussion took place in the running group recently - Lifeless Footwear!

One party was vehemently arguing that his success in his field of indulgence was not primarily due to his outstanding academic achievements but rather his aesthetically pleasing personality, charming demeanour and his utmost care that he takes on his physical appearance. With his alluring and assertive manner of handling situations, he, in his lifetime had superseded many other more qualified individuals with much more impressive CV.

The other party reiterated that even though he looked impressive and would fit the bill of every mother's prospective son in law and every CEO's manager to do his dirty job, they are some things that looks do not decide. This party, being the pacifist and leaving to-the-fate kind of fellow, stressed that some things are determined by unspecified unexplainable forces. No matter how qualified one he is, certain things are beyond control. He attributed his success in life to karma, guidance from people around him, good progressive friends and lots of hard work, the only thing he knows. The divine forces paved his way to good fortune by clearing obstacles along the way, like not getting chicken pox during an important examination. But then, a dynamic and assertive person could even fight fate......FG2.5.13

Brands, the essence of life?

We have all been told that we are all irrational beings and we do things on impulses, much to regret later on. This is crux upon which the advertising business is based on. Their modus operandi is simple, create an illusion of attaining happiness with their product when the truth of the matter is that nothing like that exists — a painter gets an inspiration after smoking a particular brand of cigarette, an entrepreneur is successful because he drinks a particular liquor and life is so easy when they use a particular brand of mobile device!

What a pity, man is still not happy.

In the running circle, on regular basis, literature is churned out about new studies which revealed that such a new product is better than the one before, how everyone had got it wrong all the while and so on...

In the 70s, sports footwear underwent a major transformation with much science and technology input. After that, everybody kind of agreed on the need for footwear to run. Fast forward 3 decades later, suddenly all these footwear and cushioning have allegedly made our intrinsic muscles of our foot atrophied and redundant. Now we are told to go back to basics, back to the cavemen days when our ancestors were roaming barefoot hunting for their meals.

Then everybody went barefoot or minimalist. Now, this people are saying minimalist is not for them after having aches here and there.

All these while, a lone wolf runner in his mid-50s whom I occasionally meet on the Sundays' long run is and has been quite happy with simple unbranded non-fancy shoes and on top of that, he just zooms past us effortlessly putting all of us, younger chaps to eat humble pie with our branded spanking new shoes.

At the end of the day, it is only the bad carpenter who complains about his tools! It is the skill, not the tool.

*Remember how India was banned from the 1950 World Cup finals because they wanted to play soccer bare-footed! (Don't know whether it is true?)*FG8.5.13

Rich spoilt brat's empathy?

So during another tête-à-tête session with my sibling regarding turns of events of late, a proposition just popped out in my mind. In order to understand the predicament of others, especially for someone in power when his decision would affect all strata of society, he has to have tasted the agony and hopelessness of poverty. Only then can he empathise with their sufferings. So that faux paus like what Marie Antoinette said to the starving peasants, during the royal banquet would not be repeated. ["Let them eat cake"]. Of course, the phrase pre-dates her era!

Rich men's kids, born with a silver spoon, without a care or worry about the next meal may not be the best pacifier of the working class. Dubya would the best example who just swished through his tenure with his clueless stare leaving a trail of destruction at every nook of the world.

But then....wait!

It may not be so clear cut! A pauper who suddenly is put on a pedestal may just end up like the Emperor and his new clothes. Like a bug who falls into a bag of rice, he may just eat away his new found fortune to death.FG10.5.13

If you can't change 'em, would you join 'em?

Someone came back and laid his back disappointedly on the sofa and grumbled, "Just should have bribed like the rest and got through the driving test like the rest. Trying to follow the righteous path, now I have to sit for the exams again!"

Then he went on to mentally count the number of driving students taking the test that day and the amount of ill-gotten gains that the almighty testers would be taking home to serve their loved ones, leaving the guilt aspect to be dealt with another day. And the dirty money would have accumulated to gargantuan proportions.

There would not come a day where a beacon of light would shine upon them to stop this practice. By then, they would have got both their feet way too deep into the muddy world of corruption. They would have committed themselves and their dependants into many ventures that their needs just keep on increasing. Catch 22 situation, damn if you do and damn of you don't.

Another instance at another place....

There are sweatshop wage earners who are coerced to work extra hours for the sake of emergencies that keep on appearing for no particular reason. Workers have nothing to say but follow as they had absentmindedly or rather desperately signed off their soul to the establishment. The agreement testimonially illustrates that their services would be called upon as and when deemed fit. Forget about incentives or crumbs, you pick the pitons that the powers-that-be decides fit for you. What? Is it not fair? Don't worry, there may be many waiting in line just to continue where you stop when you leave...

What, you as the third person, the bystander can do? To leave it at status quo as it does not affect you directly? Or be a David and bring down Goliath and the whole stinking system? Not everybody can be Gandhi or Mandela who would set aside their worldly duties to sacrifice their life for others. Most people are mere mortals. They just go with the flow and prefer not to rock the boat...FG13.5.13

May the Force be with you!

As usual things happen in waves of coincidences. Of late, quite many individuals are quite open about their beliefs and have no qualms about questioning the existence of the Almighty. Maybe, they admit the existence of a divine power or force that spins the universe but they cannot stomach the idea of God as preached by Man. Are they spiritualistic atheists?

First, in the Steve Job's biography that I am presently reading, Jobs became a non-believer (he practiced Zen Buddhism later) after he refused to accept that the all knowing God refused to help the starving children of Africa.

Then, there was another guy who questioned that no rational explanation can be given to explain the reason why his apparently healthy teenage son had to return to God after a mysterious illness. Somehow telling him that God has bigger plans and we mere mortal are at a position to comprehend the greater plans seems out of place!

The politics in the house of God also does not paint a nice picture of justice on Earth. Factions, friends with business benefits, ethnicity and other self-interests prevail over the common of doing God's work on Earth.

People are giving God a bad name! And counting contribution from the donation box is a 24-hours 3shifts' job where the workers' go back smelling of money — may not be the most sanitised smell, looking at various type of people, (the good, the bad and the ugly) who would have handled the dough and donated it to wash their sins! But then, money transcends all barriers and clears all obstacles.FG17.5.13

Om Santhi, Forever Peace?

In many religious salutations and prayers, we always emphasise that there be peace on Earth, that tranquility should prevail, that sanity is restored, that justice is done. My nimble mind goes on sarcastic thinking mode again...

How can all these things all prevail at the same time? Is it not all a balance? The good forces versus the evil? The yin and the yang? Order and anarchy?

For peace to occur on one side, there must be anarchy on the other side. For a tiger to have peace of mind and satiety, there must have chaos and tragedy in the goat family. For a new generation to seamlessly continue life on earth, there must be death and sorrow on the end of the oldies.

At one said time, there can never be complete peace on earth. Everyone is looking for an illusive utopia, a fictitious Garden of Eden which is as real as a herd of unicorns running wild or grazing in the fields.

I suppose that peace on earth can be achieved when all of us can accept that it is a balance. Peace of mind can be achieved when we accept that it is a cycle. Goats must accept that there were born to be sacrificial lamb for the dinner plate for the tiger family just like there cannot be a valid reason chickens were sent to earth other than to satisfy the appetite of meat eaters. And we just whither and fade along.... to dust for a new sapling to mushroom over...FG19.5.13

Oh, Oprah!

From the time of civilisation, human beings have tried to make others think in the same manner so that it is easy to control. Anyone thinking outside the box is considered deviant and a troublemaker out to disturb the tranquility. A uniform way of thinking and values are imbibed to all. It is accepted that red is danger and it mean 'look-out!' In the same manner, a certain response is to be invoked to a particular situation and is accepted as the norm. For example, if you find an envelope with an address written with a stamp pasted at its corner, the normal reaction expected of a person is to put the said envelope into the nearest letter box. This is accepted as how a civilised individual is expected to react.

If I were to tear off the unused stamp to use for myself and just throw the envelope and its content into the nearest bin, though logical and rational, I may be labelled as barbaric, uncultured, uneducated or under-developed mentally!

This is how the world subdivides its population. We always feel comfortable around people who act, respond and have the same values as we do. First, they came out with a uniform scripture for all to follow. To give a divine authority to it, they said that it descended directly from God via hand-picked adversaries. To ensure conformance and uniformity in governance, they gave the fear of God of devastating consequences of afterlife if His words were disobeyed. Then came the mass hysteria and mass hype of mass media. Repeated messages by various channels somehow sounded more convincing and people engulfed it as the gospel truth. A lie told repeatedly became the truth!

Fast forward to the time of telecommunication and obsession with daytime TV, reality and talk shows, now we have modern day evangelists who try to solve people's problems through public declaration, confessions and shame. People are all encouraged to think that the TV talk show compere's values are the universal values accepted by the modern world. To disagree is to be uncultured or even barbaric. There is no shame in washing dirty linen in public. Bring it on, everybody has things stashed in their closet. Why wait for *Boghi*?FG21.5.13

Banality of evil

As usual after our usual hard run on Sunday, during the breakfast of *thosai*, we got involved in our usual banter about events around the country.

This time around the subject was rather morbid, in particular about the death of a detainee by assault and the killing and unceremonial cremation of a millionairess recently. What makes a man do all these violent things to a fellow human being without flinching. Being a doctor, one of the group members could not stomach the idea of landing punches after punches and the coup de grace that tips the living daylights of the victim whilst looking straight into his eyes.

Unfortunately, I do not think that people of the medical profession are immune of this charge. Scores of heinous crimes against patients and even loved ones are testimonies of this charge.

In fact, philosophers and psychologists have pondered upon this topic since the end of WW2. Hannah Arendt introduced the concept of banality of evil where people just did evil things that they were assigned to do without questioning and thinking of its consequence as if it was just banal (trivial) thing to do.

The abandoned 1971 Stanford prison experiment by Prof Philip Zimbardo suggested that probably we all try to perform our roles too well. The prison guards, probably because of the absolute power given to them, act beyond the scope of their job with the aid of testosterone and ego. The prisoners go into submission because of their disadvantaged state and the stress hormones.

There must be some truth in Sigmund Freud's theory that man's needs are governed by their primordial primitive animalistic desires of food, violence and sexual gratification. Modernisation and culture managed to rein these unsavoury traits which are not appropriate for living in a structured society. However, when the atmosphere is conducive or desperate, when they are amongst people of similar wavelength, these unabated evil behaviours may just be unleashed to its full glory.FG9.6.13

Papa don't preach!

When I was in primary school, two of my schoolmates who were initially bosom buddies just decided to stop talking to each other. I later found out that their fathers who had gone into business together fell into disrepute which led to a massive showdown between the fathers. The animosity spilt over to the family members, hence the cold treatment towards each other. 40 years later, both guys having excelled in their respective fields of choice and their fathers had passed on, they just cannot bring themselves together to rekindle their childhood friendship.

There are some families who would continue their family feud for generations like the *Pandavas* and *Gauravas* which generated the Gita to teach Man how to live in peace with each other and in equilibrium with Nature. Sometimes, they just fight because all these while they have been fighting. The real reason is lost in time.

It is interesting to note that at the grass root level, many do irrational things. People of different political ideologies clash with each other just so that their leaders can lead a cushy life, cheating them blind and remotely showing that they care for the well-being of the same society that they are supposedly fighting for. People from different religious beliefs have no qualms in killing and torturing their fellow brothers and sisters to uphold the teaching and honour their said religion which paradoxically supposed to promote peace and tranquility.

Even EPL football clubs have supporters who would be up in arms to defend the glory of their club while the owners laugh all the way to the bank as the injured supporters rush all the way to the hospital wincing in agony after a nice battering from the riot police!

Movies are supposed to entertain and feed the mind and soul. In Tamil Nadu, however, clashes between loyal members of famous Kollywood movie star fan club are not uncommon. For all you know, the stars are all buddies trying to make a living, whilst the supporters lose many man-hours trying to prove a point which was meant for entertainment anyway.

Even there is so much of hatred and anger between the pawns at the grass root level, we do not see their leaders mauling or clobbering each other with tooth and nail! FG12.6.13

Sure, steady and steadfast!

Just the other day, whilst immersed in my weekly LSD and my brain soaked in catecholamines and endorphins, a middle aged seasoned lady runner just whisked past me. She must be in her middle age with her thick wavy pony-tailed silvery hair. Being as typical as a Malaysian can be, I followed my first impulse to compartmentalise her into her ethnicity, which I figured that she must be a Malay Muslim.

I gathered from her lone wolf individual runs that she had been doing, (I never start a conversation with her, I just assume from deductions and assumptions), that she must a loner.

She must have had detractors who must have tried to persuade her to don the chastity exhibiting head scarf. There must have been pressures for her to dye her silvery hair to something to the shade near ebony or mahogany. And naysayers must have discouraged her from running with all the fear mongering talks of injury, theft, assault or even molest.

Despite all that, she must have stood adamantly on her ground, insisting that she would do what she wanted to do.

Nobody has answers for anything in this world. Those with skeletal knowledge of a certain field would boast of this and that. The more knowledge you have, the more confused and unsure you would be as more answers breed more questions. It takes a lot of guts and ability to withstand brickbats to stand steadfast on your beliefs.

P/S. I wonder how many told 'The Turbaned Tornado' to retire at 89 and instead play hide and seek with his grandchildren when he actually embarked on his first marathon in London in 2000!FG15.6.13

Pushing the boundaries...

When you give a child a certain instruction to do or not to do something, you will see them try their luck to beyond what they are supposed to or not supposed to do. If a barricade is erected to limit their space, they would stand touching the barricade. If the barricade is a rope, they would stretch their luck as far the rope would stretch. If the barricade is solid, they would stand on the boundary and see whether if their action is reprimanded. If it is all quiet at the top brass, they may stretch their reach by stepping a foot out to test the waters.

This type of treading dangerous waters can also be seen in Hollywood and amongst teenage girls who are slowly getting comfortable with their body image and sexuality. In the 1940s, actresses were required to cover up till their necks without revealing the silhouette of their contours. Later, by pushing for changes, the filmmakers managed to get the censors to allow a little bit of cleavage. With creative thinking, they manage to bend the rules to show more and more as long the areolar was not visible. With liberal thinking of the society and demand of equality of the society, even a full Monty is no big deal anymore.

Just like that in the music industry, when Elvis started gyrating his pelvis, the world thought that Armageddon was near. Looking at the present MVs especially those involving rap artistes, we seem to have come a long way.

And this is how undergarments have evolved to become formal attire.

But then... this type of thinking outside the box is the one that propels society forward. If we got stuck on to age old beliefs and traditions, Columbus would not have discovered the New World, advances in ICT would not have materialised and A-bomb would not have been a reality.

Like in MGR's movie once, there was a comical sketch of India sending an astronaut to the moon. At the last moment, the planned launch was cancelled by an astrologer as it was the day of the new moon *amavasay*, hence it was not visible, so nowhere to go!FG23.6.13

Makes you wonder...

We, the ones leading a stable life, can sit within the comforts of the confines of our safe abodes or sanctuary discussing 'Euthyphro dilemma' - Is what is morally good commanded by God because it is morally good, or is it morally good because it is commanded by God? — But just what goes through the minds of the machete-wielding bandits who terrorise the streets of KL, sometimes in broad daylight.

Is it that survival or frustrations of modern living is so stressful that it drives them to the brinks of insanity, brandishing their weapon ignoring the cries of a toddler and an old lady in the robbery of a quiet 'mom-and-pop' kind of shop selling liquor and other intoxicants? Of course, purists may haughtily preach that such a premise would not attract the best of characters. Tit-for-tat would say the others who would bring to memory the song 'House of Rising Sun' where such an avenue was 'a ruin of many a poor boy'!

Still....

Why do they have to resort to such barbaric acts? Are they out on a vendetta against mankind, society or humanity for their failures as if society owes them a living? Are they becoming increasingly frustrated unable to keep up with the demands of the material world? The pressure of being sucked into the need for luxury for themselves and their dependant is too great that the old dictum of hard work is the stepping stone to success is so *passe*, so yesterday and is incompatible with the modern times.

'Thou shalt not steal' is no longer the Testament of life any longer. 'Thou shalt steal' as long as thou shalt be able to hire shrewd lawyers who can get you out on technicalities! They also say 'Thou shalt not kill' but it is all right to kill in self defence or in defence of the second amendments to protect your property.

Are our leaders setting a bad example of glorifying splendour and poshness? Is commercialism rearing its ugly effect on mankind?

Were their upbringing so traumatised that inflicting pain and frightening the living daylights of their fellow human being is second nature to them?

But...

Once they are apprehended and brutalised by the men in blue, all their crimes are forgotten and they become martyr. Suddenly, they will become the best son, the loving husband, the doting father who had been looking forward to the arrival of the latest offspring! Makes you wonder....

Just like the Euthyphro dilemma which may never be answered, (of course there is no dilemma if you wear blinkers to shun any discussions on this subject as if this is a non-issue as God had said so), this social dilemma can go on and on with everyone pointing fingers at each other!

FG25.6.13

Nothing sacred anymore?

Just the other day, my friend commented that during her midnight viewing of 'The Man of Steel', way too many toddlers were among the audience. Toddlers and midnight screening does not go hand in hand. Well, in *Bolehland*, everything goes 'hand in hand', 'hand in glove', 'ear to ear' and 'close one eye'!

Isn't midnight way past their bedtime?

Then you have a widescreen public announcement of putting the tone of the mobile phone in silent mode courtesy of Malaysia's favourite reason for obesity, KFC. Just five minutes into the movie, a joker would be talking at the top of his voice about his whereabouts to his caller after an equally irritating ringtone of '*Gangnam* Style'.

A typical scene in a philharmonic orchestra performance of international stature in the heart of KL... As the audience are cradled into bliss of cultural immersion, somewhere in the hall, an earth shattering techno music ring tone would shatter the serenity and the owner of the phone would rush out of the hall as if he is out to defuse a time bomb!

This similar scenario was seen in a charity dinner which I attended over the weekend. It was a modest Chinese 10-course dinner held in a modest hall with loads of history attached to the building. It was a precolonial building which had been refurbished recently and was a novel site to hold such an event. The catering was given to a small restaurant out-of-town in keeping with their cost-cutting agenda and the idea to promote SMEs. Many of the performers were doing their bit of community service by performing pro bono.

The entertainment was wholesome — performances by inmates of the charity home, famous singers and 2 stand-up comedians.

This is where the ugly side of Malaysian manifests. Perhaps, ugly is too strong a word. Ignorance, aloofness, lack of foresight or lackadaisical would be more appropriate. At the outset, the organisers had promoted Qumar as the main attraction of the event. Qumar, a well known stand-up drag queen comedienne, is famous for her X-rated below the belt jokes, was belting away with her 18+ lewd jokes. And you were wondering about in the empty space in the front of podium? Toddlers! So much so that the performer in her own jovial way told the crowd to lock up the kids!FG26.6.13

Would we run like headless chickens?

There is always someone in the crowd who is an inborn leader who somehow brings out his leadership quality in when the situation demands. It is not always a good thing as one man's action may not necessarily bring the best for all under his lead. The leader's desire to mould his subjects to conform them to his desires to toe the line is probably because the leader thinks he is one step more intelligent than the rest and that he should do the thinking. Apparently it is nothing working out well as we can see from the state of the world today. Do the leaders have a grand sense of grandiosity that they have been given the special powers by the Divine to cross the Red Sea in the Big Blue Marble?

An ant colony is known to have a complex societal system with sophisticated duties for all ants. All the 'brainless' ants are destined to their job without any guidance. The queen ants are not 'monarchs' in the real sense. They do not decree anything. They just provide the subjects, the ovaries of the community. The labourer ants just move around stupidly by chance without a boss, guided only by pheromones found on their fellow ants. They explore by accident, by chance, to discover the sweet water that is lying about there.

It is something like a new bakery shop that draws more and more customers by word of mouth which was only discovered by chance. As more people start going to the row of shops, the area becomes a hotbed for business. Then the real estate value increases, the neighbourhood becomes a township just like that. There will be order and everything will go on at its own pace. Having a leader who dictates what and how it should be done will only create resentment and retaliation. Just a thought... Life without a leader!

In the bee kingdom, certain bees are fed the royal jelly to be a queen bee, a procreator, rather than a leader. But then, unlike homosapien, you do not have good ants and bad ants. In human kingdom, everybody wants to be king and you always have bad hats who are out to spoil a good thing.FG3.7.13

Public display of private intent?

Call me a loner, a sociophobic, Grinch or Scrooge. I do not particularly fancy having a big bash for something considered private. So what if you turn 50. Anyone with a bit of luck and divine non-intervention or intervention can achieve that. Even stray dogs can celebrate theirs (birthday, i. e.) if they survive the pound catchers or being a road kill. If they still want to felicitate themselves for this, it is still something personal — not appropriate for them to brag about it to their dogs and bitches but to reflect on their personal achievements and shortcomings to shortcomings to be able to survive another anniversary.

Celebrating any personal achievement must be (er...) personal, enjoying it with the people who make it happened and the ones who were in the receiving end in the endeavour in your journey. Not that the bread man and newspaper man did not assist in your goals, this is personal. They got their dues.

Perhaps superstition, perhaps fear of jealous roving ill intended eyes, these significant events should be small and meaningful, not a public display of affordability and pomp.

We do not need a surprise 48th or that matter 50th birthday like the one in 1997 movie 'The Game' where the Sean Penn character organises an elaborate game to commemorate his rich and show-off brother's (Michael Douglas) 48th birthday. A recreational company, in cahoots with his bother, lawyer and staff brought Douglas to knees by siphoning off his money, implicating him in murder, getting him to be on his heels from the cops, drive him to paranoia that finally drove him to jump off a multi-storey office building to land on a giant glass dome which led him to a conference hall with a giant bed to dampen his fall and with all friends and relatives waiting to propose a toast there!

You do not need a public display of private intent unless you are a politician or a business where you need the public to support (or to be hoodwinked) for your private intentions!FG17.7.13

They broke down Paradise and put up a parking lot!

It is said that India is the only country that did not persecute its Jews. It is said to be ever embracing of other cultures without making compulsions. The Indian civilisation viewed every moment of time of a lifetime as a continuum, a figment of time, a drop in the proverbial in the ocean of milk a.k.a. Milky Way. People may come and people may go. Civilisations and conquerors spring and dissipate, but Mother Nature drags on through space.

This analogy is succinctly depicted in the history of Mauritius. The inhabitants were leading a peaceful life with their dodo birds and forest. Life was peaceful and the equilibrium was maintained under the auspices of Mother Nature.

Civilisations decadent of their own doings, full of disease and ill intentions had to escape their shores, like roaches escaping their hideouts after a whiff of insecticide, started crawling to their shores. Stories like these are too far too many to be unfamiliar. It happened in Surat, Cochin, Pondicherry, Macau and Hong Kong as history dictates.

For years, Mauritius laid bare uninhabited to be used by Portuguese seaman as a stop over in their exploration out into the Far East. Then came the Dutch who laid claim on the island, squandered all the ebony and killed all the dodo bird just because it was so easy to kill these stupid birds. (I wonder why Dodo Cheng picked this particular bird for her name and not parakeet or peahen which were more aesthetically pleasing?)

The Dutch introduced sugar cane which were brought in from Batavia together with slaves brought from Madagascar and Chinese convicts from Bencoolen.

Mother Nature, with wrath in her path, retaliated with a series of life-threatening cyclones. Then, the slaves staged a mutiny. The Dutch found that the Chinese were bad collies, prone to retaliation. Thinking that the island is jinxed, they abandoned their post. The French moved in where the Dutch left. More slaves were brought in to work in their sugar cane plantations. They 'encultured' the workers with the French language and culture. After losing the war to the British and the Paris treaty in 1821, the island was annexed to them. The British promised the locals not to disturb the local language and practice. By then, the French culture had been imbibed deep in their psyche. Furthermore, many of them were running around with French genes. The British introduced indentured and bonded Indian coolies into this land to work on their vast sugar cane plantations as well as the English language to run the country as its trade was flourishing. The Indians made good workers. Due to restrictive British policies and economic quandary in Bharat nation, scores of ships with human cargo ply the Calcutta-Madras-Mauritius route carrying cargo from Bihar, Tamil Nadu and Andhra Pradesh, predominantly.

Cut from their motherland, embracing into their Newfoundland, they embraced various cultures that came along, a typical Mauritian today, Indian looking (55% population), can flip flop between languages (French, English and Creole), play an important role in the administration and progress of the only motherland they know. Thanks (or no thanks) to Bollywood, their Indianness cannot be shed off. To complement their masala laced local cuisine, they have Bollywood masala stories and tunes!FG26.7.13

Never lost in translation?

A few recent events made me wonder...

In the late 70s, we could not verify when a rumour emerged that Michael Jackson had died. Many rumours came about certain leaders which never could be proved but when a rumour was told again and again, it automatically gained authenticity!

Fast forward to the iPhone age... Literally at our fingertips, information is just a few swipes away. And yet the uncertainty of certain information still lingers on.

First they would flash a sensational news, something so ridiculous that it is simply impossible to be true. Then more lay people will vouch for it in the social media with 'documented proof'. It would be followed by hue and cries asking for first blood. Only then, people in authority and some kind of stature to know the situation would break the ice (awaken from slumber?) to say something akin to 'harsh action would be taken', 'no stone would be left unturned', 'we will investigate!'. And they would recoil into their snoozing position again.

By then some other soul would say that the sensational news was no new news but had been going on for eons under the noses of the higher authorities. Then the social mob would whine that the standards have gone to the dogs. Along the way, racial remarks would be hurled.

In the meantime, the spokesperson would appear to say that he was misquoted. In spite of all the advances in recording and audio equipment and presence of journalists who can speak more than one tongue, and the ability to retrieve old recording, misquotation is quite a rampant phenomena. By then the excitement of the news would wane. People would slowly accept the fact the country had indeed gone to the dogs. They would talk about immigration but they would not as they cannot fathom the idea of not able to eat their much-craved 3 am *roti telur* at the *Mamaks'* in Adelaide!

And there will roll in yet another more ridiculous story that would sweep the former under the carpet. And life goes on...

Isn't it ironic? After all these years, uncertainty still prevails. Maybe it is meant to be that way. Man become agitated and uncomfortable with uncertainty. All his primitive bad responses like suspicion and jealousy would surface. This would make it easier for the leaders to control, play with their emotions and have some kind of horizon to work to even though they know that the horizon is just a mirage that never ends.FG27.7.13

What is life?

So this is life? After 52 years of wedded bliss, what do I have to show to myself? What am I left with? A big house which used to be a home with a hive of activities that never tend to stop, the Christmas parties that never ended, the stream of friends that we never knew we had. Now I only have loneliness as my constant companion. Solitude is my trusted friend who lassos remote almost forgotten visions of my one and only one. The bond that we shared were beyond physical worldly pleasures. Beyond the age of physical allure, our magnet attracted each other like no magnetised ferrous chunks could.

Prove of our union love is the five lovely offspring that we cared for so much. A little squeal from one used to sound like a wail to you... and the ups and the downs that we went through together. And the sickness and the health! You are the only one that I really knew.

I know I cannot be sniffling like a teenage girl over your demise. I had more than my share of happiness in my lifetime.

Oh God! I am so lonely. My shelf life is approaching its expiry. I do not wish to be a burden to the bearer of our traits. They have their commitments just like we had ours when we were in the prime of our lives.

After all the time doing all the things together, I cannot fathom the idea that I cannot touch you, feel you, question you. They say you are no more around. They say that you are in a good place and I will join you one day to continue the conversations at where we were rudely interrupted by the dreaded crab. But why is it that you appear in front of me ever so often? Why are you so silent with that cheeky smile that stole my heart eons ago? Why do I feel the aura of your presence? Why do I smell that brand of deodorant and after shave that you were loyal to all your life? Are you here as my guardian angel? Are you lonely there? Are you waiting for me?

You remember all the places that we had worked and gone for holidays together? You made it a point to bring a memento from each of your destination? Now, each and every part of these items have a bitter-sweet story to tell. Every touch of an item opens the floodgates to an avalanche of memory with you, I, the kids and our dog Boo.

So, what is life? We sprout sheepishly, spring coyly, spread majestically, stand defiantly, bow progressively and slowly wither away with no trace, leaving only specks of memories to hold on to.FG29.7.13

Back to basics

In 1988, during my housemanship, LKH, a dedicated doctor who was excellent with his ears and eyes, related to me his experience during a medical rounds taken by his professor during his medical school days. The professor was describing the methodical but laborious ways to examine the chest and to appreciate the various sounds that were audible via a stethoscope. An American medical student doing his elective posting, who was amongst them, raised his hand to suggest, "Professor, wouldn't it be easier if we just ask for a Chest X-Ray to be done?" I am afraid we have come to this. Gone are the days where a proper medical examination starts with a good history taking. After developing a rapport and trust, the ancillary tests aid diagnosis, not the way to diagnose a condition!

Now, it appears that patients or symptoms are triaged to undergo complicated tests and imaging before a proper examination is done. Furthermore, simple X-rays are deemed worthless now. Why do X-ray when you can do an MRI?

A friend was all excited when his wife delivered a healthy son after a late marriage. So naturally, when his parents, who acted as their babysitter, told them that his 4month old boy had jerky movements of the one the hands, sometimes, he flipped.

A rush to the biggest private hospital with the state of the art equipment and workforce brought him to the office of a healer. Within a jiffy, before you can say, 'POOF", the infant was MRIed and an EEG was down together with a battery of blood tests with crimson-hued sanguine filling test tubes with various colour coded more than the rainbow. After a few days' stay and a few thousand ringgits poorer, he was told that everything was A-OK. Diagnosis? "I think we will keep an eye again and do some more tests if it recurs"! In other words - Idiopathic, G.O.K (God only knows)!

The next few days were unsettling. Every grunt and every hiccough from the infant raised everybody's eyebrows and everybody's pulse rate. Ventilating with friends and relatives brought them again to an experienced paediatrician in a humble clinic without the flashy glare of new medical equipment. An old dog in this field, he resorted to the oldest trick in the book. He took a detailed history and a complete examination to come to a conclusion that the jerky movements were probably related to the improper way of carrying the baby and nothing more.

4 months after the visit, there are no more abnormal movement and everybody sleeps well in the house — father, mother, son and grandparents.

My friend, an accountant by training, realises that medicine is not a science that has to have black and white proof like the receipts that he needs to balance his accounts but is an art by itself.FG1.8.13

Nostalgia

Recently met a guy whom I last met more than 40 years ago. Yes, 40 years ago! When he was a skinny 20 something-year-old chap all sprung up to find a place for himself in the big wide world while I was also a skinny lad hardly able to read and write.

We were introduced to each through a common acquaintance and whoosh glazed the avalanche of memories like a flashback scene in a movie! Of course the memories were patchy and sporadic. The more you tried to think about it, a few more just pops up. That chap was quite amused and sometimes embarrassed with some of the things that I remembered about him.

They say that little things excite little minds, so the little things that he and my uncle did stick permanently on my mind. The sight of with face full of shaving foam was new for me then as my dad never used foam. They used to laugh a lot then while shaving. It was followed by a splash of aromatic liquid from a cute bottle which I came to know later as 'Old Spice' after-shave liquid.

For hair grooming, a little scoop of *Tancho* with the index finger, rub on the palms almost obsessively, slide over the hair, 10 minutes of grooming and voila you are ready to go. This part was just part of old memories of a bygone era as he had lost his prized crowning glory quite early in life. On the other hand, my uncle is still faithful to his *Tancho* Pure Vegetable Nourishing Pomade after all these years.

To uncle B, you sculptured the idea in my young mind of how a macho man should be — tall, intelligent, opinionated, articulate and suave! FG20.8.13

The other side of poverty?

How often have we seen people with pleas for help? We grew up hearing these kinds of melancholic wailing and sobbing and 40 years forward, nothing has changed. Still the same old, same old, helplessness and hopelessness. Something is just not right. These small people are walking the tightrope of life with no social safety net below them. That is why we have leaders to be their mouthpiece to demand their place in the sun, on earth. If you do not see any change, something is wrong somewhere in the system, the delivery or the subjects!

Now, just the other day, as my friend visited his regular den in his usual Chinese restaurant, the usual Myanmarese helper came to take his order. But this time, helper told him that that was his last day there and that he was to be going off to US with a green card and that the next round of drinks was on him.

They sat down to hear his story. He landed in Malaysia as a UN refugee without the ability to utter a single word in English. He started helping around in restaurants, helping and doing odd jobs. On the side, he started learning English. He also started a provision shop to cater for fellow Myanmarese's needs. To further boost his income, he did some money-lending for a fee. At the height of his 'career', he used to earn up to RM20,000 per month; and that is excluding the bribes to the authorities (police and immigration) who harassed him incessantly, pilfering up to RM5,000 in a month!

He was 28years old when he came and in 12 short years, he made himself a fortune and was heading over to the land of opportunities. It only makes one wonder what he will achieve there!

Does one have to live in fear of prosecution to succeed in life? Are natives at a disadvantage compared to refugees? Do we have to be refugees to succeed? FG21.8.13

Rabid attachment to her furry little animals, still!

Heard an interesting podcast recently...

There was this 15-year-old girl in Wisconsin in 2004 who became febrile and started losing her coordination gradually. Exhaustive medical investigative procedures came to zilch. And her condition was deteriorating fast. She was in and out of a coma.

While engaged in small talk during the visit by her old paediatrician, the mother mentioned about their visit to the church the previous month and how the animal lover part of the girl helped a stranded bat in the church. The bat was injured was flying helplessly banging into the glass and missing the exit. Her Good Samaritan deed earned her a bite on the hand which the family nursed it as per a usual wound. That struck an alarm... Bats, bites, rabies...Unfortunately, rabies had 100% mortality rate. The doctors could not do much but put her in a dark room, minimise stimulation, supportive care and slowly ease her path to meet her Maker.

Left with Hobson's choice, the family kept on doing the only thing that kept them sane after seeing their springy teenager slowly wither away — prayers and more prayers.

Then an infectious specialist offered an experimental form of treatment. The rationale of treatment was that rabies does not actually cause structural damage to the brain. It paralyses the vital functions of the body before our own antibodies are able combat the offending intruder. So, if there was some kind of way to maintain vital functions and organs, the body can produce enough antibodies to fight the disease. They started antiviral treatment and ventilated here for 2 weeks.

After many tense, hopeful and false alarm moments, she slowly recovered. And she continued recovering till she finally passed college with flying colours, albeit not 100% yet. And she is now working with bats and other animals aiming to be a veterinarian!

Unfortunately, the success of the same form of treatment had not been replicated elsewhere, although some success was seen but not 100%! So, what happened? Were the parents' prayers answered? After all they were all regular church-goers but then why being bitten by a bat in the church in the first place? Is this some kind of divine mirth or divine comedy or errors of divine proportions? Errors corrected by sending a healer with the knowledge to rectify? A device to garner more support from the congregation by flaunting of His powers?

Is it because she may have been partially immunised by a lesser strain of rabies? Or the current strain is less virulent? Literature had suggested people living in close proximity with animals reputed to carry the virus had survived in anecdotal unconfirmed reports.

We can all believe in what we want to believe... At the end of the day, she and her family kept their faith and it seems stronger now.

Another discussion point in the podcast is the use of this modality of treatment to be made available to all victims who had missed the window of opportunity to receive the immunisation or symptoms have emerged. Unfortunately, there is the cost factor which needs to be considered. Guess you have to be born in a rich family or country to be bitten by a rabid animal!FG23.8.13

What say you?

Heard an interview with the founder of AirAsia about his childhood. Apparently, his father bought him a one-way flight ticket to study in the UK when he was a teenager. He landed in a boarding school and had to literally swim out of the deep end to survive. What he initially thought was a punishment turned out a blessing in disguise as he can weather any kind of tumble which had made him what he is today. He calls it Darwinism that propelled him to success!

My brain started thinking again when I heard of Søren Kierkegaard's fiction 'Fear and Trembling'. It is a highly controversial text which described the anxiety that went through the mind of Abraham when he heard God's call to sacrifice his son, Isaac. He described the anxiety that he must have had in the three and a half day journey up a hill and the splitting of firewood for the process.

And it both cases, the sons just submitted themselves without a fight!

What makes the fathers so cocksure that what they are doing is indeed in the best interest of the child or of mankind?

Much too often, we have seen kids who were thrown into the deep end just drown. Some keep deep resentment against their parents, blaming all their failures to their parents. Others give up the fight by indulging in destructive activities or worse, intractable depression.

So, are you going to take the path of least resistance, the path much traveled by others? Or are you going to a gamble, take the responsibility of the future of your kids in your own hands by venturing into something like home-schooling or packing them off to boarding school?FG1.9.13

Wiser or going in circles?

At the beginning of last century, the period in the time of a child's life called childhood did not exist. People like Tom Sawyer did not have a time in their life that they can reminisce as childhood. Kids at that time just grew fast, learnt as much and as fast as they could and matured fast, in time when they are physically developed to perform the duties of an adult. Nobody bothered, and it was not a problem, that their tender years were not paved with love, affection, comradeship and groupies. They did not become deranged psychopaths ala Norman Bates. Even as late as the 70s, nineteen-year-olds were donning military fatigues and marching to war.

In the Eastern culture, children were to be seen, not heard. The children were basically void of emotions and were just growing vessels who were supposed to be grateful to be born, fed and prepared for the future.

Then came the modern way of bringing up children. These vessels suddenly had become sensitive fragile *mimosa pudicas* that became everything that their parents thought they would not become. And to top it all up, they squarely blame their parents for all their failures in life even though their lives were indeed a bed of roses as compared to their parents and the generations before them.

The Asian parents took this idol worshiping of these little Napoleons one step further. China's one-child policy, put these oversized pampered brats on a pedestal, dancing to their every whim and fancy. Combined with the desire for their children to outdo their neighbours' child, their life essentially became centred around their offspring. Every effort was taken to shield them from eventualities and cushion their every fall.

After all these years, on the contrary, the Francophile way of bringing up children dictates that they should be left to grow on their own like wildflowers, learning things as they go on. They should not be made the centre of attention but rather be let to learn the roles and duties as adults as the children's role is just assimilate into society as adults, nothing more.

Hey, we have now gone a complete circle. We were doing it right all along only to be advised by experts that we were doing it wrong and suggested a new method which is actually a mirror image of our old ways. Ironic!

This is also true in other fields, our diet, for example. After steaming, broiling, grilling and frying our food all this while, some are now eating their food raw as our cavemen ancestors used too.

Pet lovers are also feeding raw food to their loved one. My cat who has been consuming pellets of food all this while would get a shock of his life and run for his life if I were to throw a raw fish at him! Don't ask about catching mice, scaredy cat!FG5.9.13

Perfect sense

Growing up in RRF, Amma tried all the ways that she knew that could impart the values that could mould her son into a knowledgeable individual. One of the ways that she carried off her duty was reading aloud the proverbs and quotations printed on the daily leaf of a Tamil calendar. This calendar had a daily chart of good and bad astronomical times together with daily saying of the day. The leaf of the calendar is torn daily and voila, another gem comes out.

Mother read me about JFK's 'Ask what your country has done for you...' long before I knew about American foreign policy, about 'turning the other cheek' from Gandhi and Jesus, and Socrates' call to think critically and question intelligently. I would then in turn rebut with some wise crack ridicule of the sayings, but it must have helped in thinking outside the box and making cynical remarks

In the growing and trying age of a teenager, quotations were a big deal. Teachers' autographs on annual school magazine were treated as gems. LHS' 'plough hard while sluggards sleep' and 'cows may come and cows may go but this bull stays here forever' were inscribed permanently at my reading corner!

The Gen-Y may have missed all these while they were growing up. Like they say, a poor man and unhappy man are philosophical men. Our parents, from the doldrums, have many gems that they have learnt in the course of trailing the pebble-stoned path of life.

Anas, a fellow Free, had complied some of life lessons from his parents that make perfect sense today, even at the time of 4G and Google! FG12.9.13

One man's meat is another's ...

Back in early 90s, whilst I was still a green horned newbie at the art of healing in Malacca, I was approached in the course of my daily dealings, by a lady who despite her outwardly ultra conservative appearance of being dressed in a hijab, looked in the eye and asked whether there was any way that her 3month foetus could be screened for Down Syndrome.

From her dressing, it did not require a rocket scientist to guess her views on prenatal screening and termination of pregnancy.

After a protracted discussion, I discovered that her previous child was a Downs and needed multiple surgeries for heart septal defects and Hirschsprung's disease even before he was one. Seeing the puny one cut open and pricked repeatedly was just simply too much for her to stomach. And the monthly follow up the Capital City just drained here physically and financially. Even before she could recover from the trauma of having a special child, in rolls in another pregnancy (through the act of Man and The Divine Powers) and the ensuing uncertainties. Rather than seeing history repeating itself, she was willing to undergo whatever test even a termination of pregnancy if warranted, than to deliver a Down Syndrome baby despite her religious convictions and country laws because she had first-hand experience of a special child.

It is easy to judge others using our life experience as a yardstick of how everybody else should live. When a similar malady strikes us, all the rules and regulations, which in normal times would be fought tooth and nail to be upheld, just goes out of the window!

This reminds me of a Lat cartoon strip published in the local dailies at a time when moral policing was the flavour of the month (it still is). It was a caricature of an elderly husband and wife couple in their 70s. The husband was reading aloud about the banning of Muslim girls in beauty pageants. The wife replies that it is improper to expose too much in public. To this, the husband replies, "I wonder who was the 1947 Miss Ratu Ronggeng? And the wife bows her head in embarrassment!

It goes on to say that we make rules and regulations for others to follow but when we are the affected party, somehow the bar is lowered or the goal post is shifted!FG14.9.13

50 going 17?

31 years ago, they all left to start the journey to their future, armed with the scroll of their knowledge. In their long treacherous and arduous journey, they must have swum through many sharks infested water, weathering through inclement weather. Some would have hit the jackpot; some into bottomless pit; some through bad decisions of life; some with incurable maladies; some through painful divorces; some trapped in the clutches of the black dog; some ventured into untested territories and God-forsaken places; some happy; some sad and some were ashamed of their absence of achievements.

The idea of getting together at 50 was mooted about a year when YTH got a handful of people together for a simple meal. It was followed by a series of small meetings here and there. The killer shot materialised when my better/other half schemed my 50th surprise birthday party.

All salutations to geeks who started social medias.

With the help of emails, WhatsApp, FB and mobile communications, the number of attendees kept on snowballing. The excitement was set to motion via WhatsApp and FB Group. The number of participants swelled to its maximum number and the alert button kept on bleeping. The messages kept on coming by the minute and suddenly the 50 years olds were acting like 17years olds, gazing at their smartphones every other minute and overtaking their children in the number of messages received on the social media.

Old stories and photos made their way to rekindle old fond memories. Our brilliantly creative art prodigy, DTBT, took a trip up north to snap brilliant pictures of the Alma Mater from various angles to further set the mood going.

Finally on the day of reckoning, close to 80 people zeroed on the venue of PFS '63 GTG Five-O from near and far — as far as both ends of the Peninsular, Sabah, Indonesia and USA. JT took 10days leave for his busy paediatric practice just to join the fun. Fun, a rocking good time they had. Seeing each after 30 years brought laughter and smiles that which no laughing gas, SSRI or LSD could. All the accolades and prefixes were out of the window. Everyone was on first name basis, as they always knew. There was so much so roars of laughter that day that the restaurant would probably have second thoughts if we were to have our second gathering there again for fear of driving patrons away.

Everybody was 17 again, retelling and reliving the teenage escapades. Untold stories about their pranks with teachers and friend came to the surface. Poking jokes at each others appearance was also another favourite talking point. Megapixels after megapixels of pictures were taken again and again to immortalise the union.

The shower of joy lingered on until way past the closing time. The fellowship continued later at various eateries around town in smaller groups.

For more than 4 hours, the 80 odd 50-years-olds were acting like 17-year-olds like how they were some 30years previously. Every good thing must come to an end. All when back happy for while, back to face reality of life and its intricacies.FG15.9.13

Be imaginative, they say!

The management gurus will always come in say that in order to stay in vogue with the ever changing times, we have to re-invent ourselves. To stay relevant, we have to re-brand, re-train and to stay afloat with the flow.

Err... It doesn't sound right of you are an accountant and you start getting creative in your accounting. What about your trusted medicine man who starts becoming imaginative with his treatment modality and decides to experiment with new treatment avenues just to be different, giving a new meaning to the name of his office — the practice. He gets creative to make you more sick than you really are! And when things go wrong, he would say, "Oops, I'm sorry" and carry on with his next client/ patient/victim. Of course those in the artistic arena would benefit and survive from regular face-lifts. Their clients are easily bored and forever yearn for something new and fresh.

Fresh face actors, avant-garde inventors, revolutionary designers and attention craving performers need to shed their exoskeleton every once in a while to turn heads. Even lawyers have to repeatedly think of ingenious ways to dodge their clients' wrongdoings (the truth does not come in the equation) by creatively creating loopholes or doubts in the legal framework to sketch an element of doubt for their 'pathetic' clients to escape punishment!

Even conmen and thieves are becoming slicker these days. And the Nigerians with money stuck in frozen accounts... Do I need to go on?
FG23.9.13

Why these intermediaries?

Conversations in a trip through the journey of life....

HL: You know, I have had it up to here with the chief priest of the temple. I have religiously been going to this temple for God knows how long but when I need help, the chief priest gives me the runaround. Sometimes, I think he only serves the rich and famous, not a poor nobody like me!

FG: Why don't you ask his assistant to help you?

HL: His assistant rather has his boss do the consultation for fear of hurting him.

FG: What kind of out-of-this-world help that you are seeking that only the chief of chieftains can help?

HL: No, just wanted him to help me with my astronomical stars and charts so that I can do the necessary prayers!

FG: For what?

HL: Huh? So that I can do a proper prayer for blessing.

FG: For what?

HL: Huh? For blessings!

FG: Do you believe in God? Do you believe that He is omnipotent, omnipresent and omniscient? If you do, then you must realise that you do not need to tell Him anything. Least of all, you do not intermediaries to tell Him your problems because He knows. He knows what you want, what he has, what you do not, what you need and even what you think! He is supposed to be a God for all. So, I think you can communicate with Him directly, why not?

FG: Nobody knows the purpose of this journey. Some claim to know it all as if they have had a direct audience with God or have seen what is there on the other side. But, believe you me, we are all just as ignorant. Nobody knows what is in store for you, for me, for each one of us. We are all just sailing clutching to whatever that he says, she says...

HL: But still...

FG: Aaah...We are here...but not quite on the other side...FG25.9.13

Only the good die young!

So at the funeral pyre, the crowd sobbed at the passing of a likeable 53 year old lady who succumbed to the devastating effects of the malignant crab of an organ which held the seeds of life (not death).

The family members and friends have been prepared and even relieved to see her go. Seeing her organs fail one by one to be supported by modern science and pain (oh, the pain)... Death was the saving grace. After stopping all medical interventions and returning home to the comfort of the familiar company of her family members and family home, in the echoing chants of prayers, she breathed her last breath.

One relative who was perplexed by the turns of events confided why she should just wither away so soon, being a seemingly kind lovable religious vegetarian and all, at an age where she should be enjoying the fruits of her life struggle. She finally came to terms that this was one of those unexplainable things in life that nobody could decipher. The only thing she could do was to do good, pray hard, do the necessary medical tests and hope for the best!

....The evil-minded devil's advocate in FG got him thinking...

Maybe, the dearly departed was so lovable that even God wanted to have her close by his side! If not, why do you see so many seeming evil man and women still roaming the world? Would not a bolt of lightning just strike at the right spot to jolt them into place? People who had allegedly done great disservice and atrocity to humanity, should they not be eliminated early to maintain peace, law, order and sanity on Earth?

Chin Peng, who is gripped strongly by a big group of the people in this nation lived to a ripe age of 89. There are even some plotting devious plans of dominance and ill intent against his enemies at this late twilight of age. So, my friend, this adage of doing good to live longer does not hold water. On the contrary, only the good die young. Furthermore, living on Earth is supposed to be the punishment of the soul in the cycle of karma!

When you pray, are you communicating with a bigger Being who would change the course of your life after taking pity on your plight or getting fed up with your constant harassment? Is it not just a monologue or a self-pacification to give encouragement to counter the daily challenges of life?

The more you think of things like these, the more confused you would be. People with limited knowledge probably with vested interests would tell you this and that attempting to cow you into submission with talks propagating siege scenario. So, the best thing for me to do is to run and clear my mind...... 42 here I come...Only the good die young, so be a bad*ss!

In their last moments, people show you who they really are...Heath Ledger as Joker. FG29.9.13

His time in the spotlight

What is success? How high do you want to go before you say enough is enough? How much do you want to be in the limelight? How high is high enough? Have you reached the zenith? Have you found what you are looking for? Will you ever?

It is all a matter of perspective, whether your life is half empty or partially filled.

If you sit down and analyse, you must have a tale to tell. It could be small or it could be big. If you dig deep enough, even if your life is not even half complete, you must have achieved something, anything, if you look hard enough!

This I discovered during my last meeting with long lost childhood friends.

On the outward, they may not look as glamorous or flamboyant as our typical mindset depict, they indeed have something to brag about. A small footstep for the rest of mankind but giant one indeed for him and from where he came from.

Everyone will have something nice to be mentioned in their eulogies!

Or maybe you are still looking for the elusive pot of gold or the mythical Prince Charming to saunter along and sweep you off the feet to ride into the sunset. Dream on.... When you get up, you can see things much more clearly then!FG7.10.13

This is what social studies and humanity is all about!

Just the other day, somebody saw a piece of newspaper lying on the table as she was about to sit down to enjoy her usual cuppa of *teh tarik*. The newspaper struck her as being unusual as she was written in Arabic script. On close scrutiny, she realised that it was a newspaper meant to satisfy the intellectual needs of the expatriate Pakistanis community in Malaysia.

At one look, she thought, "Wow! The Pakistanis have become so bold that they have their own publications."

But then, it is only evolution...

Humans are social animals. They are not machines who would work 24/7 for the prosperity of his bosses without having little vices here and there. These little vices and outlets are his only ways to maintain his sanity. Literary indulgence is definitely one way for him to keep him abreast with happenings back home with the satiety of not neglecting his homeland.

When a country takes in human capital from abroad, she does not only squeeze his sweat for work, she also inherits the baggages of his social and animal needs. She should have plans for medical support and plans for his extracurricular indulgence of sowing his wild oats.

The early immigrants who came to this country also went through this cycle. Pretty soon, the Pakistani workers, just like the many immigrants before them, will see no reason to go anywhere than to stay in the place that they had toiled their sweat, blood and even life for. That is how nations are built anyway.FG13.10.13

They only want your money

I heard an advertisement over the radio the other day enticing its listeners to visit their medical centre which they boast of being a forerunner in the field of preventive medicine. The ad cajoled further by highlighting the fact that prevention is better than cure. Yeah, sounds quite novel and logical but why am I not convinced?

You want to prevent lung cancer and other respiratory ailments, refrain from inhaling those noxious tobacco and industrial fumes. Afraid of looking like Sivaji in 'Vasantha Maaligai', jaundiced and all, drink modestly to keep liver diseases at bay. Avert life style diseases, embrace healthy styles! Sound easy and logical enough.

But why is it that I am not convinced when a business person tells me that? Why do I feel that you just want to make a sick person out of me to tell me that I have this and that? I will be more worried of a disease that I may have a condition which may not bring me down and may earn me a label. Thanks to your zillion screening procedures that you extend to a zillion healthy individuals in the hope of finding a zillionth chance of picking out an abnormality which in turn would demand more tests and more tests until you drain me dry financially and drive me blind flabbergasted with statistically bombastic jargon and predictive values. And put me at risk of risking my life through your tests but cover your posterior by asking me to agree to it anyway, under duress, by telling me that it is a simple procedure but I may die but I still want it and I know the complications and consequences. If you do not find me a physical ailment in my apparently carefree life, I may need to congratulate you of your possible success of driving me into one but of the loony bins!

You may tell me that the frequency of my nocturnal thrust which is no concern to you but to my loved one alone is insufficient. You may show me that my urges fall in dangerously low centile of healthy living based on some obscure Sunset Boulevard kind of celluloid living and prescribe me this and that. You will say that my medications may interact with the new medication that you are about to prescribe (which I may need in the first place), and tell me that I would need a more expensive medications.FG17.10.13

Chicken's Invite? (Ajak-ajak ayam)

In the Malay lingo, the phrase 'ajak-ajak ayam' refers to an insincere invitation. Of course, many of us invite for courtesy's sake but then the invitee may think that the invitation is for real! How does anyone know? Inviters and invitees must be smart enough to take the cue that one party may have gate crashed with ulterior motives or the other may not want him to join in the first place!

Easily twenty years ago, my family was invited to a toddlers' birthday party. As my children were toddlers too then, we were requested to come early so that my kids could run around play in their big compound. And that the host said she would arrange series of games for them to enjoy.

So there we were in the early evening at a house that resembled very little of one immersed with joy and celebration. Instead, we were greeted to by a house devoid of activities and no guests. The host was still out shopping her last minute list and her helper was in knee deep with her preparations of cleaning up the premises. Time dragged on so slowly.

The host sauntered in smiling as if she had struck the lottery and asked us to look around as if nothing is the matter. Guests (younger kids only) were sent by parents to run around the compound. Children, being children, were running around in circles in the humid tropical evening like how a dog would be trying to catch its own tail. Unlike a pig, they were all sweating and clammy. And the host was still lost in her work as the dusky sky was slowly engulfed by the twilight of darkness. Feeling thirsty and hungry (did I mention no food or beverages were served?), we politely informed the host that it was time for us to leave. I was taken aback when she curtly said, "Ok then, see you around!". No, hang on there, Just a minute, We'll start when more guests arrive, nothing.

And we headed to the nearest food court for our own party! It was a memorable party, no doubt, as we still laugh about it and tell ourselves how to be a gracious host. Lessons in life...

Then there is another story... I do not know why I befriend these people. Maybe I am too nice or simply too gullible! So, this guy persistently kept on insisting that we should all go out as a family for a meal together as he had been to my humble abode many a time for dinners.

After many clashes of dates, my wife finally managed to arrange a dinner at a nice Chinese restaurant. The day came and there we were, my family only. My friend, the supposed host dragged himself in almost an hour later, in piece meal-first his wife, his kids and finally the man, complaining "traffic jam, traffic jam"!

After the cursory pleasantries, we dug deep into the chow.

As the curtain call rolled in, the talk became redundant, laboured with many draggy sentences. I thought it was customary for the host (my friend) to call it a day or ask whether there was a need to order more desserts. But hell no, he and his wife just got up and thanked us heartily for the meal, good luck, good health, bla, bla. And guess who took the tab? It was not even a chicken's invite (ajak-ajak ayam) as the restaurant served seafood only!FG19.11.13

What maketh a human?

So it is yet another run, my personal competitive run #35 since I took the plunge into my first run in 2009. This time around it is the Adidas King of the Road 16.8 km run, third time running. As I was running along the mammoth monolithic man-made structures amidst the mixed affluent and the not so affluent part of the suburbia, I realised that nothing about the race had changed. The wannabe runners with their *'gaya muthusamy'* way of branded dressing and gizmos filled to the brim, heart monitors, sweat head-band, logo flashing florescent compression suits, Gel Kinsei (the Bentley of the running shoes) etcetera, etcetera. Even the loud mouthed hooligans with nonsensical hurls and catcalls at the 18 km mark were there this time around. Only, they had gotten their stereophonic bass beating high trebled high fidelity systems to complement their rowdy act!

So there was nothing new, it was just same old, same old... And as I was running and thinking what to write about the run, it came to me. Why not write about the dressing of some of the participants, I asked myself?

Some dress to flaunt, some want to flaunt but cannot due to certain social and cultural restrictions. Some flaunt anyway (because they can and they want to) whilst others modify their dressing to flaunt the law to be acceptable and to cover the restricted taboo zones.

Like they say, sarees are worn by people like Mother Theresa and sarees are worn by sex workers in the most remote area of India. What may the difference, the modesty versus the alluring inner desires? It is the composite act of carrying oneself and speech that complement the whole package, is it not?

So, I chuckle to myself and ask myself why all the effort to colour code, to enhance the contour and leave none to our imaginations and let it all go to waste? Just a thought whilst I continue the run....FG20.10.13

Nationalism, Racism and Humanity

There have been some talk of late on the inhumane treatment of stray dogs by the city pounds. Then I heard of an NGO who is advocating counselling for children of refugees/illegal immigrants, that they should not be placed in the same place of incarceration as adults for fear of traumatising these gentle souls for life. But then, I thought of most of the immigration population all around the world had done well for themselves and for the country that accepted them as guests. In fact, history has shown those who do not roam the streets but grow out of relatively stable societies, with affluence, structured social structure and without a care in the world may end up as raving lunatics.

Then there are those on the other end who are out to squeeze out the last drop of blood and sweat of their foreign workers. Even though they gave their life and soul to the development of the country, these workers are considered lesser human beings by many. They were not born here, they say. I was here earlier, say others. What would happen to their children, you would say? Surely by then, the offspring would have learnt the local lingo and customs. And other things would be mentioned that suspect their loyalty, their race, their whatever. If the workers fall ill or get debilitated en route to elevate the status of the nation to one of the first world, the country feels that the non-productive worker must be bundled back to his native country rather than letting him hog the system and over utilise the already depleted resources in the public hospital.

The other day, a friend, living in an up market guarded community was relating an incident that happened recently. Two occupants of above average intelligence and socioeconomic strata (obviously neither of common sense and humanity faculties) were involved in a meaningless tiff. Animosity brewed gradually over trivial matters like one neighbour's dog peeing in the other's compound. Then the other became unhappy when the parking arrangement of one's vehicle impinged on the other's compound. One thing led to another which finally ended up with a noisy stand-off!

We cannot even care for each other fellow human being, but we seem to be more emphatic to animals! Ironic... More like moronic!FG28.10.13

Blind Justice?

So you think the truth will always prevail? You tell me that justice is impartial and is always fair. Is it just me or why is it that I think that it just a farce, just created to pacify a crying child. It is never fair. Justice is blind, deaf, mute, dumb and everything in between.

So, there I was, driving like a good guy, crossing the junction after ensuring that the road is clear. In fact, the cars at the T-junction waited for me to cross. Out of nowhere, comes a motorcyclist weaving through the traffic in between cars to crash directly to the side of my car. No warning, no honk, just like that, like a death wish.

And there I was trying to help him out to be up on his feet. Somehow, I felt the whole accident was staged. Out of nowhere, people appeared to the site offering various services — towing, insurance claims and unwarranted less than 2cents' worth of opinions.

And when, I, as a diligent citizen, made my police report, I was told that I was not totally off the hook. After listening out my story, the investigating officer suggested it was also my duty to ensure that nobody comes my way when I drive!

I was there, I know what happened!

And my father tells me of a civil court case where the presiding judge decreed that in a case of an accident at a junction, even if the traffic light is green on his side, the onus is still on the driver to ensure that there was no oncoming vehicle. What a load of crap? The law is blind alright! FG8.11.13

No pain no gain?

The jury is still out on why runners from a certain part of Eastern African, especially of a certain tribe in Kenya do extremely well in the middle and long distance races. People of the Kalenjin tribe who comprise 0.6% of the world population have the honour of holding more than 40% of the world honours in distances of 800 m and above, all the way to the marathon. Many theories have been suggested for their lion's share on these records.

The familiar reasons that have been told to us are their physique, training in high altitude, their low socio-economic status and running as their trump card to freedom, bla, bla...

Now, I heard of a new quasi-genetic explanation for their superiority — their tolerance to pain!

In 1968 Mexico City Olympics, the unforgettable heroic saga to the victory of a certain athlete, Kipchoge Keino, started the flood gates of subsequent champions emerging from that side of the world. After the preliminary rounds, Kip was to partake in 3 events, namely 10,000 m, 5,000 m and 1500 m. He collapsed during the 10,000 m finals. His doctor diagnosed him to have cholecystitis (gall bladder infection) and advised him to call it quits. Kip defied doctor's orders and ran the 5,000 m to win the silver medal. Again the doctor discouraged him to run another race. The gallbladder was apparently at risk of rupture, so the story goes! In spite of the stinging pain at every breath of fresh air, Kip persevered.

The 1500 m finals of Mexico City Olympics turned out to be a tale of human endeavour. Jack Ryun of USA, the then world record holder for the event with his 'kick' was favoured to win. Starting as last in the first lap, Kip zoomed past everybody to, not only to beat Ryun but to break the Olympic record with his gall bladder infection. There was a 20 m gap between him and Ryun.

A theory suggested for their tenacity is the ritual of the Kalenjin tribe adolescents had to go through as they came of age. This ritual is an elaborate ritual of circumcision with skewers and tying the prepuce in a bow tie fashion. The boys' faces are splashed with mud that dries up. During the circumcision, the boys are not allowed to grimace as evidenced by flaking of mud on their faces. Failure of this test would result in severe beating and loss of licence to find a partner, hence reproductive opportunities. They are required to run everywhere with the pain. Women are required to undergo their own circumcision rituals.

In the long run, only those with high pain threshold had been selected to continue the progeny!

The newer generation of Kalenjins, of course, do not wish to be tortured this way. Even their parents are quite happy with their offspring having the cut into adulthood with modern analgesic techniques. Does that mean that the Kenyan runners would one day eventually lose their prowess?

So, no pain no gain. Of course they would be aches and they would be pains, only the ones who persevere will live to see the finishing line....
FG9.10.13

Sitting ducks, are we?

For years and years, many seemingly unimportant information are written in case notes of patients. Many apparently worthless piece of news is recorded diligently. Who actually bothers about the weight of the placenta during delivery? Many routine things are recorded faithfully at a spinal level without any grey matter involved.

Even when a doctor 'clerks' your illness, at the back of his mind is to record salient features of your interview. Sometimes, he acts more like a clerk trying fulfil his duty of completing the mandatory questions and forms. Don't even bother about the nurses! By the time they retire, they would written all the Vedic scriptures a thousand times over.

Why all this obsession to write? I always wondered.... And I saw how many particulars are retrospectively filled and many descriptive posterior covering documentation occur when an unfavourable outcome happens. All are done in the hope that they, the attendants, would not be likely pinpointed and penalised when the day of reckoning if it happens, one day!

Hey, then it all makes sense. Those in the medical profession are just sitting ducks writing day in and day out for one day, if the patient that they had cared for, has a bone to pick, their nitty-gritty cherry picking attorneys can scheme through with a fine tooth comb to corner the practitioner, who acted in good faith and God as their witness, to appear as a buffoon and a conniving psychopath with the benefit of hindsight! The attorneys would appear like all knowing smart alecs highlighting the elementary facts of life!

So that is what it is......FG13.11.13

So you think you made it!

Perched high up on skyscraper, placed on a hill overlooking the lowlands of common people and the iconic bridge to mainland, amidst the clutter of cutlery in the continental restaurant, indulging in high calories' diet with no guilt, sipping the freshly squeezed orange, brain immersed in endorphins, it sure feels good like a million dollars to know that you had conquered the challenges that life had to offer, albeit in our own small ways.

We made small baby steps to face the giant face of life and came out smelling not of stinking sweat but sweet smelling roses. We persevered, we fought the fight, endured the pain, ignored the heartbreaks and followed the path of least resistance. Like James Brown said, "It feels good, it feels nice". Even the unsweetened black coffee tastes sweet! And the bread as we know it has a funny foreign-sounding name.FG24.11.13

Better late than never?

So, there I was rushing through traffic trying not to embarrass myself by being late. Looking at my watch periodically, I just wanted to ensure that I do not walk into the hall with the bridal entourage instead of before them. Not that it had not happened before!

I remember, many years ago, in my hometown, where everything was a lazy affair, my family and I were invited to a friend's parents' wedding anniversary which was celebrated in a glitzy and pompous manner. In keeping with the high-brow nature of the function with distinguished guests and all, the host decided to start right on the dot.

Talk about right timing, we just made our entry just when the spotlights went on and Cliff Richard's 'Congratulations and Celebrations' started playing. It very much took us by surprise. We were dumbfounded in a 'deer in headlights' moment.

So were the guests who were expecting to see the special stars for the evening!

Anyway, coming back to the present times, I finally made it to the wedding reception hall. This time, the surprise was on me again as the hall was practically empty! The invitation quoted that dinner was to start at 7 pm and there I was at 7.30pm.

After a good half and an hour of looking around from top to bottom and from side to side of the hall and the decorations, guests started strolling in. My friend who was supposed to join me coolly sauntered in at about 8.30pm just when the function was starting. As a matter-of-factly, he sneered at me for coming so early for a Malay wedding. He said that it is an unwritten rule that things are to start at least one and a half hour late. So far, I have only heard the Chinese complained about their wedding dinners not starting on time. Even the Indian wedding receptions are better, half to an hour late.

Anyway, when the function actually started, everything was forgotten. Everyone was merry-making and having fun rather than brooding about wasted time.

So, the next time, it would be still a one and half hour delay. I would be wiser. I would also go late. And the trend would continue. Nobody is going to start a function when nobody is in attendance. There would be the royal couple but without lowly peasants, the royal couple would just a couple without the lowly subjects to fete them up to high heavens!
FG28.11.13

We don't dress our women!

Just the other day, I was watching a Youtube clip 'The God Delusion' by the world's most famous atheist, Professor Richard Dawkins.

I was particularly fascinated by one scene in this man's crusade to convince his audience that the institution of religious actually brings more disharmony to mankind. In that scene, Dawkins was interviewing an American secular Jewish man who got his divine calling and had embraced an ultra-conservative form of Islam. He was residing in Gaza. Upon being asked about the state of affairs of world today, he went ballistic. He blamed the evil of the world on the Western civilisation.

"You dress your women like whores and send them to the streets, you expect the world to be a better place!" To which, Dawkins coolly told him, "We don't dress them, they dress themselves!"

I think that statement says a lot of things. You set a certain set of rules for people and say that some are more than equal than others and expect people to follow them forever and ever till the end of time. Unfortunately, suppression and repression has a threshold. After a certain point, it loses its elasticity and reaches a point of no-return!

Social experiments in animals have shown them reacting violently when one is given preferential feeding over the other. Recent outpour of emotions over the demise of a fellow worker in an unrelated bus accident in Singapore is also testimony of a group of unhappy workers who felt short-changed in the flow of development and the sea of economic prosperity. It is not enough to tell them this is what you deserve as Man, being Man, will always strive to be at higher place and is forever searching for that freedom, happiness, liberty, truth, nirvana, *moksha*, whatever you call it....FG10.12.13

Don't judge me!

Dear Thelma,

I am a 19-year-old lady with very low self-esteem right now. I am writing with the hope that you may empathise with my predicament. Hopefully, you can help me justify the big action that I am going to do right now.

Growing up in the interior of Sarawak, education was not a priority. Carrying on clan's tradition and continuing the women's roles in the family was paramount to the existence of our gender. As the importance of education and need for self-empowerment were not impressed upon us, we were raised to believe that we were born to serve the men folks and keep the home in pristine condition and not to stress up the men of the house. Going to school, which itself was a bore, a chore and a burden to the family, I found the long journey to school on raft and foot a nuisance. Hence, I was pleasantly and naively surprised when I joined the band of girls who started vomiting in school, not due sub-optimal preparation of canteen meals but rather because of bludgeoning dose of placental hormones and HCG on the medulla oblongata!

At the speed of lightning (very very frightening me), I saw my carefree days of childhood crush tumbling down like a deck of dominos. I was paraded through a ceremony to give a name to our lusty at the spur of the moment escapade. Very soon my physique ballooned out of proportion unimaginable even in my wildest nightmare!

At the speed of lightning too, I discovered that the man of life was a two (or maybe three) timer and also the man of another woman before me and had offsprings to prove his virility!

As I discovered that as my petite body bloated up with oedema of pregnancy, my affaire d'amour with my 'The One' came crumbling down. I was just another one of the statistic of the many helpless victims of 'The One'!

A protracted pregnancy and labour ended with an offspring which essentially killed my childhood. Free time for me was folding diapers and cleaning the house. One year went on... My long lost aunt appeared from nowhere to change my life. She told me to take charge of my life. She persuaded me to crawl out of the cocoon that I have built for myself and change my life. She peeled opened my eyes to see the world more than just brooding over my misfortune.

With a renewed zest for life and the glitz for the good life, I made a drastic make over of myself. Off I came to the Peninsular for life anew.

The blinding lights of the city brought me to heights unimaginable by a village lass like me. In due time, it brought to me the acquaintance of Mr Z. The showering of gifts and attention must have drowned in his sea of love. Pretty soon the sweet fruit of passion begin to rear its ugly head. The spinning whirlwind of dizziness with accompanying sickness without motion soon ensued.

Suddenly reality hit me smack on my head! History seems to be repeating itself, yet again!

What kind of a mother am I?

One unplanned unwanted child growing up in wilderness like undergrowth, unattended to, without love and attention, without role model to follow, without a mother, unwanted and shooed away like a house fly! And now, as if bringing one wild flower to the world is not enough, I am here with another, out in the world so cold. Unsupported and unable to stand on my own two feet. How many times am I going to be the source of offspring who are a nuisance to others? What can I do? What should I do?

I want to start living as a wife and mother like anyone else, married and settled down. My partner, somehow, has other plans. He cites young age and need to improve his economic status as sufficient reason to terminate our art of love! Am I just a pawn in the game of love and sweet nothingness?

It is easy for the uppity high-browed individuals to judge me, that I deserve what I got, that I am short on the religious faculty. It is easy to judge. To err is human, be in my shoes and you will understand....

Right here still waiting.FG21.12.13

Life is short?

Heard about an internet dating service that promotes sexual affairs. Their tagline says it all, "Life is short, have an affair". They allegedly have over 20 million subscribers to choose from to have a fling, discreet, safe, yada yada yada...

Of course, people are up in arms on both sides of the fence for and against legitimisation of such a site. On one hand there is the argument that one should be left to do what one please as long as it does not hurt the other party. We should not criminalise affairs as man, who by nature, are polygamous and nature encourages selection of the best for continuity of species. Whether we like it or not, infidelity is going to happen, just as corruption and cheating. It is always better to do things in the open than doing it in a clandestine fashion. They often quote the therapeutic effects of affairs and spouse swapping to release sexual tensions and mismatch. On the other side of the fence, the naysayers argue that affairs are cheating and people are bound to lie, to be hurt, etcetera. And the question of religious sanctions and morals are also roped in. The non-believers would always question why religion is always brought in the equation! The usual explanation is that something as uncertain and incomprehensible by feeble man as life and its dos and don'ts should not be questioned. They substantiate their support by quoting texts from holy scriptures of impending doom to our civilisation and these were some the symptoms. The union of man and woman has always been sacred and intriguing to man from time immemorial that ceremonies, festivals, rituals and public declarations have been emphasised. The forces of nature and God have been invoked to bless this union.

So, how? Is sex and companionship so indispensable in human survival that affairs are mandatory in continuity of species? Companionship and comradeship does not need to involve opposite genders always - I do not mean the physical nude tactile type! Are the just trying to sell their 'clever' business strategy to strength their (the webmaster) relationship with their bankers?FG23.12.13

The tale of two tails

Just the other day, a visitor who visited me passed a remark in the passing. She was looking at my cat who appeared looking far into the horizon crouched at the glass window of my house. She remarked that he could be looking at all his stray friends on the other side of the fence and envying their freedom and their ability to roam and go anywhere as they please any time of the day. And my cat would be engaged in forlorn glances brooding over his helpless situation.

I instead told her that my cat's friends on the other side, on the hand, would instead be gazing at him with eyes full of envy. He sits in the comfort of the house, aesthetically pleasing environment shielded from the cruel forces of weather and nature, with love overflowing all around, soothing tactile stimuli to caress and rub, sheltered from noxious sickness, protection from prancing predators and people discontented with their presence and mating call!

That is life isn't it? One not happy with one's own life and would die to be in the other's life, thinking that it would be all greener on the other side. Expectations only lead to disappointment but acceptance to contentment....FG24.12.13

Lotus feet of the Lord?

The latest catch phrase or latest hip lingo to use in speeches seem to be to include 'leave all your troubles worries at the lotus feet of Lord and surrender yourselves'. Hey, they remind me of a camping song we used to sing in school - Pack all your troubles in your old-kit bag and smile, smile, smile...

Unfortunately, the song 'pack all your troubles' was a propaganda song of World War 1 to motivate the youngsters to sign the life away to the cause of the war all in the name of nationalism and world peace. Is it not ironic that man has to go to war to maintain peace!

I suppose, in the same way, leaving all your troubles at the divine lotus feet is akin to sweeping the proverbial trash under the carpet. It just gives us the confidence to clear our mind to gather resources to strategise our next moves to rid the trash that form our source of worry.

It may just be a soliloquy or monologue similar to a listening ear or a shoulder to cry on, just is there for visits. You can come and go as you please... They say that about pubs too — you could come and go! You spend too much time and you go wayward!FG28.12.13

History repeating itself?

I must be appearing like a painful unfriendly doom prophet to people around me. Pretty soon I would not be surprised if people run away from me to keep me at arm's length rather than engage in a tête-à-tête with me.

Why?

Just the other day, a guy whom I know, was boasting of the new management team in the company he was working with. The team had been recently changed. The company that he had been working for so many years used to be one of the last bastions of multinational companies managed by local businessmen. After many business wrangling and buying overs, it came to be run by a famous foreign company.

He was singing praises of the management of the new company, its efficacy and ease of getting things done. And he went on and on...

So, I told him how 3 centuries ago, a certain group of businessmen presented themselves with exotic gifts and proposals to elevate their lifestyles as well as ease their lives. Then came troubles over troubles. And poof! The businessmen became their bosses.

And how some clergymen came to natives' land with their Bibles. And they closed their eyes in prayer. Poof! The clergymen held the land and the natives, the Bible!FG30.12.13

Of foie gras, food and fond memories...

I grew up amongst elders who constantly complained about the lack of taste in the food prepared by the then younger generation. The frequent banter that they indulged whenever the elders meet is the reminiscence of the mouth watering palatal stimulating dishes that their elders used to prepare back in the days. Sometimes I used to think that these people were indeed gluttons and lived to eat. One of them include my father and my maternal grandfather. The latter literally sold off his ancestral property just to satisfy his taste buds and hypothalamic satiety centre. They used to recollect the times when the aroma of chicken curry cooked in one person's kitchen used to fill the whole neighbourhood and how 'simply out-of-this world' food generally tasted.

I used to think that taste never changed. I thought their remote memory of input of olfactory nerve to the limbic system just reignited their nostalgic childhood memories. Until I heard the story of a man in Spain who reared geese to prepare them for foie gras, the natural way without the notorious force feeding which is often spoken about.

A journalist well versed with fine dining decided to trace this eccentric man, Eduardo, to his farm to interview and see for himself the truth of his claim. Eduardo has his own beliefs on ensuring succulent juicy fat geese liver. The goslings are left to roam wild in an unfenced field exposed to various selected grasses. Of course, security is a concern as he lost 20 to 30% of his flock to predators and wanderers. He does not touch the geese as it may loose its protective sebum. The flock is left to roam freely and happy.

Geese have an inborn ability to gorge themselves in preparation of winter. They eat and eat if they are happy.

At the end of the interview, the journalist had the chance to taste his product. To his astonishment, the dish did not need artificial flavouring. The foie gras did not need additional seasoning as all the various flavours were allegedly provided by the food that the geese fed on. According to Eduardo, modern farming had destroyed natural flavours in food.

I suppose there must be some truth in what the old folks were saying when we were growing up. In order to feed the ever increasing population of the world, we managed to increase the production of food at the expense of taste.FG3.1.14

Best thing since sliced bread?

I was made to think that I was missing the world, that I was outdated, that I needed something to commensurate the amount of time I spent on blogging and that I should learn how to spend for myself too, to pamper myself. I was made to think that I was important and was missing the sheer pleasure and ease of the greatest invention by man.

I went on thinking that I was stupid for not joining the bandwagon. The masters were at work with time-proven business psychological methods of Edward Bernays. Eventually, I started thinking that my mundane life would suddenly morph forever into a psychedelic colour filled Strawberry Fields. I decided that I had to have it at all cost.

And I took the plunge...I got my MacBook Air...

Now that I have got it, I have come to realise that life is still the same. There are no flying confetti and rainbow paved pathway. I still have to think and compose with my brain and type intelligently. It is just like art and craft. I have to create the art but craft of performing is different. How different? Just as familiarity breeds contempt, absence make the heart grow fonder..FG8.1.14

All things will/must pass...

A coincidence happened a few days ago to convince me that all things will pass and not to get upset about things. And it also persuaded me to look at the other side of things. Somehow, wearing the other person's shoes, the problem does not look like a problem anymore!

 A few days ago, my neighbour's puppy started barking incessantly. Prior to that, nobody in the neighbourhood even knew of the existence of a dog in their backyard until the eventful day. Calls after calls rang off the hook of my neighbour's phone complaining about the nuisance so much so that he became phobic receiving calls and stopped answering them.

Almost like magic, during a casual conversation with my sister living 300 km away a few days later, she was complaining that her neighbours were unhappy with their loss of sleep over the continual barking of her dog. She was at wit's end trying to get to the root of the problem with no avail.

Back in my neighbourhood, the barking ceased. It could be one of the follows — dog died/put to sleep/whatever offending the creature was removed/dog just stopped barking/in somebody's cooking pot! Whatever it is, my neighbour never saw his neighbours the same way again after all the hurtful words hurled at him at the spur of the moment.

On the other side of the 300 km end, my sister zeroed it on the fact that the dog must be feeling cold after an overzealous grooming. After probably the disappearance of the initial irritation and adaptation, it stopped whining and in the next few days and everybody in her neighbourhood were all smiles again.

And life goes on.... Hurdles, tragedies, ailment, loss and calamities are just obstacles that we have to pass through in our voyage of life. No point getting upset as all thing must pass. Sometimes we pass with them too but we may be in a better place (so they say)......FG9.1.14

Who needs thinkers?

The Eichmann trial had often been critiqued for being a witch hunt, looking for a scapegoat rather than trying to get to the root of the problem. A problem far bigger than Adolf Eichmann transporting prisoners to Auschwitz, more than just sending the lambs to the slaughter!

Hannah Arendt, writing for the magazine New Yorker, herself a Jewess who suffered imprisonment by Nazi, who was expecting to see a gruesome looking mean dude at the trials, was quite surprised at the simple looking civil servant who was more interested in completing his given task, at the dock. He was oblivious to the sequelae of his actions. Arendt coined the term 'banality of evil' and proposed that evil done unknowingly by an unthinking person is the worst kind.

That got me thinking....

Again and again, history has shown of people choosing a leader and following his directions blindly. The Germans elected a monster through the legal means who rocked the whole world to realise his megalomaniac dream of creating a pure-bred Aryan race. The ever mild-mannered Japanese are also guilty of turning a blind eye to their regime which raped and massacred half of the world.

Looking back, these nations would like to forever erase that dark tainted part of their nation's history.

But then, to achieve a certain agenda, a leader has to have ways to influence the masses to do things in a particular fashion so that their mission is accomplished. The masses must be seen to be doing their given tasks without questioning all in the name of glory of the race, nation, flag or religion. They must be spineless working at spinal level like zombies. Thinking is not allowed.

If everybody starts thinking and questioning, the target would not be met and what you would have is pure pandemonium.

On the other hand, these unquestioning loyalty and war did produce some milestones in the human civilisation. Advances in air transportation, engineering and energy are the testimony to this. The large big step forward is also marred by the fact that they are savvier of ways to annihilate each other.FG30.1.14

Nobody owes nobody nothing?

Just the day I was thinking...

Unlike my dog in childhood, Rexxie, who used to get all excited, jumpy, tongue waggly, drooling at the sight of any of the family members as they return home, Felix (the cat) is not the least bothered.

Returning home after a hard days' work, you think that looking at some(one) who is all excited about your return would *just make you feel all right*. But Felix at the corner has other plans... He saunters casually in a relaxed fashion, strutting his stuff, gyrating his hind legs (guess that is why they call it catwalk) walking haughtily with his nose held high (*like inhaling imported air*) looking away from you without a care in the world. At that moment, he does not need anything, only his breathing space! Just leave him alone (*stop dogging him around!*) pun not intended...

He does not need you right now. You have bought his chow, his litter bag, his playpen, got his veterinary needs fulfilled. He is big and strong, he does not need you now.

That is the same story about life. Nobody owns anybody. Everybody fans for himself. At the desperate time of helplessness, nobody can help you. You have to help yourself. You have to swim yourself to shore, you have to fight the waves, shark and the wind.

Nobody owns anybody in this modern world except if you are in the human trafficking business. Your merchandise that you own is human flesh, bone and feelings that go with it.

Slavery supposed to have died, has it really?

And then there is something called emotional blackmail where some Indian mothers know just strings to pluck to strike the chord of self-pity and helplessness! These strings of control are subtle ways to control the subjects and cow them to submission...FG6.2.14

Burst my bubble!

Dear Thelma,

Sometimes I feel that I am breathless. I can't breath. I feel that I have been forced to do what I do not want to, or rather what the society wants me to do. And I have been shortchanged!

I grew up with lots of dreams and ambitions. I wanted to be somebody, away from these misery and constant tone of melancholia and sad songs that seem to be the background score of our daily life. I wanted to be free. I wanted to escape from the clutches of poverty.

Since young, only X seem to understand me. Coming from a similar background, he could relate to how I felt. Only thing that he is a male and I, a female.

Over time, our feelings changed, from one of empathy and understanding, it metamorphosed into something intimate. Our raging hormones which just spurred from nowhere eventually pushed us to cross the boundaries set by society. Suddenly, there was no barrier, no shame. The boundary guarded and protected all this while was now breached.

Why is it that I feel so guilty? I have not done anything wrong or have I?

Something so good cannot be so wrong! Now there are people telling me that all my big wonderful mountain high dreams have to take a back burner. The fence of decency had been breached and the law of nature must be respected. Our bond must be formally sanctioned by the forces that be. We cannot just go on happy without public declarations.

That was 3 years ago. Now with 1 infant screaming day and night and another quickening in my body, my dreams seem like a distant planet — visible but unreachable.

As if they had an audience with the Forces of Nature, they restricted my reproductive function. Contraception is a 4-lettered word in my in-law's family. I thought I was in a hell hole but now I am in a dragon's den, from frying pen to fire.

Why do they keep bringing me down? They put the fear of God and unheard cryptic scriptures to cow me into submission.

If religion was made to transform human from savage to a sage, why is it that there are savagely exerting their authority over me?

In front of eyes, my sandcastles came crumbling down.... Just sandcastles in the air that popped like a bubble.FG13.2.14

Just a thought!

When our offspring wrong on us, we forgive them. We tell them it is all right to make mistakes as it is part of growing up and maturing. When they look into our eyes and lie through their teeth, we say we understand them. When the young ones show disrespect by uttering hurtful words, we swallow our pride and tell ourselves that growing up these days is hard unlike in the good old days. We do all these because we are considered all knowing and have seen it all compared to the young souls that we brought to this world. Their shortcomings, in a way, are our shortcomings. They are in our mould and we provided the nurturing!

We do not expect them to sing praises of us or to mention the gratitude of us in every little word that they utter or under every breath. It may suffice to remember who is the boss around here. The steady state, tranquillity, sanity and equilibrium that had taken aeons to reach need to be valued, savoured, appreciated and maintained.

This goes through my devilish mind whenever I am in the company of pious (or holier than thou) people who invoke the Divine in everything they say or do. There must be something wrong in the way we pay our dues (respect) to the Almighty. I do not claim to have all the answers and neither do I want to ridicule those who find joy and solace in what they are doing.

Is it not that we are expecting Him to behave like Tony Soprano or Don Corleone, demanding to be surrounded by acts that accentuate His grandiosity and be surrounded by yeoman who would bend over backwards to please Him? I do not think our Maker would want to be treated as such! He would not want to be 'apple polished', put in high heavens, to be sung praises all the time. Too much praising as always is a turn-off and can be nauseating. A spoon of sugar with your coffee is nice. Put two, it is tolerable, put ten and expect it to be pushed out of your system! Are you cajoling the Powers-that-be to somehow alter the course of the universe to suit our self-interest without taking to consideration that every bit of our action and reaction has an equal and opposite reaction? Is it not being selfish? The rainy season is welcomed by the umbrella maker but not by the farmer who intends to harvest his crop. Or are we just following the example set by our leaders and their assistants who find absolute joy in showing allegiance to and hanging around the tails of their superiors with the hope of having a bone thrown at them? FG14.2.14

Above us only sky, amongst us bigots!

You tell me the world is a smaller place, that there are no borders but only in our minds, that Lennon prophecy of there is no country will soon be reality. You say that globalisation is bringing us that way. I beg to differ.

People are flocking together. People with small minds are flocking together with fellow feeble minded individuals of the same calibre. They are trying to see the difference amongst us rather than rejoice the various journeys that we take to reach our destination. Don't they know that all roads lead to Rome (or Jerusalem!)? Even amongst themselves they aspire to further subdivide and claim superiority over the other. It is always 'they' and 'us'. Even though all DNAs are all 99.99% all the same and they have not found the sequence for stupidity, they still claim that they are 'the chosen one'.

They live in a cocoon contented with they have and swear that there is nothing more that need to explored as they been enlightened a millennia ago.

In social medias, as if these man-made divisions are not enough, they have made groups by alma mater, by ethnicity, by sub-ethnicity, etceteras ... And they have hostility against each other, forever trying to find the difference rather than similarities.

Are these all effects of being in the comfort zone for far too long? Are they begging to put in place with a wave of calamity to strike them? History has proven again and again that man will only unite when they have an unconquerable common enemy. It could be a mammoth natural calamity, common abhorrence against an incorrigible tyrant, pathetic living conditions or absolute hopelessness when all of common human dignity is at stake!FG19.2.14

No right, no wrong!

Don't know why, this week, two of the people just went on rattling about the problems they were having with their kids. Not to solve their problems but to ventilate, hoping to hear that they had not done it all wrong but they did all right. To hear that they did what was right at that specific frame of time, in that specific situation, with the resources that they had. Looks like everyone is in the same boat, expectations on the duties performed. The receiving party, however, feels that it is their birthright to be given on the platter. Through thick and thin, the providers provided, feeling that the responsibility was theirs to shoulder (ain't too heavy 'cause it is their flesh and bone).

What they expect in return is gratitude and respect that they had given their elders. But then, times change and values change. A gratitude in the medieval times is returned with life, in the spanking new technology-driven 21st-century world, it would be a 'like' in your Facebook!

What the provider really want is for the recipient to be able to weather the storm which may strike at any time in their unpredictable lives and also to be a steadfast rock for future dependents! That's all.FG24.2.14

Lackadaisical attitude, that is all

I wrote some time ago about errors in signboards, the atrocious state of English Language in the country and the lackadaisical attitude of people in power to ensure perfection or near perfection in whatever they do. Well, it looks like the country is only filled pompous over-fed individuals who just delegate their duties to their subordinates, sleep on their job and just live off the hard work of foreign hands. Lately, it was brought to my attention of two notices that brought quite an embarrassment to the people who were given the responsibility to carry it on.

In the first instance, a congratulatory greeting ended up emitting the wrong vibes. A simple misplacement of letters gave an embarrassment that stunk to high heavens. (from TAHNIAH to TAHINAH, as *tahi* denotes faeces, *nah* is a derogatory and half-hearted way of offering something). As the message was supposed to be a congratulatory note to a very powerful man, many heads are set to roll.

Trickling down to ground level, even in the supermarkets, labelling of goods are left to the imagination of immigrant workers to coin out new words in the Malaysian language. Mosquito traps are hot selling items these days due to the public panic of dengue fever. In one supermarket, it was dengue (or denggi in the Malay language). The supervisors must have left it to the menial workers to design the labels and this is what they got... A label displaying an RM29.99 device to eradicate jealousy and ill thoughts. You see, DENGKI is just that!

Unlike our forefathers who were generally hardworking people who only believed in the mantra of hard work as the only to success, we are slowly evolving to become a nation of laggards and want to live in pomp and splendour. Because things have been relatively easy thus far, everyone thinks that it is their birthright to expect some kind of special treatment. The new form of slavery is dependence on foreign labour. Little do we realise that what happened in the 'Planets of the Apes' may indeed become a reality. The apes who were initially recruited to help around the home eventually became too smart. One spark started a mutiny and pretty soon the world was ruled by generations and generations of apes of worsening brutality!FG7.3.14

The art and science of knowing of your limit!

When you reach a certain age, everybody around you who apparently shows concern on your well-being will give you unsolicited advice asking you to slow down and take things easy, that now is the time to savour the fruit of your labour and the sweat of your hard work. They would often quote you instances and examples of apparently healthy individuals just dropping dead like flies after a seemingly trivial chore. The way they coax (or put you in a corner), they seem to be cocksure of their facts and pretty soon plant the recurrent seed of doubt, uncertainty and fear in your brain. Admittedly, no matter how much goodness there is of a better living condition in the afterlife, we rather grow old, sick, wasted, unwanted and shoved around than die no time sooner, preferably never! We all want to hold on to our dear lives!

You will slow down, fearing for the worst, the unknown enemy. You become sluggish, puffed up, unfit and fat, poorly coordinated and a ticking time bomb. When your pin is unhooked, you disappear, become another statistic and everyone will move on with life, looking out to dash the hope of another health-conscious middle aged man.

Man would not have reached where he has reached now if he had stayed in his comfort zone, fearing the unknown. There would not be any of our ancestors who would have walked out of the African continent to explore newer pastures, no tomatoes in Indian cooking as tomatoes are native of Mediterranean land, no spices in cooking (the European wanted to find alternate route to lay their hand on these black gold), no preserved foods until refrigeration came around, no pleasures of smoking as the first puffer would have been petrified to inhale, no simple pleasures in life (scared of retribution in afterlife), no new World as we know it as Columbus would have been stiff dead to topple over at the edge, no Fauja Singh running till the age of 101, no Arnie and no Arnie for post of Governor of California if he were just contented with green card, no space exploration, above us only sky, not to incur the wrath of the unknown forces...

True, everybody has their potential and threshold. No pain and no gain they say. You certainly do not want to push yourself to the limits and beyond and to realise too late for goodbyes. It is an art to know your limits. Use the sciences and the signs to reap the maximal benefit out of activities.

I remember hearing a story in my childhood. A sage meditated for months to get his wish granted. He did not want to drop dead but to be given ample warnings. The Gods agreed.

The sage lived close to a century and died in his sleep. In heaven, he questioned the Gods for not keeping to their words. The Gods, in reply, denoted that They kept their side of the bargain! The greying, receding hairline, the kyphosis, the joint pains, the reduced effort tolerance, the failing eye-sight, the slow thinking processes and so on.... The sage, the wise one he had been, had just failed to notice!FG9.3.14

Keeping up with the Joneses?

I remember an uncle, a close family relative and a retired civil servant, who spent a lot of his retirement time watching old Tamil movies. I found that quite amusing as none of his kids have an iota of the outward appearance of embracing Indian culture. They did not speak any of Indian dialects, watched only English language TV/movies and even sneered at the comical sing-song way of how movie stars delivered their dialogues. The uncle's reason for indulging in his pastime is for the meaning life lessons and heart rendering song lyrics that it had to offer.

I found this ironic as my parents were looking up at the way they brought up their children and we were asked to emulate them as much as possible. They were envious at their children's command of the English language and their skill in playing instruments. Not wanting for us kids to lose our mother tongue, ironically my mother would insist that we spoke Tamil at home. Outside the house, however, we were barred from speaking in our mother tongue as Tamil was not considered as a language that would 'draw intellectual discourse'! In the neighbourhood that we were living, only people from the underprivileged background would converse in Tamil. Hence, the ability to converse in English would make one step above the rest, so she professed! We were from the city and it was the 70s. People were all trying to improve themselves economically. Tamil, as we saw it, was not going to lead us anywhere.

All the way to adulthood, I encountered many who hailed praises of the Tamil language, of how it is one of the oldest surviving language and how has a separate word for every situation. Even in the modern scientific scenario, there is a readily available word for use. If in the English, the word 'love' is used to denote various types of affection between man, God, woman, animal, food and so on, in Tamil every particular act of love has a specific word.

Having said all that, if one were to listen to any Tamil language interview on cable TV from Tamil Nadu, 50% of the sentences are laced with English. As if, spiking English word makes the conversation more intellectual. Of late, even advertisements are using many foreign words instead of readily available Tamil alternatives!

Recently I saw a caption which advertised the title of an afternoon matinee slot on Raj TV, a cable TV. It read in verbatim, not translation

— சூப்பர் (super) ஹிட் (hit) மேட்னி (matinee) ஷோ (show). I am sure there must be a suitable translation for that in Tamil (தமிழ்)!FG10.3.14

Defensive mode

We are all living in a world where everybody is just waiting for another to make a mistake whilst at the same time everybody is just so careful that their posterior is not exposed and hence vulnerable to abuses.

Whenever a misadventure is encountered, the first response is mum! Nobody talks to anybody as anything you say will be used against you in any situation just to fry your goose. Silence is golden whilst the conniving officers of the law scheme out devious plans to dissociate yourself any plausible repercussions. Truth, justice, liberty you say? What is that? When you are persecuted and crucified for an event that even be beyond your control and your rice bowl is jeopardised, to hell with doing the right thing. It is the right thing all right, for yourself and your dependants. By admitting mistakes, everything would be pinned on you conveniently. In this world of fault seeking and destiny defying population, no one will empathise with you or have sympathy for your predicament. The time for Truth (a.k.a. God) to set things straight is long gone. We killed God long ago with our advancement in technology. There was a time when we were quite green about things around us. We had once marvelled at the splendour of many breathtaking events in our lives — how the sun was eaten by darkness; how the wrath the Mother Nature belched out boiling molten rocks whenever we thought we had wronged and how God punished the fornicators by inflicting incurable diseases!

When Man found a plausible manner to explain all these God sent events, he stopped blaming God for everything. He instead held each other responsible for misadventure, negligence or gaffe, depending on which side of the fence you are! And the sharks have no intentions to bring peace on Earth as it would affect their rice bowl and drinking chalice too — a tool of their trade.FG11.3.14

What drives you?

Of late, I have come across people who have indulged in activities which would be frowned upon. Nobody in the sane mind would ever, even in their wildest dream, consider some of the things that these people would do. The more you interact with these people, the more you will realise that they have a tale to tell, and a sad one too!

One guy was happily married to university sweetheart till she was diagnosed with the big C. Her health deteriorated as quickly as the news sunk in into the family. Even before the family could come in terms with her impending demise, she left Mother Earth. The guy, devastated with the whole turn of events, was a flicker away from being engulfed by the black dog. He did what most sane people do in situations like this. He ran. Like Forrest Gump, he ran and he ran like he had never run before. At the age of 50, he completed his first marathon and there was no stopping him. The euphoria of the post run high appears to be the only thing that conserved his sanity. The addictive endorphins just kept him pushing his distance. Recently, I heard that he completed the gruelling 100 km Hong Kong Ultra Marathon in 29h30m! He kept his feet on the ground and did not leave his future to the stars!

Yet another person went through another earth shattering moment in her life. A full grown adult son took his own life! If the trauma of losing a loved one was not enough, the worse was narrating the whole event again and again to well-meaning friends and relatives. The worse was the self-appointed creative rumour mongers who spun tales, spiced up stories on the turn of events. Not only these people were doing a disservice, they do not realise that news gets around and reaches the unintended recipients, like herself! The pain was simply too much! Like something God-sent, she was introduced to a Guru.

All the various brain waves that she was exposed to through various sessions of meditation and self-realisation helped to rewire her dendrites. She is now standing tall and calm in the sea of uncertainty. The Guru was her anchor when her going was rough.

Naysayers will always ridicule and highlight negativities of people's various indulgences. They are quick with their so-called 'credible information from the horse's mouth' but they should walk a mile in the sufferer's shoe to feel the pain.FG15.3.14

Pull up your socks!

I remember a mate in school who thought that his teacher was commenting on the loss of elasticity of his school socks whenever the examination results were out and he was reprimanded on the outcome! Of course, over time he came to realise the real meaning of his teacher's message and he is now all grown and is somebody in society!

For so long, the civil servants of the country have been working with a chip on the shoulder, thanks to the legacy left by the colonial master as CSR to the natives, knowing very well that their services would not be terminated. At its worst, they would be transferred to another department. It did not matter anyway. They were not there to learn or do their delegated jobs. It is their part time job, really. Their real job starts after office hours. With so much life of comfort, with the powers that be bending over backwards to cast a safety net to cushion any form of hardship, they had it good.

So, when a crisis of magnanimous international magnitude strikes, they were caught embarrassingly inefficient with their pants down. Many standard common sense protocols were let to slither through. The 40 years of hibernation in a stuporous zombie like life form has been exposed bare for all to see. If the civil service is bad enough, the armed forces were malaise to react to an unidentified flying object in its air space. It is reminiscent of the book which had no publishing licence for years but was only banned after its contents offended certain quarters of the society!

Wake up roll call. As a true Malaysian, do you know how embarrassing it is to display what is the best of brains in the country groping helplessly stringing sentence which confuses its listeners on whether he is speaking in the present tense or past?

But, you justify... That it is a unified organised plan to belittle and ridicule you.FG16.3.14

What has divinity got to do with it?

We have always blamed divinity for all of the follies of man — the land-slides, the accidents, etcetera. On the other hand there are these fights, the holier-than-thou attitudes, the delusion complex that it gives, the ability to cow fully grown Man to zombies to perform atrocities with legitimate justification and promise of better 'living' condition in the after-life. They would later walk on with impunity as they know what they did is good in the eyes of the Divine.

Interestingly, I know many who use it for their own benefit. After indulging and overindulging in items of palatal pleasures from mid-October (Diwali) all through Christmas and New Year, they thought their liver and gastrointestinal systems needed cold turkey treatment. The liver, particularly, had to commence their housekeeping and refurbishment activities. The intoxicants which were consumed in the name of feting clients to tease out the contents of their wallets and securing project had to be purged out. What better excuse than to invoke the name of divinity for personal gains? They decide to observe an extended Lent via solemn abstinence from meat and alcohol all the way from New Year through to Easter, a good 3 months of relief to the liver!

By then, people might lose interest in his company or would beg for his company to be a party animal all over again. Hey, nobody is going to force you when you bring in the name of God in it! A perfectly legitimate excuse!FG17.3.14

The neutralisation

In the course of my daily duties, in providing advice to partners who came in proud to display the result of the union of their love or their lusty clandestine activities, I cannot help but notice that quite a number of them have contrasting personalities. True, opposites attract, men are from Mars and women are from Venus but quite often each from different poles, North and South, Night and Day, Beauty and Beast.

Sometimes I wonder how they reach common grounds.

Occasionally, it is a scenario of a beast with a beauty or the hog with a hunk. One may be articulate, the other clueless on social etiquette. One smelling of an English Rose Garden with Parisian perfume while the other with halitosis worse than an overnight fermented ashtray. One warm and charming whilst the other cold and vicious. One educated and cultured, the other lacking in simple basic social skills. One may be looking for a green card, what about the other? One mesmerised by outward beauty, the other internal which may be eternal?

Rod Stewart sang 'Some guys have all the luck' but I would say, "Do not despair!" All this 'luck' would all fizzle out over time.

What may have started as a union of convenience may soon turn stale when the reality of life pounds its thrashing bits by bits? And as the appeasing view may also be hit by forces of nature, ultraviolet ray and the loss of elastic fibres.

Some accept it as the evolution of the times whilst others may go many extra miles to turn back the clock or at least slow the ticking hands of the face of the clock of time...FG20.3.14

Preys pray?

I have a friend who was devastated when his only son was afflicted with a scary form of cancer. He was aggressive in offering whatever humanly possible to nip the disease to the root of things. He has thus far successfully dodged his son's disease. At time of the initial denial phase, my friend made a vow at the spur of the moment that he who stop doing his divine duties indefinitely if his son did not escape the grab of the dreaded crab. So far, 2 years on, the Gods have not lost a devotee!

Then back to the present time, a plane goes missing. What are we told to do? To pray and invoke intervention of the unknown as the experts do not know what else to do!

How is prayers going to change the fate of things that had been predetermined through the synchronised chaos of the butterfly effects? Whatever has happened to the ill-fated vessel had already happened. Our interventions or coaxing of the Forces is not going to undo what had already happened.

What prayers could invoke is the comfort that we are actually trying to do something when all other earthly avenues are exhausted. It shifts the blame from a human side towards the unknown. In the end, everyone would just accept whatever the outcome is and take things as it is and reassure themselves that everything happens for the best.

What matters to us most in 10 hours may not mean too much at 10-days interval and possibly laughable 10 years later.

When caught in a corner and the situation is hopeless, a miracle may not happen but people will accept and move on.

If an outcome of the situation we are praying for is not a desirous one, does that mean that we have not prayed hard enough or it is that we had invoked the wrath of the Gods or do we it just accept that everything happens for the best? Is our prayer going to alter the path of the universe or adjust the orbits of the stars? Probably not. Then it would create another mammoth catastrophe which is bigger than life itself. There would not be anyone there to pray anymore or to pray for, would they? FG23.3.14

You can't dance or is it a difficult dance?

A surgeon does a surgery and runs into problems. The surgery can be considered routine but in life nothing is routine. A mundane day may turn into an eventful day and a highly anticipated event may be a non-event. Such is life.

The surgery is over but one by one what can and may happen after surgery or anaesthesia happens. What is the justification (excuse)? Do you say, it was a difficult surgery? A seemingly routine procedure that was anything but? Murphy's law was the order of the day? Do you blame the anaesthesia, anaesthetist, the obese patient, the operating milieu, the technical difficulties, the subordinates or God?

Whenever anything goes wrong, the accusing fingers will point directly only at one person. That person would be the surgeon. The world does not expect an apology or self-mutilating honour preserving Harakiri type of reaction. They just want to know what actually happened and the circumstances the misadventure happened. The one thing that they want to hear is the truth, the whole truth and nothing but the truth! Your whole credibility would crumble and shatter to smithereens if and when you are found to be hiding or even deviating from the truth. If you are not forthcoming with information at times of misery, how are you going to truthful at times of happy ending?

And I am not talking about medical misadventures here....FG25.3.14

For the love of God

First they gave the physical appearance of Man to Him. They gave Him our hues and variations. To give Him power and awe us, they increased certain capabilities, appendages, arsenal, power over beasts...

Then they dressed Him like us. They gave Him human traits, likes, dislikes, moods, rage, wisdom... All the traits that we feel to have and yearn for more. And they feed Him, bath Him and sing praises of Him. In other words, they personified Him! That cannot be right.

Some force which is way beyond our capability, wisdom and power donning our same traits and attire? And the 'boys club' that propagate and encourage these thoughts and beliefs? Or do they have vested interest?

You build a wall of superiority complex around you. You tell yourself it is for the masses who are not as enlightened as you. It is a point of reference for them to focus and understand something quite abstract like the arts. You do not need intermediaries to connect to Him as He is supposed to know your thoughts and even intentions, so why need middlemen to put forward your requests? Just cut the red tape.

Why hail all our salutations when He is there to protect you? Or punish you too (the loving one)? Why the formalities? Cut the crap.

But you tell yourself that you are one notch above normal being. That you understand the ludicrous of the above and they are all symbolic. It is to help an average man who cannot fathom the concept of Nature, God and Universe. Just like it take certain finesse to appreciate something as abstract as art and beauty.FG26.3.14

You say there is nothing wrong

Your boy, a toddler, plays with dolls, you say there is nothing wrong.

You girl, plays with guns, you say there is nothing wrong.

Your office staff dressed down to office, you say there is nothing wrong.

A doctor comes to duty with jeans and slippers, you say there is nothing wrong.

Your child is defiant of your orders, you say there is nothing wrong.

Your kid does badly in school, you say there is nothing wrong.

With his bad grades, he wants to do a professional course, you say there is nothing wrong.

He doesn't have the grades but the passion, you say there is nothing wrong.
You choose the back door to appease him, you say there is nothing wrong.
Then he fouls up, you say he did nothing wrong.
You cut corners and you say there is nothing wrong.
And yet you say, the country is coming to the dogs.
That is the status of the present world isn't it?
Like you tell the whole world about your feelings, like there is nothing wrong.
And yet to complain there is no privacy,
Yes, yes, there is something wrong...
You're just a special kind of stupid! FG29.3.14

I want it all?

I want it all and I want it right now! That seem to be the mantra these days. The next of kin of the ill-fated plane wants to know all the nitty gritty details down to the technical details of the search thus far. They feel that they are being taken for a ride. Too many rumour mongers and conspiracy theorist are out there every ready to spin yet another spanner questioning the legitimacy of yet another finding of experts. They say information is king but is it really?

Looks more to me that ignorance is bliss. The more you want to know, the more there is to be found out. When the roads are aplenty and the directions are aplenty, one is bound to be lost and maybe caught in a maze or a roller coaster!

The patient wants to know all the minute details of the operation that she is due to undergo, right down to the rarest of complications. Murphy's law, being Murphy's law, may strike at a time when we least expect. I wonder what she really wants to know. I remember an incidence in a University Hospital some 20 years ago when patient empowerment and medical litigation was rearing its ugly head. A lady was scheduled by a Senior Professor for a rather major cancer surgery. A day before the planned surgery, she was reviewed by an anaesthetic doctor to ascertain her anaesthetic risks. The doctor did his due diligence and rattled off all the possible problems that she could encounter in the long and tedious surgery. In not so many words, he told her that she may die on the table after looking at the myriad of medical ailments that she was having. She created such a ruckus in the ward that evening when she adamantly refused surgery. The senior Professor had to rush in to pacify the mortified patient. Anyway, everything went on well and she cruised to recovery.

A recurring theme in my favourite TV show of the 90s, X Files, was to find the 'Truth'. The 'Truth' always remained elusive and Agents Fox Mulder and Dana Scully spent their whole sane life trying in vain to discover it. They were repeatedly told that they cannot handle the 'Truth'.

Many questions only open the door to more questions. So are we just going to take everything that is given to us? If we had not sought out, we would still thinking that we are the universe and everything revolves around us. Well, many amongst us still do!FG2.4.14

The animal in you!

Imagine you are just another one of God's creations. Just another one life form amongst many - nothing special about you - not the chosen one. Not created in His mould!

You have been having the grandiosity that the world revolves around you. That you are superior over other creations and that you are complete with senses to think, sympathise and empathise. Err... You got it wrong again. The zest, the spontaneity, the emotional display and meaningful response are also displayed by them (the others), albeit in their own vocalisation.

On the other end, animal do not exhibit human qualities like killing each other for no particular reason, other than for food, territory or mates.

Just like the concept of an alpha male in the animal kingdom, we also have set preset hierarchy to place some people in a place superior to another.

In the video recently released by a European animal rights' group, the behaviour of animal try to erase the notion that animals have no feelings. Non-lactating cows, worthless from an economic viewpoint, were initially caged for months waiting to be culled. After the animals rights group fought for their rights, they were released into the fields. See the joy of these supposedly lowly unthinking beasts basking in their newly found freedom. They are seen jumping in joy in the air, rubbing their faces and bodies on the ground, caressing each other and running around in sheer glee. See the joy, see the emotion. Who says animals are devoid of emotional expressions?FG9.4.14

Economics: Amma's style

Back home in childhood, money was always hard to come by. Many a time, we, as children, wished that those frequent squabbles between our parents over money (lack of) never arose. As part of economising and savings, Amma used to ink down a monthly budget for the family. Sundry goods were always enlisted and bought in advance from a particular shop, with cash of course. Amma made it a point never to buy on credit as she believed that it would always spiral out of control. She learnt her lesson well, thanks to her father who singlehandedly burnt off his whole family fortune in a single generation!

When I look at the budget that she had penned, it would appear as money was just enough - No place for unexpected misfortune or malady. Of course, she would supplement her income through her sewing skills. Pretty soon she carved a name for herself amongst the occupants of the low-cost flats we were living. When the coffers started welling, never overflowing, she would give out loans to pathetically poor and uninitiated inhabitants of flats who turned out to bad paymasters and I would be summoned to be the debt collector!

Her bank was gold. With the little savings, she would buy gold ornaments. To me, it appeared like a waste of resources, paying for the workmanship and risk of theft and I would express my displeasure and absurdity of displaying openly her wealth for prying eyes and jewel thieves to see. Well, she looked at it differently. It was her status symbol, to be put in high esteem by her neighbours and friends. In case of emergency, she would quietly board the bus to pawn her priced jewel at a particular pawn shop near Prangin Bus Station. She was not dependent on anybody for alms. Periodically she would peruse the pawn chit to make sure that she does not miss the pawn expiry date. When times are good, she would proudly redeem her jewel. Otherwise, when the tide is high, it would be another 6 months' lease. Hold behold, the day she missed the pawn expiry date. Everyone in the house would be in the line of fire for no obvious reason.

This, I think, is the economic dynamics in most South Indian low middle-class wage-earning family in Malaysia a generation ago. The family on the outward may look patriarchal but deep down when it comes on to dollars and cents and the daily running of the household, the duty falls on the wife. Answerable to the head family, in spite of the meagre income, she somehow stingers here and there to ensure non-collapse of the family economics. She could use her ingenuity and living skills towards this end. She would sing the song of melancholy and hopelessness even in the best of times. Come dire straits, she would somehow needle out money here and there out of thin air!

So, it all boils down to management. And that applies to all fields that we indulge or given the responsibility to take care.

In a lush equatorial country like ours with rain in abundance throughout the year with rainfall of close to 100 inches a year, we still have to keep up with embarrassing headlines of water shortages and water rationing hogging our newspaper. That why it is a water management board is there in the first place — to manage water and ensure supply during a dry spell, not just cut water supply of non-payers or just put up water disruption notices. You cannot blame in on the rain, the lack of it, contamination or simply God. Period.FG11.4.14

What are you good for?

The Jains are kind of obsessed with not hurting animals that they just shoo a mosquito rather than squash it. Of late, quite a number of people are caring for the welfare of animals, physical as well psychological wise. Unheard careers like dog whispers, veterinary acupuncturist have secured their stronghold in some societies.

Now, you may say all that is fine but how is a mosquito (also an animal) contributing to society and should be given due respect? All that they do is to spread disease. In the last census, half of world population from Stone Age have died from mosquito-borne diseases especially malaria.

True, only female mosquitoes bite humans as they need nutritious proteins for their potential offsprings. And that mosquitoes are also found in the Arctic Circle but they only help to germinate wild orchids.

Maybe the mosquitoes are doing us a favour by competitively protecting us from more severe diseases. Or that they are protecting the green lung tropical forests from intruders to supply oxygen to the atmosphere.

Now that we still continue our deforestation, they must have come back with a vengeance. They too have migrated to our backyard to become city dwellers and give us dengue.

The solution? Mosquitoes are not the culprits here. They just happened to be at the wrong time at the wrong place with wrong genetical make-up to make themselves vectors of diseases. Just that their bodies form a great reservoir for certain protozoa and arboviruses. The real culprits here are the organisms (protozoans or arboviruses), not the vectors, the messengers. Don't kill the messenger! The diseases spread if a mosquito bites an infected person only.

We should strive to get to the bottom of the problem, eliminate the real causative agents.

Addendum: Does it answer my children's justification of having chicken in all their meals? Their excuse is that there could not be another reason for God to have created chickens other than to garnish the dinner plates! They could not find another reason for their existence in the ecosystem!!FG26.4.14

Remember the time?

Remember the time in history when the first merchant ship landed in Surat and the year 1509 when Lopez de Sequeira landed on our shores with gifts and praises. The locals bent over backwards, as the local culture dictates, to please the guests and make them comfortable and feel welcome. The guests fondly referred to as 'Bengali Putih', did not fulfil their part of the bargain of being a gracious visitor but instead became their masters. Life, as the locals knew it, was never the same.

Fast forward 5 centuries later, the whole country is excited that the most powerful man on the planet with the official authority to annihilate the whole world with a press of a button decided to grace his presence in this land. Media has gone bonkers hailing the visit as the next best thing since 1966 when his predecessor came here to signal to the Eastern Block that we were proxies of the Uncle Sam. So, keep out!

So, why the honour? Is it because Big Brother wants to ensure his little one is doing all right? Is it like how we have to visit our loved one every so often to show that we do care about them?

Is his visit going to straighten our dismal human rights' record, our achievement in topping human trafficking list, poor media freedom and the mushrooming of state sanctioned ultraist groups? Dream on.

In the immortalised words of his predecessor known for his clandestine activities in the cloak-room than the oval office per se, "It's all about the economy, stupid"!

The poster boy has arrived to exude his charm or twist arm the leaders to sign at the dotted lines of the TPPA (Trans Pacific Partnership Agreement). We have reached a crossroads where the leaders would have to decide whether to enrich corporate America, to safeguard its citizens or benefit (enrich) themselves via spillover effect of the deal.FG28.4.14

I'm loving it?

When you are young, you are told to choose the field of study that you like because that is going to be your bread and butter for the rest of your life. You are told to dwell into something that have a passion or aptitude for.

Then you have people who are cocksure on what their calling is in life. They would go at all lengths to achieve their desire. They tell themselves that they were sent to Earth for that mission. Even if they were not qualified to pursue their dream, they would try to get in through the back door at all cost. They would oft quote Walt Disney on the powers of dreaming and the power of positive thinking. "I think therefore I am"!

So, does that mean that if you choose some career path that you so desire, you are set to be loving it all through your life come what may. The ups and downs of the profession are no hindrances and all can be taken in all its stride?

I thought people, by nature, are easily bored. Today fashion is tomorrow's junk, what is lovable today is loathed next week, today's match made in heaven is next decade's ugly divorce, today's ally is next confrontation's enemy...

Even businesses reinvent themselves to stay relevant and lure people's interest. Artistes frequently re-brand themselves to be liked. Chameleons to this end include David Bowie and Madonna.

Not every individual has the mental strength to stay true to their cause like Florence Nightingale or Mother Theresa. Even Mother Theresa might have asked herself whether what she was doing was really worth it! Imagine, after weeks of counselling, giving positive outlook on life and averting her from attempt of suicide after being abused by her husband, Mother Theresa must have felt like pulling her own hair when the victim decided to return to her abusive husband, yet again. Nightingale, with the number of corpses piling up with a skeletal staff and limited medical supply, did passion solely keep her going?

As for mere mortals, the candle would eventually burn out, long before it burn itself away....

Most people do the job they do because they have to do something. At least they can do what is expected of them, a full grown man, to bring home the bacon. Maybe, besides the vocation that they are involved in, they are not capable, brave, intelligent or street smart enough to do anything else to bring home the killing!

Maybe the first years of doing something you love will make you go on by your sheer desire and satisfaction. With time, with challenges becoming too few by far, dead ends and frustrations in many forms setting in, you have to find ways to motivate yourself to keep that fire burning inside.FG4.5.14

No child's play!

There was a time when little children were persona non grata. They were just running around with not much to do but to grow and take over the adult roles. Their duties were none, no structured education was planned. They were eternally grateful to the elders who provided for them, taught them skills and ethics. Once they became teenagers, they entered the workforce and continued the cycle of life.

With the worse of economic times, with war and loss of parents, they were left to fend for themselves. They matured fast to survive.

Then came a time when they had to be prepared for adulthood. They had to be 'initiated' to be ushered. Education became a pre-requisite. Structured lessons were laid out. Some of the lessons they learnt were never used at any time except during examinations. They still needed to be 'prepared' for the world. Things that they learnt were thought to be useful at some time in their life or career. Some even found their passion and continued with the things they were exposed in school.

Then the desire to expose all them to all form of knowledge arose. It was hoped that the hidden talents would hopefully be exposed and the kids would make a killing later in life or even made it their life.

Then the pressure (no more desire) to ensure that all knowledge known to mankind is parted to growing brains. Parents felt guilty or inadequate for not providing all these avenues. Some even felt that they had failed miserably as parents for not opening their minds in activities which invoke stimuli from the right to the left parts of the brain and anywhere in between.

If a generation ago, Benjamin Spock's childcare was the second-best bestseller in the US after the Bible, now child care manuals can fill a whole library, covering obscure topics like gluten free diet, TV free childrearing, etc., etc.

It is understandable if parents feel inadequate and overwhelmed of entering parenthood. It looks like they want to do well with no place for error. The path is set and everyone has to toe the line.

It is no child's play. The exercise of child rearing which started as an economic commodity to replace the ageing workforce has evolved. It has become an economically draining experience but an emotionally satisfying one provided you do not suffer from postpartum depression or become a lunatic trying to prepare them into adulthood.

What started as life as a child with no childhood to talk about has slowly evolved to a period of childhood that never seem to end. That is if you define adulthood as taking responsibilities of your actions.

Just heard someone telling his 18-year-old son the other day, "Congratulations, son. You are now 18 years old. You can go to gaol now if you caught by the police!"FG11.5.14

The trouble is...

"The trouble with the world is that the stupid are cocksure and the intelligent are full of doubt." Bertrand Russell

That is the trouble, is it not? People are so cocksure that certain things must done in a certain way and insists that others follow suit or malady may befall upon them. And the naysayers do not have the courage to support themselves steady on their vertebrae to oppose such views as they themselves are not cocksure about their convictions or is it because they are wiser but do not want to offend? At the end of the day, the louder, the mightier and the vocally gifted would rule the world. The real truth would lay dormant, pacifying the feeble into submission, living on hope the elusive truth would one day came afloat to reveal the final revelation. Till that day, the cheats, bigots, idiots and evil would reign...

An old Tamil proverb consoles the oppressed in this manner, "The king's justice is immediate but the justice of the Divine is worth the wait!" Now, the problem is that the king wants to mete the Divine's justice on Earth!

If there were a God, I think it very unlikely that he would have such an uneasy vanity as to be offended by those who doubt his existence. And He would not like to be apple polished all the time! Imagine your children singing praises of you every time they think of you. Annoying, right? FG17.5.14

Play the Game?

First, it was simple. Everybody did their predetermined duties in society. It started with the noblest of intentions, to relieve the suffering of mankind from the elements of nature. The exact pathogenesis remained elusive, putting a lot of mysticism, astute observation and trial-and-error into it. The bewilderment of the ability of the healing man earned him a place high up on a pedestal. It soon became the only humanly thing to do — not to deny the science and wizardry of the healers to the sick and downtrodden.

As not aliments were amenable to the advancement of medical sciences, many saw it as an outlet to serve mankind. The frustrated, the forlorn, the individuals who have given up conjugal wishes and the jilted saw it as an avenue to be a servant of Almighty to do His work on Earth to serve the outcasts of society.

A doctrine was draughted for practitioners to hold dearly to their heart, an oath to serve humanity and first not to do harm. The pleasure of serving humanity was considered suffice to even mention any other forms of remuneration.

Society evolves, priorities change. A predominantly agricultural based society was slowly suckered in into an industrial based society with limited skills of being able to make what they needed. The Industrial Revolution had slowly transformed the society into a consuming self-centred society who lives only for themselves. Gone with it were the values that glorified the advancement of society and mankind. Everyone was for himself.

The healing profession also evolved. Service beyond self, physicians heal thyself are phrases from a distant past. Now, just like their counterparts in the loan shark, tow truck and legal businesses, the healers have turned 'ambulance chasers'-like finding problems when there are no problems to start with. Working with probabilities and statistics, they excel at creating the paranoia of worrying of the unknown and uncertain.

And the art of healing which was perfected by the sciences has been hijacked by the finances and numbers. The lure of striking it rich compounded by the morbid fear of death has lured the vultures of businessmen, hyenas of insurance companies and wolves of associated services to join the foray. FG20.5.14

It is the economy, stupid!

So, there I was having a tête-à-tête with a friend who use to hail from the land of Karma sutra where the people could take you for a spin in more ways than you can shake your head. As I thought that the results of the recently concluded Indian elections would excite her, I started asking about the results at her home state. In Tamil Nadu, in spite of the bad publicity that Amma had many elections ago with the extravagant wedding of her adopted son, she literally swept the state this time around. Her nemesis failed to win a single seat. Over at the national level, the feared Hindu nationalist party won by a landslide. To be fair, Modi was cleared of wrongdoings by the court and the buoyant economic progress in his home state is the catalytic factor for his win. Many tragedies involving high-level corruption, high profile national shames and stagnant economy of late had people going for a change.

So, my friend, when asked on Amma's victory, she nonchalantly asserted that the feel good factor won her over. Many of the poor folks were given monetary support. Rice was distributed freely to the needy. Senior citizens were given alms. Saving interests were higher for the elderly. With no major natural catastrophe to worry, she rode high to victory. At the end of the day, it is the economy, stupid!

Man, over the ages, have experimented with a system that is apparently fair to everyone. They tried to unshackle themselves from the dependence of wealth and power. They tried to create a utopia where all man is equal, where human qualities are appreciated and the Law of Nature is respected.

Unfortunately, time and time again, man have failed, miserably, sometimes. Feudalism, communism, fascism, religious fundamentalism all met with the same disappointing fate.

Maybe, it is ingrained upon us to be rebellious. That is how we, as a human race have come thus far, from the plains of Sub-Saharan Africa. Deep inside us is the desire for instant gratification.FG23.5.14

Waste of money?

Economics was easy when I understood that you have to save and you cannot waste. My Form 1 teacher, however, confused things for me. In an essay about the pros and cons of space expedition, he disagreed that it was a waste of money. As a matter of fact, he said, nothing is a waste of money. Money does not go anywhere out of the world to be wasted. It simply changes hands. The money at the side of the transaction could still be used for 'meaningful' reasons.

My nimble mind was never the same again. Money was no longer just income and expenditure. For that matter, everything had the other side which is not necessarily the wrong one.

Money and wealth are not going anywhere, just changing owners. So, the recipient of the monies are still able to put it to 'good' use. Just then, their priorities may be different. They may like to keep it in assets which may be useful for the next generation. But the building and running or maintaining the well being of the assets will generate economic activities. But then the bone of contention is that the minute 1% of the population seem to be possessing the lion share of economic control.

The structure of any societal build-up makes it that 1% of the population is always one step ahead in terms of intelligence and leadership qualities. This selected few are not only smart but devious and sometimes psychopaths.

Whatever it is, economics on a global scale is a different scale from that of an individual or family where what you spent is what you get. And what you spend and don't have will land you in lots of problems, no matter how easy the lure seem to portray it to be.FG26.5.14

Smirk?

To the question 'What is the one thing that you would like your child to have', one of the many responses was confidence. Confidence would take them a long way as they know that what they are doing is right. They would march through life knowing jolly well that that is the way, the truth and how it should be. Really?

May not. A certain amount of conviction is needed for one to do anything. The confidence that he has the knowledge to drive from point A to point B, the confidence that what he is doing today will reap benefit one day, the certainty that he would get up tomorrow as he lay his weary head to sleep...

On the other hand, a certain amount of uncertainty is needed to ensure that the loose ends are checked. It is normal that he is unsure whether he has offed all electrical appliances and rechecks them as he embarks on his long journey, he double checks his facts before he puts his life and name on a document and so forth.

We sure do not want a conceited fool who is cocksure about everything and overconfident that his 'yet another new venture' would see any daylight. Too often than not, we have seen again and again of fools who are only fools in the eyes of everyone else except the person concerned.

That comes to the question of what type of environment do we provide to the kids as they grow up meeting the challenges of future? Do we encourage them with showers of praises so that they would be bold enough to stand out on their own feet or do we plant the seed of doubt so that they would occasionally turn around and reflect themselves before they make an ass of themselves?

Sometimes it reaches the level of 'ad nauseam' to see parents praising to high heavens their children's seemingly feeble feats!

But then again, the seemingly great men in the history of mankind had weathered failures after failures to pursue their dream knowing and confident deep inside them of their cocksure confidence in themselves that they are right!FG2.6.14

What is right anymore?

As we wobble along in our vessels in the sea of uncertainty, we make our rules as we sail along perhaps with strong conviction that we indeed have the right formula to reach our destination in one piece. Not only reach our destination in person but to finish strong and be respectable in our finish. Some have dogmatic views on how the journey should be done whilst others are contend being followers, following the path oft taken by others, the path of least resistance assured of success barring untoward misadventure.

I was thinking of our friendly debate of recent. What initially started on the merits and demerits of students squealing on the misdeeds of their teachers developed into something more profound.

What constitutes whistleblowing and what is being an obedient subservient servant of the system? Are the rules different for the adult and the minors? We are told to have self-respect, fight the good fight against tyranny and injustices and follow the path of righteousness. Is the playing field different for the young minds?

A child complained to the Principal about the teacher who had had used what was in the student's vocabulary a foul-sounding word and one thing leads to another and the teacher is reprimanded.

Is that a good move on the student's part that hails salutation and felicitation or is that setting a precedence for many more unhappy encounters with the authorities to come in the future?

No doubt, some rules border on ludicrousness and have not evolved in tandem with the change of the times. If one were not to obey rules set by the powers that be, there is bound to be anarchy. Growing and maturing generally involves following regulations to ensure everyone gets a place in the sun.

How is the process of learning going to take place if the awe and respect are not accorded to the guru? The master forms like a mould upon which students try to emulate and try to garner knowledge. No one is perfect, but if children are allowed to constantly ponder upon shortcomings of the master, I do not think that the transfer of knowledge can take place, suspicion on the side of the recipient and apathy on the side provider. Just a thought, not a formula.FG10.6.14

Warped morality, you say?

You contract something that smells like a sexually acquired communicable disease. You get it treated with your trustworthy friendly doctor and you get back into the hype of things. As a responsible modern metrosexual individual, what is expected of you?

Your moral conscious would bug you to rummage through your old faithful little black book to sieve through the contact your exes to inform them of your predicament and advise them to sort out the issue. Perhaps they had caught a bug or two during the good old days, the way you were! Sometimes, your duty does not end there but you may be needed to arrange an appointment with your doctor and even accompany her to such a visit.

Imagine the awkward scenario where you accompany your ex into the doctor's consultation room and you feel like a fly on the wall whilst the doctor rattles off enquiring about your ex's recent extra-curricular activities and he is not talking about her training for next half marathon! Sometimes, you have the urge to immerse yourself into the mirage world of your smartphone but social etiquette intervenes.

Hey, the modern man would say that is how a modern man should behave. He has to take responsibility of his actions and is his moral duty to inform the receiving party of possible exposure to something sinister. A moral duty, you say, but is it morally right to leave a part of you all over the place akin to a member of the canine species marking his territory? Morality, my foot!FG14.6.14

All born evil?

I heard of a theory put forward by a psychologist recently that we are all born evil! Deep inside we are born, not as clean slate but as a chalice of evil overflowing through our every orifice. Of course these helplessly cute tots are not able to perform any of their evil deeds because of the sheer size and incoordination. The psychologist, however, proposes that upbringing is the one that modifies these literally 'inner demons' to be doing things acceptable in the society. The caregivers guide us through our daily guidances to mould us to be useful members of the society, to conform to what is accepted as the norm. The social etiquette and logical reciprocal course of reaction to any action are engrained into us through repetitive conditioning. This Pavlovian reaction helps to maintain sanity and ensures that even the weak and downtrodden get their place in the sun.

Come a moment of desperation, a mob, famine or pain, these inner demons will come to fore. They will be exposed in full glory to ensure that their hosts come out tops. It is called the survival of the fittest. So niceties are only preserved for peace time. Your forever smiling pleasant neighbour may just turn against you when the situation is ripe and the instigating environment warrants it to. Beware!

*P/S. I stopped fighting my inner demons. We are on the same side now.*FG19.6.14

A nation in tatters?

Deep inside us, all of us know that this piece of cloth is the one that binds us together to maintain peace and harmony so that all of us can do our own things without any fear. We also know that this cloth, in spite of being just a piece of cloth, is no ordinary piece of cloth. It is a testimony of our sovereign nation. It is the same piece of cloth when hoisted upon being raised after winning a medal evokes a tear or two in the eye of every true blue Malaysian.

Scenes like these, the national flag in various states of neglect and disrespect are common sights these days. What was hoisted in *Merdeka* month last year is left to weather the elements of nature all through the monsoon months and this is what you get... A faded *Jalur Gemilang* flying majestically as its threads tatter away in shreds.

So, what are you going to do about as a loyal citizen? Are you going to make a citizen's arrest or just look the other way?

Looking at the number of mad people working around amongst us, do you think it is a good idea to handle the perpetrator head on? Make a police report which would be lost among the pile of junk which would eventually make it to the recycling man's compound? Or blog about it? FG22.6.14

Do we know, really?

In a silly internet poll recently, it showed that my personality is that of an influential person! Influential?

Even with the sinuses clogged with phlegm of influenza and my thinking faculty clouded, I still describe myself of anything but influential. Firstly, I am quite lethargic of influencing anybody of anything which makes me neither a salesman, a visionary dictator nor an industrialist who would transform the world we live in. I am also not influential enough to move mountains or 'arrange things' with my contacts like a chess master moving his pawns. On the contrary, I visualise myself as one easily influenced (fall prey to/suckered) to others' sob stories.

I like to think that I can be such a good role model that I can influence others to the path of glory! Maybe that is wishful thinking. And you think you know everything and about anything.

Just the local leaders and foreign think tanks who basically hoodwinked the world into thinking they were in grasp to all the information laid before them and finding MH370 was just a matter of time.

And the paternalistic political leaders who think they know what is best for their subjects. What about the religious leaders who think they know all the purpose of our existence on Earth. As if they had an audience with God, they choreographed our every gesture insisting that God like to be worshipped like this and like that.

Why not just put all the cards on the table for mankind to judge? But then the element of mystery and mysticism would be lost. Their importance would amount to nothing if the element of the unknown is lost.FG23.6.14

Then what?

My brother from a different father and mother sent me a mail recently about a certain Mathematics tutor from Patna, Bihar, who would tutor students pro bono for them to pass the coveted Indian Institute of Technology entrance examinations. He handpicks a group of 30, motivates them, arranges hostel facilities, cooks healthy meals and literally drills them day and night to achieve 100% pass rate.

The students swarm in from remote and impoverished regions of the land to slog it out for about 7 months with the sole intention of passing the test. A pass, to them, is the panacea of their woes. A rewarding career and perhaps a post in a multinational company or even an overseas posting is a sure way to uplift their living conditions and of their immediate loved ones.

The spill-over effect can be seen even to the relatives whose background and caste is irrelevant anymore. I can relate to the hopeful eyes of the illiterate parents who put all their hope, putting aside their difficulties and poverty, to educate their offspring. In the year that the documentary was shot, 29 of the 30 students passed.

So what happens afterwards? The teenagers go on to IIT, get a comfortable job, parents continue their tortuous job albeit at a less strenuous pace. Then what? They get married, perhaps stay in a big mansion or migrate to a developed country and enjoy the fruit of their labour. They themselves would have offsprings. After growing up guarded against poverty and shielded from the harsh reality of needing to acquire street-smartness and survival skills, they would think that it is their birthright to demand luxuries that their parents offered. Whatever they missed, they did not want their children not to have.

On the part of the children, hard work and motivation would be alien vocabularies. They would talk about enjoying life, having a complete life, not to miss out on finer things of life and the now well renowned phrase of that it is their life and they can live any which way that they please!

In the immortal words of Confucius, wealth in a family would only last 3 generations. And the cycle of life would go back to square one!FG25.6.14

No, thank you!

Maybe I am becoming a grouchy old man looking at negativity rather than the brighter side of things. Perhaps I have a sour puss face with a perpetual frown that turns people off. Could it be that I am a nag? Or maybe my appearance and demeanour do not warrant salutations.

You do your transactions, you pay your bills and what do you get? Silence. You end up thanking them for fleecing you off your hard earned money. You pay them and thank them. How did it come to this? Whatever happened to mutual respect and social etiquette?

You may wonder why do I keep on going to this same outlet in spite of their lethargic treatment of customers. I should just take their business elsewhere. It is not that their spread and splendour of their delicacies outweigh any shortcomings on their part. Neither am I performing a social experiment to determine the number of visits they need to reciprocate wishes. It is by mere convenience that I often land up grabbing a bite or two when I am on the go.

This is what happens when our people refuse to break their back but instead sublet their business to foreigners who bring their style of communications, hygiene and standards to our land. Some countries bring in helping hands to help around but set the standards that they want from the outset.

Here, nothing like that happens. Everything happens on autopilot. Instead of bring the country one notch higher than the backwaters that our ancestors who found this place, we seem to be content seeing our country spiral back to the standards left by people from the lands of volcano spirit, shamans and have more passports with their photos than they can count. Each passport has a different name so much so that they cannot remember their parents' given name anymore.

We are still waiting for that someone to whip everything back to its place. Superman, where are you when we need for you. Instead, what we have are many *Suparmans* only!FG8.7.14

Just another day in real life!

Now that the nights are spent in slumber land, the eyes are becoming less congested and the mush in the brain is slowly clearing up, I can write. It is amazing how a game, after all a game, can exert so much effect on events around the world. Perhaps, it was meant to be thus. Average Joe being side-tracked by events that are clearly not going to determine the fate of mankind, as, they, the capitalists create a sense of urgency and fascination amongst the lay people and laugh all the way to the bank. If not, how would you expect a supposedly non-profit organisation like FIFA to have 5 billion USD in their account, leaving a trail of heartaches as they count their loot. And the money is for the development of world football, really?

Soccer is just another tool for the powers that be to achieve their agenda. Back in the 1930s as Brazil was developing as a nation as the white masters, black slaves and the mulattos joining hands to develop the nation, the powers that be decided that football would be the unifying cement something like how ANC used rugby to unify a young post-apartheid South Africa. Brazil became all excited with the young mulattos and their fancy footwork. They were initially a second tier team following the shadows of great teams like Uruguay and Italy. With a lot of hope, they hosted the 1950 World Cup. With their high-scoring games in the initial games, they were set to win the Cup easily then. In fact, the papers on 15th July 1950 printed pictures of the Brazilian team with the caption 'Tomorrow's World Champion'!

What followed shook the nation for years to come.

Brazil lost the game to Uruguay in the final game 2-1 to a devastating crowd who were prostrating in grief. The Maracanã went completely silent when Uruguay hoisted the cup! The ghost of 1950 Uruguay had started. The players were ostracised for years to come. Some went into depression. The mention of the ill-fated game angered many citizens. The ghost was finally buried in 1958 Sweden final with the new kid of the block, Pele. It then went on to 5 World Cups and have the bragging rights of being the only country to win outside their continent.

The prelude of this World Cup (2014) included massive demonstrations by the poor homeless as the disparity between the haves and have-nots escalated over the years. Grandiose commercially non-sustainable projects like the Manaus Stadium angered them further. The Government was thinking of hoodwinking the public by giving the 'feel good' euphoria showcasing their samba hospitality to the world. They thought this would nicely fit in as the country was due to move into a fresh set of elections.

Looks like history had repeated itself. If the 1950 loss to Uruguay 1-2 was a national tragedy, how would the ghost of 2014 be exorcised? The team, which has a long following the world over, hailing from a land where football is a religion, were humiliated by Germany 1-7 in a highly emotional semi-finals. It took 8 years in 1950 before they turned themselves around. Now, how?

As the World Cup comes to an end, the nation has to pick up the pieces, feel the emptiness left after a month's high of activities and pacify the forlorn nation who has to sort out the bread and butter issues too. The politicians are also seeing stars. Are the people going to return them to their seats or is it time for them to pick up their money and run?

The lesson the lay person would learn would be, 'Cows may come and cows may go but the bull here stays forever'! The guests would have returned. It is time to clean up, get back to life and get back to reality.FG13.7.14

Go, find excuse!

every time you
tell your daughter
you yell at her
out of love
you teach her to confuse
anger with kindness
which seem like a good idea
till she grows up to
trust men who hurt her
cause they look so much
like you
to fathers with daughters — rupa kaur

I came across this card which was sent from a daughter to her father on conjunction with Fathers' Day. Not a flattering message, I should say. Looks like the daughter seem to be blaming her failures in life and the recurrent wrong choices in choosing partners squarely on her father, the contributor of half of her chromosomes. Just because her father did not mollycoddle her but instead showed her the reality of life, she looks at it as an abhorrent. She must be thinking that real dads are like the TV sit-com dads who would take all the tantrums of the young ones and also apologise for their own shortcomings. Dream on. Adults in real life have too much ego and have an important role to play nurturing them through the hard knocks of life unlike their Tinseltown dads who play their 30 minute role, smiling all the way to the bank.

You say you came to learn that someone who hurts is same who loves through your father's actions. You sound like a smart girl — able to appreciate the finer subtleties of the language and poetry. You are probably smart because of the way paved by your father who ensured that his daughters were no second class citizens, the right to education just like his son, your brother. Now, you are big and strong and smart, you are smart enough to bounce off all the misgivings of life on this man.

Didn't the man act hard on you to correct you, to put you back on track, because you almost went astray? Is it because of his guidance that you able to maturely assess your failures and analyse of your own shortfalls? May it not be his drilling that made you still standing tall despite the calamities that you had to encounter in your short life?

It is easy to find fault. Anyway, there is never a cookbook recipe for parenting. He may have done what he thought was best for you. Perhaps that made him the man he is, able to provide and care for you and your family. For every 10 bad points you identify about your father, there must be 20 more of the contrary.

Remember, when you point your accusing index finger at others, invariably your last three fingers would point at your good self. The thumb may point to ground (nature) or up (sky, God)!FG17.7.14

But, that is not the real way...

Now how often have we heard people sitting high up and looking down saying, "Yeah but that is not the real way of doing it! They are not doing it right. There are specific ways of doing it. The Truth is all there in the scriptures!"

Yes, and yet no religion is *not guilty* of it.

The animals are supposed to be respected and are said to be also creations of the Almighty but the way they are abused, culled and hunted, it appears like their sole purpose of existence is to be eaten, hunted and be bullied. They say that their religious way of justice is God sent and is cast on stone. If you look around, their justice is made to look so disconnected from the train of thought of contemporary man. If you do not have a living example to follow, how can you proclaim that your system is the best. We need a sign. We need a living proof of the superiority of the merchandise that you are trying to sell us!

Your religious leaders allow atrocities to be carried out on fellow citizens. Yet they advise middle path as the best way to reach Enlightenment. Even your saffron robed holy men partake in these atrocities in the name of justice. Others of the same faith, however, admonish their actions by saying that their brand of seeking the truth is deviant.

You say God works in mysterious ways but yet you take it upon yourself that you must do His work on Earth. And you self-appointed yourself as the chosen one.

You say everyone is sent to Earth for a specific reason but how do you know that what you doing IS the reason you are sent for? Perhaps, you still have not found you are looking for.

You think you know everything and you know you are right but what if, just what if, you were wrong all the time? You cannot undo what you did to them, can you?

Are you trying to show your might as might just might be right and buries the rest?

Since we are all groping around trying to understand the things that surround us, why not give peace a chance? Maybe when the storm had cleared, you can see clearly then... You do not want yesterday once more.FG18.7.14

Puppetmaster or dice thrower?

As we straddle along the boat of life as it manoeuvres itself or we manoeuvre it along the river of life, we sometimes wonder why some things happen at all. Are they random occurrences or are they planned move made by the king chess-master? Are they just chaotic activities which somehow coalesce to give meaning and pattern? Is it all a game by the dice thrower for the fun of it? Does the puppet master enjoy seeing His inventions cringe and wail to their heart's content?

In 1983, when tensions were high across the Iron Curtain after USSR downed KAL007, a Korean civilian plane, Stanislav Petrov of the Soviet Union made the unconventional decision of not alerting his superiors when the warning alerts screamed of a launch of US inter-continental ballistic missiles into the Soviet Union. The SOP then was to launch missiles in retaliation. And time was of the essence as every ticking second meant annihilation. At that crucial time, Lt. Col. Petrov decided to become a human rather that a lean mean killing machine. Something told him that the warning system was flawed and the US were not sending 5 missiles to Russia! His inaction, even though militarily unacceptable, did, however, avert a nuclear war and possibly World War 3!

Fate reared its ugly head in the life of Sanjid Singh Sandhu. Sadly, he perished in the ill-fated flight of MH17. He was not even supposed to be there. He just filled in for a friend. Aviation disaster had earlier escaped his wife when she swapped her roster not to work on the fatal MH370 flight on 8.3.2014 at the last minute.

Many who escaped the mishap miraculously by a twist of fate — missing the flight, changing their schedule at the last minute and so on. They praised the Maker who saved them but what about those who perished? Preferential treatment or there is a higher order which is beyond human comprehension?

Life is full of dichotomies and alternatives, so is its outcome. Life becomes too complicated if we keep on thinking what if, what if. Nobody would be brave enough to face the world and do what they need to do for continuity of life if they are fearful if the outcome is not in their favour. A man got to do what a man got to do.FG21.7.14

A storm in the teacup?

Now that the dust has finally settled on the vilification of Kiki over her outburst and overreaction over the fender bender that is hardly worth discussing, sometimes I wonder how I would have reacted in such a situation — on either side of snafu.

I would not be surprised if I had flipped if I were Kiki with the brand new spanking French beau after years of being contented with the only automobile affordable that is forced down my throat with my meagre pay. After paying all the unnecessary additional payments to secure my lucky number and with the smell of new car still lingering on my tunic and skin, it is pure heartache to see it being defaced, albeit its triviality. Putting all that aside, I would have acted inappropriately if a stressful event had occurred prior to that fateful encounter — an unfair statement from someone close, an abusive client, committed a big mistake at work, getting up on the wrong side of the bed, a bad hair day or whatever that would make anyone flip.

I do not, however, condone any of her actions by any means.

Regarding her seemingly racist's rant, come on admit it! We, Malaysians are racist by birth, by default and by force by the powers that be. How many times have we try hard to compartmentalise a new colleague or acquaintance into the common ethnic group in the country? It has become almost second nature to us to instinctively utter a totally inappropriate statement, racial wise, by stereotyping one by race. In the heat of the moment, Kiki did the same.

Perhaps her mistake was that her anger took a mighty long time to subdue. And to be caught on tape. If there was no evidence of the whole event in cyberspace, it would just be another unglamorous event occurring on a daily basis in the streets of Malaysia, another storm in the teacup.

What happened afterwards was even more laughable! The trial by social media, the vilification, exposure of personal details, the show of lack of privacy and how our life can be bear open for others to see, the crucification, the unwelcome stardom and the mania that followed does not augur well for us in our endeavour to portray to the world as a developed and mature society.

The biggest lesson learnt from kerfuffle is that 'Somebody is always watching you'... I am afraid to wash to wash my hair, when I look up, I see somebody standing there, somebody's watching me now! Who? The IRS!!!...FG22.7.14

The evil that lurks...

Deep inside, we are all the same. Despite our seemingly outward differences and self-inflicted desire to be different, deep entrenched in the crypts of our sulci and gyri and between the creases of our DNA, we are all one. Our desires, our inner, our likes, no matter how much we deny or suppress, it is pretty much the same.

We may impose restrictions on what we should eat and should not. It would only last that long. The inner drive would prevent it or suppress our desires to taste the forbidden fruit but at the same time we change the goal post to suit both the regulations. A vegetarian yearning for fish came with fish textured soya minus the odour, prawn-like crusted soya to be sizzling in a wok and so on. Kebab and teriyaki lovers replaced meat with cheese on skewers. They keep their faith and their taste buds happy.

With the aim of keeping social problems of uncared children, society imposed strict rules and penalties for its subjects pertaining mixing of the carnal kind. Again and again the virtues of monogamy and responsible parenthood had been impressed upon their offspring. Society imposed draconian rules and even inhumane punishments to cow the society to fall in line. In spite of apparently outward manifestation of conformity and piety, the primal need to sow the seed and immerse in the joy of union of the sexes thrives in all. In spite of the strictest law cast in stone, the animalistic desire prevails again and again. Of course, all laws are made to be broken, they are also amended and manipulated to please their fancy.

Traditionally, the female gender has been left with the unenviable task of running the household as the men left the caves for long spells in the effort to hunt to provide for the society. The nomadic tribe had the same arrangement. As the organised religion came to fore, the gender roles reversed. The society took a patriarchal stance. The female partner became subjugates to do and not to do. With evolving times and demand for equality via bra burning, something had to give. However, the hocus pocus pseudo-scientific cockamamie excuse for protecting the weaker sex still manage to con them to submission. The fear of God, as usual, works all the time to win the male's place in society.

We make our dresses to appear modest and civil. We may claim conservativeness in our drapes so as not excite the faint-hearted. But deep inside, there is an eternal desire to be noticed, to stand out, to be praised of our looks, our beauty albeit skin deep. Even if the mandatory sensitive areas that need to be covered are so, the hide and seek game continues. Even the covered areas are highlighted and enhanced with accessories to enchanter the eyes of the beholder.

We can hide, we can deny but deep inside our primitive primal desires lurks like a caged animal waiting to be unleashed. When conditions are ripe when he perceives himself to be off the radar, this demonic desire surfaces. But then... he can say, "I was weak, I was tempted, in my lowest ebb, the Devil with his devilish ways won. I repent. After all I am human, I err!"FG24.7.14

My look at feminism

As Man started walking on the savanna plains of Africa, either after being banished from Garden of Eden or when their primate ancestors had to come down from the trees to look for food, they became gatherers and consumers of what nature had to provide for them.

Soon they explored themselves and each other to discover that the female counterpart was indeed a mysterious creature. The pre-historic men were indeed quite curious about life, energy and all the wonders that Mother Nature had to provide. The female gender had the special chalice, receptacle, that could generate life.

They were definitely awed by its ability. As it was their practice then to show their respect to mysterious energies around them, like the thunder, sky, fire, wind and water, they created goddesses who could control all the elements of nature. They even thought that nature and Earth must be matriarchal in origin.

Things were going fine. They rule their roost while the men went on long expeditions in search of food.

Then the society became farmers and stayed put in villages. About that time, monistic beliefs which was particularly patriarchal in outlook emerged. They imposed various restrictions and subjugated the weaker sex to be subservient to the so-called laws of the Divine.

With the passage of time and availability of knowledge, the enslaved fought back with a vengeance. They came back strong and now have shown superiority in many fields. The oppressors now continue their suppression with their cock and bull stories of divine decree. When the name of Almighty is invoked, the oppressed, fearing the wrath of Herculean proportions is left with Hobson's choice but to submit unconditionally.

After going through turmoils after turmoils, the fighters have now taken an 180-degree turn. The feminists feel that they do not need handouts but are able to fight on the same level field with the aid of handicaps. Enters the anti-feminists movement...no,no, we want to be pampered....FG3.8.14

Shortcomings and trimmings...

Unless you have been living under a shell away from the evils of social media, you should be aware of the brouhaha of late of the cyber display of the advertisement publicising '2014 Penang's International Nude Sports'. Let us leave the merits and appropriateness of flaunting one's modesty for others to judge to theologians and esteemed philosophers to argue it out. I was particularly intrigued by some of the comments posted by supposedly learned members of the public. Some criticised not because of their brazen differing morality standards but rather because they were not impressed with what they saw. They commented that it is an embarrassment when they exhibited their seemingly unimpressive bodies, visually unappealing.

We, as a society, seem to have been brainwashed into believing that the human body is supposed to look like what is seen on the celluloid screens of Hollywood and Bollywood. Anything disproportionate to that standard is unacceptable. Period. Not fit to be recorded.

Welcome to the real world. Yes, the human body is not meant to be in perfect symmetry. Yes, it is meant to sag, have unsightly blemishes, cellulite, wrinkles and scars. Yes, life goes on after a mastectomy, a double mastectomy and disfigurement of birth defect or burns. Yes, they also come in various shades — white, pink, yellow ochre, shades of brown and ebony. There is no need to feel green or feel blue. Only the yellow will chicken out with reality.

For your information, most Hollywood stars have than one double — one for each part of close-up shots of their body part. A Malaysian had the dubious honour of having his calf used as 'leg double' of Brad Pitt's puny ones, unbefitting of the role of Achilles that he played in the 2004 movie, 'Troy'!FG11.8.14

Seize the day, Carpe diem!

You think you have got it made. You think you are perfect. That is what everyone aims for. And we all yearn to be THE one. Many want to leave their legacy behind, something for their descendants to feel proud of. Mythology, told repeatedly over time from ear to ear over the years, got spiced up and snowballed to portray characters which are infallible, invincible, just, powerful and elevated to demigods and God statuses.

As usual, my mind got thinking....

That could explain the many 'great' men (*mahaans*) and avatars of God who had graced and walked the land we stand on. Not to belittle the great deeds that they had done, there must be blemishes in their otherwise pristine time on Earth.

When Robin William passed on recently, the internet and social media were fluff with a flurry of messages praising him to high heavens. Many thanked him for his comedy and making the world a happier place. One even praised him in his role as a motivating teacher in 'Dead Poets Society'. If not for that film, he would not have enjoyed literature that much and pursued that line of career. Some highlighted the pathetic and helpless situation of being trapped in the world of the black dog. In spite of duelling with manic-depressive illness for a good addiction of his adult life, he still managed to live a full life.

The passing of an individual is always remembered by the good deeds done by them. The public generally like to put a lid on their shortcomings, thankfully so — maybe not for all - Hitler, Stalin, Atilla the Hun etcetera.

Wikipedia checkup did show a few unsavoury conduct the actor exhibited. Besides his substance addiction which could be attributed to his illness, he had been the cause of his own marital disharmony. Imagine, how a pregnant wife would feel when her husband is sued by his extra-marital tryst for infecting her with herpes!

In spite of all his shortcomings, he must have been good in other ways. He still has a cordial relationship with his daughter and string of grieving fans. Rest in peace.

Life is a symphony with crescendos and fortissimos. The joy of music that emanates is precisely from these troughs and ploughs of notes.FG15.8.14

Merry making with Mary or marry her?

In the traditional Indian society, wedding is considered as a panacea to all social woes. Son loafing around aimlessly? Son does not take things seriously? Son very irresponsible and childish? Get him married, everything will sort out itself, they would say.

Rodney Dangerfield, on the other hand, had said something to the effect of 'Once I got into this institution called marriage, I stayed institutionalised!'

Call me old fashioned but I have been brought up to think that people declared their private intentions publicly before they get cosy privately. Or at least that was how it was portrayed to be.

Being privy to being a confidant of people's after hours' activities and private lives, I know that that is never the case, maybe of late or perhaps all the time just that people were discrete about it. People do not need that piece of paper to approve their biological urges. After all it is only natural. "The birds and the bees do it, why can't we?", they would say!

Then why have the paper, pomp and announcement at all? Well, the wife can change her name, especially if her maiden name is tainted with a criminal record. The children can have a surname and the wife and kids can have a legitimate claim on the property if there is any.

Who needs the licence anyway?FG16.8.14

Maid to serve?

Whatever happened to Tamil mantra 'your job is your God'? Postmen clung on their postman bags even when their vehicle plunged into a ravine. Secret service agents stood steadfast in the line of fire to protect the symbol of sovereignty of a country even ignoring their own lives. Humanitarians flock to war-torn or epidemic hit zone to care for the needy. Servants rather take abuses than invoke the wrath of their employers.

We are talking about a different time zone. Unless you have travelled back in time in a time machine, you would realise that things have changed drastically.

Perhaps some the examples mentioned above are remnants of the feudalistic era or leftovers from the practice of caste system of division of labour based on their familial tool of trades. It can also be a figment of what Pol Pot and his revolutionaries were trying to propagate. The ideology that man were made to serve nature and we do not need technology as Mother Nature has it all for us.

There used to be a time when certain things were considered to be out of bounds when a person is at work. Some things are obvious. Thou shall indulge in any intoxicating beverages whilst at work, unless of course, you are from the upper strata of the workforce and entertaining clients and make them lose their inhibitions in order to secure businesses in your favour is one of the scopes of your work.

Generally, you do not like to see a person in uniform puffing away at his post. Nor should he be seen fiddling with his smartphone or seen busy entertaining his caller rather than vigilant on the task he is assigned to.

But then, values change. The honour of being in a job and the pride of carrying his duties to the virtues held by generations before us has lost its lustre. In the present world where everything and anything goes and is possible, there is nothing wrong in turning up at a lecture in beach wear. It only shows that he is innovative and is open to ideas. Well, as long as the work gets done.FG25.8.14

All-or-none law works in science, in life?

Everybody has some goodness in him. Sometimes, he thinks he is doing the right thing. Well, from where he is standing, that is how it looks to him. He has to protect his own interest or that involves people around him. He says charity begins at home. When a family is taken care well, society and humanity will take care of itself. His servants may agree to his action and those at the receiving end of his actions may abhor. The victims may cry for help and may curse for him to burn in the eternal flame of hell. They would refer to history and scriptures to justify their actions or inactions.

At the end of the day, at the end of life, the sums of things done in a man's life can never be either black or white. It can only be in shades of grey. It seems totally unfair to gauge the goodness (or evil) of one's action using a 2D yardstick with pre-set rules which never changes seasons over seasons and generations over.

Surely at the Pearly Gates, the dichotomy cannot be so straight forward. The deeds done in a lifetime cannot be all be easily classified — thumbs-up or thumbs-down. And it seems unreasonable to be given a new slate just because you repent at the last minute after a trail filled with heartaches, misery and disappointments. An all-or-none rule works does not seem the plausible way of doing things.There must be a halfway house between heaven and hell.FG6.9.14

We lack superheroes?

The actions of King Rama, his consort Sita, his brother Laxman, his humble servant Hanuman have been used as the yardstick of how a human being should live his life. King Rama and his principles on natural justice, respect of power and upholding of promises; Queen Sita and her virtues of a chaste wife exemplified by her conduct; Laxman with the meaning of true friendship and Hanuman with undivided subservience to authority. The conducts and misconducts of the aristocrats and noblemen in Rama's courtyard form the pillar of what Hindus the world over use to run and not to run their daily lives.

Man, the losers, were always awed by their captors. They would try to emulate and assimilate the cultures of their new found victors as their own. That would explain why we speak English and not don our sarongs to work.

So what I am saying is...Everyone is a role model either directly or indirectly to his subordinates. A child, no matter how much he despises his parents, will eventually pick up the subtle cues from the elders. So goes to the common man in the streets. His priorities are set according what he sees from his leaders and people in power. In the modern age of ICT and TV, pop and movie stars fill in the gap as well.

If the idols display traits that seem to glorify wealth, prosperity and the good life without hard work, that it would be. Money becomes the aim in life. If stars can be okay with shameless lifestyles and call it living the life, so be it too. Like in the case of the broken window theory, when the lethargy of enforcing law and order is the rule of the law, noble attributes that differentiate man and animal take a back seat.

That my friend is the real reason why the young 12 year-olds need to re-sit their public examination papers. The people entrusted with the duty to maintain the cold chain of secrets had failed repeatedly because they fail to appreciate the need to maintain integrity in their line of work. Guess they have all their priorities twisted....FG13.9.14

Evil by whose standards?

Now, what is education and what is it to be learned? Is it the ability to regurgitate in verbatim what is written by page and chapter without actually understanding what is written or recited? Or is it the ability to understand that there may be two sides of the coin and allowance must be given to an alternative perspective to what has been accepted as the truth without batting an eyelid?

I do not think that one becomes stupid or is a trouble maker by questioning what seems to be a no-brainer.

Year in year out the effigy of Ravana is burnt with so much pomp and vigour to signify the win of good over evil with the help of the Gods. Ravana is painted in hideous hues and is vilified as the epitome of everything that is evil on Earth. After fasting and praying for 9 days to signify the greatness of the matriarchal forces of Nature, devotees celebrate their victory of staying true to their endeavour by symbolically burning something that is synonymous with evil. Who is going to argue? The scriptures innumerates numerous misdeeds that had been done by Ravana, the Demon and his equally demonic sister. They were accused of upsetting the tranquility of Rama's exiled household.

But then... History is written by the victors...

The remnants of the untold history of the losers insist that Ravana indeed was a cultured emperor of 10 kingdoms as well as the one who had mastered the knowledge of 10 holy scriptures. The 10 heads in his representation of him is the symbolism of his supposed grandiosity. He was an intelligent physician, a talented musician (veena player) and devout Shiva devotee. His subjects enjoyed peace and prosperity under his rule. Poverty was unheard of. Even peasants in his rule used golden utensils in their daily household usage! — so they say.

Even today, he is hailed as a hero, a demigod and is worshipped in many parts of India. Temples and statues had been erected in his name in northern and southern parts of India.

They assert that the whole bad publicity came about because of vested interest of certain superpowers over the other. Ravana is said to be the last of defiant kings who resisted the hegemony of aliens or invading forces from the North. Or was it another deathly clash between Vaishnavites and Shaivites?

Again and again history is re-written to justify the tyranny of the victors and to put them in a better light.

... used the Ramayana to radicalise the Tamils in southern India against Brahminical supremacy and the domination of North Indian Sanskritic culture. For him, Rama, Sita, and all the rest of them were northerners without "an iota of Tamil culture", but Ravana, the king of Lanka or southern Tamil Nadu, was a Tamil. **Periyar E. V. Ramaswami** FG20.9.14

What gives? What it takes?

Since King James I/VI united Scotland and England under the same umbrella after his mother was abdicated, imprisoned and eventually beheaded for treason, Scots had always been feeling that they have been short-changed. The impression that I got when I was there is that the Scots were just waiting to break free from the union.

The recent referendum outcome obviously proved me wrong.

Come Monday, it is back life and back to reality. The naysayers and the yay sayers have to bury the hatchet, hold hands, walk into the sunset and be embroiled in the daily challenges of life.

That is life. No matter what differences we had harboured against each other and the outcomes that may despair us, we have to carry on with life with a straight face.

To all the people who think that we are being hypocrites by not standing our ground and rejecting all kinds of actions that contradicts our belief, I say get real. At the end of the day, the equilibrium and sanctity of the institution has to be preserved. This can also be said of a family. A family member may have certain strong beliefs on certain subjects. By comprising and adjusting his decisions to accommodate the desires of other members, it is by no means indicative of a weak leadership or sucking up to populist sentiments. Life is a game of give and take. It is a game of tug-of-war where the final outcome is determined by what gives and what it takes!FG22.9.14

Can you handle the Truth?

There he was standing undecided what to buy. He knew exactly what he wanted to buy. He knew how everything worked, right down to the low down nitty-gritty details. He knows where the nuts and the bolts should fit in. He knew what is the latest gizmo in town and what is the newest 'kit on the block'. And he knew how much each item costs. In short, he knew the good, the bad, the ugly and anything in between. But yet, he cannot decide on his latest gadget that he wants to lay his hands on.

Item A is superior in one aspect which is less efficient than item B but is more pricey as compared to item C which in turn is more durable than item D and the list goes on. At the end of the day, he is at his wit's end on what to do next. The thought of losing his hard earned money to a substandard merchandise is unacceptable in his book. So he waits. The trouble is that this is not the first time he is caught in this type of quagmire. Again and again he feels fleeced as he always knows that there is something better out there!

His neighbour, on the other hand, never had his life so good. With his newly gained windfall, life cannot be better. He sees something, he likes it and he buys it. Simple.

I guess that why they say ignorance is bliss. Things are easy when you are ignorant like what the Beatles said, "Living is easy with eyes closed!" (Strawberry Fields).

Surprise, surprise. Even in the 3rd century BCE, the fear of information overload was suggested by Seneca the Elder who lived during the reign of Augustus, Aurelius and Caligula. His son, Seneca, a philosopher, served Nero but was forced to commit suicide when he was accused of conspiring to poison the Emperor!

This fear was highlighted again when Gutenberg's printing press took the world by storm. It was thought that man's ability to absorb all those vast information and to be able to make quality decisions was suspect.

Words like 'information glut,' 'infobesity', 'infoxication', 'data smog' were thrown in as time went on and ICT opened the floodgates of information.

A learned man can be a confused one. The thin line separates the ingenious and the insane. Many things were left unanswered to be discovered by ourselves and for us to draw our own conclusions. Perhaps, the level of ignorance amongst us is the only quality that help us to be level-headed and be level on the ground we stand on. Ignorance is the driving force that makes the human race want to explore and makes us reflect upon ourselves and our fellow earthlings.

FG says that deciding to buy something is like ordering in a Chinese restaurant. After finalising on your order, you would realise that the Joneses at the next table have a nicer more palatable-looking spread and you wish you had ordered the same. The same can be said about life partners unless it is decided at the end of a shotgun! It all comes in a package, the good, the bad and is all at how you look at it.FG28.9.14